*The Inland Ground*

# The Inland Ground

*An Evocation of
the American Middle West*

REVISED EDITION

Richard Rhodes

*Illustrations by Bill Greer*

UNIVERSITY PRESS OF KANSAS

Some of these essays originally appeared in periodicals: "Death All Day" in *Esquire* under the title "Death All Day in Kansas"; "Harry's Last Hurrah," "Behold, How Good and How Pleasant It Is for Brethren to Dwell Together in Unity," "An Artist in Iron," "Watching the Animals," and "Cupcake Land" in *Harper's Magazine*; "How I Rode with Harold Lewis on a Diesel Freight Train Down to Gridley, Kansas, and Back" in *Audience*, © 1971 by Hill Publishing Company, Inc.; "The Farther Continent of James Clyman" in *American Heritage*.

Excerpts from *At Ease* by Dwight D. Eisenhower, © 1967 by Dwight D. Eisenhower, are reprinted by permission of Doubleday & Company, Inc. Lines from "A Primitive Like an Orb," from *The Collected Poems of Wallace Stevens*, © 1954 by Wallace Stevens, are reprinted by permission of Alfred A. Knopf, Inc. Selections from the writings of Jesse Howard are quoted by permission of Mr. Howard.

Published by the University Press of Kansas (Lawrence, Kansas 66049), which was organized by the Kansas Board of Regents and is operated and funded by Emporia State University, Fort Hays State University, Kansas State University, Pittsburg State University, the University of Kansas, and Wichita State University

Library of Congress Cataloging-in-Publication Data
Rhodes, Richard.
    The inland ground : an evocation of the American Middle West / Richard Rhodes ; illustrations by Bill Greer.—Rev. ed.
        p.  cm.
    Inclues index.
    ISBN 0-7006-0498-7 (hardcover)—ISBN 0-7006-0499-5 (paper)
        1. Middle West.  I. Title
    F351.R58  1991
    977—dc20                                                                91-26020
                                                                                    CIP

British Library Cataloguing in Publication Data is available.

Printed in the United States of America
10 9 8 7 6 5 4 3 2 1

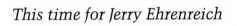

*This time for Jerry Ehrenreich*

# Contents

# *Preface*

THE INLAND GROUND WAS MY FIRST BOOK. I BEGAN
writing it in 1967, when I was thirty years old; Atheneum published it in 1969, when I was thirty-two.

I planned it as a book, not a collection of essays. It was supposed to be a series of "takes" on the Middle West, each chapter examining a different subject but all the chapters, considered together, forming a montage that would evoke what
seemed to me essential about the region of the United States
where I was born and grew up and still lived. Unfortunately for
its critical reception I discovered along the way that magazine
editors, always hungry for stories about the mysterious region
of the continent that lay between the coasts, would pay me to
publish the chapters separately as articles, essays. I was supporting a wife and two small children; getting paid twice for
the same piece of work seemed to me a champion idea, but
enough chapters appeared in magazines before the book was
published that many reviewers assumed *The Inland Ground*
was a collection and dismissed it accordingly. I don't remember
how many copies it finally sold. Not more than five thousand,
I think. I don't think Atheneum printed more than that.

Oddly, it's still the one book I've written that most people
around Missouri and Kansas seem to know. I meet someone at
a library or in the back of a lecture hall and they say, "I liked
your book," and I say, maybe a little impatiently now ten books
down the road, "Which book?" and they look at me strangely
and say, "*The Inland Ground*" (or, sometimes, "*The Inland
Sea*," a reasonable mistake, just as *A Hole in the World* sometimes comes out *A Hole in the Wall* or *A Hole in the Head*). It
also seems to have wandered off across the landscape like those

stones that skitter around the desert on their own when no one's looking. Someone told me years ago that he'd come across a copy in a used bookstore in London, though there was never even a paperback, much less a British edition, and when I mentioned to an editor recently that I'd given away my last copy long ago, she sent me one a few days later that she turned up at a used bookstore in Boston.

Despite these migrations, *The Inland Ground* isn't a book many people have had occasion to read. It appeared almost a generation ago, obscurely. Several of its chapters, the more journalistic and least successful, had become dated. When the University Press of Kansas offered to reprint it, I proposed assembling a new edition instead. I deleted the dated chapters, added several that were originally published elsewhere, reviewed every word (and changed a few here and there) and wrote this preface. Bill Greer drew illustrations for the new chapters in the elegant woodcut style of the old. The result, I think, is a successful renewal; the Midwest has changed less than the rest of the United States, and these examinations of its people and institutions still seem to me to reveal something essential of what it is and how it came to be that way.

I WANT TO SAY ALSO HOW THIS FIRST BOOK HAPPENED for me personally, how I got started writing, because people who are starting out themselves almost always ask, and knowing how writing a book and publishing it happened for someone else makes the process a little less obscure and terrifying. Part of what I have to say repeats what I wrote near the end of *A Hole in the World*, but there's room here to add to that brief confession.

Before *The Inland Ground* I'd published newspaper articles and book reviews. I'd come to believe that writing fiction was something I might do, might even learn to do well, but whenever I tried, the writing emerged either mawkish or flat. I was afraid. I was afraid I had no right to speak. I was afraid I might fail. Crucially, because of the violence of my childhood and the rage that violence engendered in me, I was afraid, grandiosely and delusionally, that if I revealed my feelings in writing I might somehow destroy the world.

I was working in those years in the public relations department at Hallmark Cards, Inc., in Kansas City, Missouri. I wrote the Hallmark daily newspaper, *Noon News*, every work day for two years running. I wrote a newsletter for salesmen and articles for company magazines. I wrote press releases about new products. After four years in public relations I moved along to become editor of a small line of gift books. I learned from these experiences, at which poets have sneered, that writing is writing—getting the Spam to the front lines, to borrow a memorable phrase of William Burroughs's—a craft that may or may not be afflicted with genius. Learning to adapt it to whatever purpose comes to hand is always valuable. There are infinite gradations of rhetoric, from the Hallmark *Sales Bulletin* to *Finnegans Wake*, from greeting-card doggerel to *Paradise Lost*, and every gradation is a useful tool to add to a writer's kit.

Conrad Knickerbocker (see Chapter 14, "A Friend's Suicide") was my boss in the public relations department. He was starting out as a professional writer himself, a little farther along than I, bootlegging book reviews for the *Kansas City Star* and the *New York Times*. I cornered him in his office one day and asked him how you become a writer. He squinted one eye closed in embarrassment at such a naive question, pretending he was Popeye—he was as mercurially comic as Robin Williams—and said, "Rhodes, you apply ass to chair," the best advice about writing I ever solicited. On Knick's recommendation I started writing book reviews for the *Star*. At home I worked on a novel, a very bad, Faulknerian novel, about a college love affair.

Knick left Hallmark for the *Times*. The news came back of his suicide. I waited a decent interval, collected together my best *Star* reviews, sent them to the *Times* with a letter evoking my dead mentor and the *Times* started offering me books to review.

From there I branched out to the old *New York Herald Tribune*. The editor of the *Herald Trib*'s Book World section, Richard Kluger, noticed the mini-essays on the Middle West that I fitted into the interstices of some of my reviews. When he moved on to become an editor at Atheneum he called me up one day, out of the blue. He said no one had written anything new about the Middle West since *Winesburg, Ohio*, and asked me if I'd like to try.

I was terrified. I was thirty years old, unhappily married, depressed, visited daily with such intense attacks of anxiety that I was drinking, on the average, half a fifth of whiskey a night, nearly anoretic and, since Knick's suicide, flirting with suicide myself, imagining that if I crossed over to the other side I might meet Knick. I didn't understand that I was suffering from posttraumatic stress disorder (the term hadn't come into common use yet, nor had it been applied to the aftermath of severe child abuse), but I'd had the good sense to seek help. I'd started psychotherapy twice a week with a good man trained at Menninger's. That work of excavation and healing would continue for seven more years.

It was lucky that I'd found my way into therapy when Dick Kluger's offer came along. I was able to muster the courage to take Dick up on it. I didn't know how I'd write the book he proposed, but I knew offers of book contracts don't grow on trees. Dick had asked for an outline; I sent him one that the table of contents still faithfully reflects; the Atheneum editorial board approved it and proposed an advance of $3,000. I accepted and shortly after I signed the contract the first check came.

Spending the money before I'd earned it helped force me through the eye of the needle. It helped that I had signed on for nonfiction. Reporting on the Middle West was closer to what I'd already done than fiction would be and farther from the black center of my fear. Truth is safer than fiction. "Don't tell *stories*," authority figures accuse us. With nonfiction I could deny responsibility for the stories I told—after all, they were *true*. I could reveal myself indirectly by my choice of subject and my interpretation of what I learned. I wouldn't have to invent. So I imagined, or pretended.

I wrote two chapters I didn't much like, one on a Kansas City foundation executive, one on Kansas City's pretensions to high culture—not surprisingly, the two chapters that dated soonest and that I've removed from this revised edition. I struggled to do anything more. I began to worry that I couldn't make the book work.

Six months into therapy I started eating and started writing. How that happened I'll quote from *A Hole in the World*:

> Then a friend of mine suggested I go with him to north central Kansas to follow a coyote hunt. We bounced across wheat fields in pickup trucks with wheat farmers who occupied their idle winters coursing coyotes for sport. Their greyhounds and Russian wolfhounds bayed from boxes built onto the truck beds like camper shells; they dropped the dogs close in for the kill. They didn't use guns. Their dogs tore the coyotes apart. On the way home from coyote hunting we stopped off in another part of Kansas to watch an evening of illegal cockfights. Men, women and children with fists crammed with gambling money screamed from the bleachers while fighting birds down in the cockpit caparisoned with bright plumes stabbed each other with three-inch steel spurs. Back in Kansas City after those bloody witnessings I reread Ernest Hemingway's *Death in the Afternoon*, got thoroughly drunk and splashed some of my violence and my horror of violence across the page. The result was a chapter I called "Death All Day," the first fully open writing I ever managed. I knew what it was; my hands shook from more than hangover when I read it. Kluger knew what it was and sent it on to *Esquire*. Don

Erickson was editor of *Esquire* then, a Kansas City, Kansas, boy, like me. Don sent Art Kane out to photograph the fighting cocks and published the piece with fanfare.

I felt as if I'd cleared a choked spring. I've written well and badly in all the years since that first breakthrough, the water has run muddy or clear, but the spring that began flowing early in therapy has never since been blocked.

To write was to speak. To come out of the clotted silence of my inarticulate rage. In therapy I'd found a place where I felt reasonably safe, a place from which to begin. The other chapters in *The Inland Ground* followed all in a rush. I'd collect the information I needed, calling in sick at Hallmark when necessary to steal the time for a story trip. Then, writing at night after work, I'd usually get drunk to jumpstart the piece. I thought I had to, and maybe at first I did. I always edited sober. My analyst waited several years to offer the insight that writing drunk—trying to control all the levels that work in a piece of writing and fight intoxication at the same time—had to be harder than writing sober. By then, a couple of books along, writing full time and making a living at it, I was ready to understand that he was right. I started writing fresh in the morning and felt like a banker opening up a full vault.

At the time I wrote *The Inland Ground* I thought I knew why I chose the subjects I did, but reviewing the book now, twenty-two years later, I'm struck by the number of chapters devoted to father figures and the nearly total absence of women. I was looking compulsively for fathers and brothers in those days, trying to recreate the time before my father remarried when he and my brother Stanley and I had shared a single room in boarding houses, a time I mythologized. I also wrote about famous and talented men because I was looking for heroes on whose works and lives I might model my own. (Those were the years when I dreamed myself in their company as well—vivid, realistic dreams hanging out with Eisenhower, Khrushchev, Jack and Bobby Kennedy, whoever was in the headlines or in a book.) I deliberately modeled *The Inland Ground* on William Carlos Williams's *In the American Grain*, one of the neglected masterpieces of American literature. I didn't know my mother, and the woman my father married when I was ten, my stepmother, had been the violent instrument of my abuse, so I'm not surprised I wasn't yet able to write about women. I never really have been and perhaps never will.

In these peculiarities I was different from other thirty-year-old would-be writers. In other ways I see I was cut from the same cloth. I was damned sure of my cultural opinions, surer then than I am now. I projected the pain and anxiety and insecurity I felt out onto the world—or did those abrasions sensitize me to recognize the darkness I found there?

Obviously I felt safer writing about the past than the present. That revetment served me so well that I started from behind it on my second book, which Dick Kluger also risked commissioning. *The Ungodly*, my first novel, was to be an historical novel (truth is safer than fiction) about the Donner Party, the midwestern pioneers who emigrated west in 1846 for California but were caught in the Sierra Nevada by early snow and forced to eat their dead to survive the long, terrible winter. "The story that follows is not a history," I asserted in a brief introduction to *The Ungodly*. "It is a work of fiction, written to other ends. Yet I have attempted to include, and nowhere to violate [sic—what an odd verb] every known historical fact."

Well, the book that follows, now revised, is a work of nonfiction, but it's clear to me all these years later that it also was written to other ends. All books are, however much their authors may claim objectivity. Among the small gift books I edited at Hallmark, my favorite is a collection of paragraphs selected from among the writings of Ralph Waldo Emerson. A large, impersonal corporation paid me well when I was a young man to sit at my desk one month and read, carefully and thoroughly, the collected works of a classic American writer. Emerson's aphorisms still pop into consciousness when I need them and I still look them up in a reference copy I keep of that little Hallmark book. Here's the aphorism I just thought of. It makes my point about the ends, conscious and unconscious, to which books are written: "People seem not to see that their opinion of the world is also a confession of character."

I had to grit my teeth to type it, though, because the opinions that follow are still, despite judicious editing, the opinions of a young man. But there's good work here and it's worth another round.

Glade
February 1991

*The Inland Ground*

# 1 / The Inland Ground: An Introduction

THE MIDDLE WEST WAS LAND BEFORE IT WAS PEOPLE, A broad inland ground. To the south, alluvial; to the north, glacial; to the east, forested; to the west, dry and barren of trees. A vastness, a wilderness. Once an ocean floor, now the basin of a great river. Rimmed by mountain ranges. Only slowly settled, and not settled yet. A place of many places, too many for one book: what follows must be only a sampling, Kansas, Missouri, something of Nebraska and Iowa. The black dirt and prairie west, the Middle West I know.

Many, when they first saw the prairies, looking out from the forest of the Middle Border, called them a sea. That is how they

3

would look to seaboard eyes, but they were a sea you could walk on. Their essence was their boundlessness: they extended to the horizon, hardly interrupted by trees or hills. Onto such blankness each visitor could project his own interior landscape, and did, some calling the prairies the Great American Desert, others the Garden of the World. Both were right—are right today about the entire Middle West, culturally as well as geographically. Culturally a desert, if by culture one means the high European forms; culturally a garden if by culture one means the broad vernacular forms, if one means sources, if one means the talented young. A coyote hunt has its aesthetic, as formal as any bullfight. Missouri on the Mississippi produced both Mark Twain and T. S. Eliot, not a bad list for any state's canon. Iowa grows poets as sturdy as its corn. Independence, Missouri, raised Harry Truman, and Abilene, Kansas, raised Dwight Eisenhower. And the Middle West has delivered its young to the great turnstile cities of the East and Far West long enough to qualify, like Great Britain, as a region suffering from the emigration of its best minds.

Like Florida, with its interior swamps and its circumferential ring of cities, the United States itself is polarizing on its east and west coasts. The Middle West is not yet losing population, but neither is it gaining at anything like the rate of increase of the two coasts. It is a region most coastal people fly over, and even the natives who live here, more and more of them, speak of moving away. The Middle West's cities have aged; its farm population has declined; and only its anonymous suburbs, as in the rest of the United States, have temporarily prospered. At what terrible expense to the human spirit who can say?

And perhaps the Middle West is not a place at all, is too dispersed over the vastness of its lands to generate any sense of permanence in its children. We were never a steady people, but moved on to the next range of open land if we didn't like the land we settled, or had used it up. Our western range was among the last land to be settled in the United States. Pioneers preferred the difficult and dangerous pilgrimage to Oregon and California. Iowa was settled soon enough, but Iowa has never seemed to me to be typical of this region: more a demonstration farm than a place; more some cosmic public relations project designed to prove that God's in his heaven and all's right with the world. Missouri joins all that is worst—and best—of North and South into one Gothic rural ruin (except for St. Louis, a French city prefabricated in New Orleans and shipped up the Mississippi two hundred years ago by fur traders); Kansas sits as strait-laced as some country church; Nebraska stretches out flat and parsimonious and plain; but Iowa might have been buttered, it is so sleek. And how many different places have I already mentioned, and hardly begun to mention all the places of the Middle West?

My Middle West, which this book is more or less about, with some important omissions and some wanderings off over the hill, was Kansas City, Missouri, and Independence, Missouri. It is a country lake in Kansas as I write. During the years of World War II, we—my widower father, my brother, and I—moved all over the east side of Kansas City, a lower-middle-class area which is now part of the city's black ghetto, living in boarding-houses and occasionally a real home. I was cared for by German immigrants who believed in education, hard widows who knew how to bread a meat loaf, middle-class mothers in need of extra income, and spinsters heavy with love. If anyone raised me, my older brother did. We lived in the streets, flattening bottle caps on streetcar tracks, walking the high parapets of outdoor billboards, occupying vacant lots, wandering the huge storm sewers that drain Kansas City's rainwater into the Missouri River. We saw *Lassie Come Home* at the National Theater on Independence Avenue and cried, and later saw *Frankenstein* there at night and hardly dared the shadowed walk home. Old Mr. Gernhardt, a German immigrant who took in boarders to make ends meet, told us of helping to build the Al-Can Highway and sang "Mademoiselle from Armentieres" at the piano until Mrs. Gernhardt stopped him.

Unable to find a school library book in my fourth-grade year, I stole a five-dollar bill from my father, bought a box of kitchen matches and a package of notebook paper at the corner drugstore, and rode by bus and trolley on a school morning in the wintertime to Swope Park, determined to become a wise and much-consulted hermit there. Climbed the wooded hill to a clearing behind the bronze statue of Colonel Swope, wadded up the notepaper, and lit it. Found no warmth but some wisdom, retraced my path back to school and accepted the principal's mild scolding and my father's amusement. He paid for the book.

We tended no Victory Garden, being renters only, but collected grease and flattened tin cans to help the war effort. The Manor bread man drove through the neighborhood three times a week in a wagon pulled by a horse and gave us—a gang of children long ago dispersed and their names forgotten—day-old sweet rolls. And though my brother and I were lonely, those days seem now some paradise for the city and for me. The war occupied adult attentions and eliminated distracting luxuries: with little gasoline available to automobiles, the streets were ours, and a glorious afternoon in midsummer might be magic as simple as a hike up the hill to the Velvet Freeze ice-cream parlor for a butterscotch sundae.

Later, my father remarried, and all our lives for a time became painful. Still the city spared us. Told to leave the house in the morning and not return until night, we biked to the eight-foot trailer of an old woman who lived in a vacant lot beside a creek. She had a cigarette-making machine, and would roll cigarettes for us along with her own. Once she baked a moist raisin cake on her hot plate which the three of us ate at one sitting. In her prime she roamed the back roads in her trailer taking portrait photographs of country people. Now she was old, and lived on the little money her son could send her.

And other distractions: school friends; long bike tours to green city parks; watching the doughnut-making machine at the Katz drugstore; reading at the library; selling Christmas cards door to door to earn a chemistry set; swimming at the city pool.

And abruptly, when I was twelve and my brother fourteen, in the summer of 1949, we were removed to the country, to a boys' home run under a private trust, the Andrew Drumm Institute in Independence, Missouri, and found ourselves farmers. Neither of us took easily to farming, having lived in the city as urban Huckleberry Finns, but we had no choice, and so we learned that work, never with the inborn sense of routine that a child raised on a farm possesses, but with some fair imitation of it.

Began cleaning chicken roosts for chores, leading the old mare in and out of the barn to raise and lower the hay hook, straightening whole kegs of nails salvaged from a razed shed, hoeing the twenty-acre garden, picking strawberries, planting potatoes, filling up, when the train bell atop the smokehouse called us to supper, on heavy country food. Learning, later, to plow and disk and mow; to feed cattle and clean the barn; to cook for forty people and clean the dormitories; to cut down trees; to weld; to speak in public and conduct a parliamentary meeting; to operate a mangle and a steam press; to drive a school bus and a farm truck; to show a steer and a sheep; to butcher cattle and hogs and chickens; to can tomatoes and cut meat; to paint fences and build a barn; to call hogs and terrace a field; to deliver calves; to dock lambs; to put up silage in the sweet sweaty silo and grind corn in the violent hammer mill. Learning besides to play football and baseball and basketball; to run track; learning plane geometry and algebra and world history; learning vocational agriculture: the anatomy of farm animals, their diseases, their breeding, seeds, crops, fertilizers, woodwork, metalwork, electricity, plumbing, engines, farm machinery.

Feeling at times, in the isolation of adolescence, despair of my past and despair of my future, but never able to sustain such despair for long because the land and the animals and the work always called me back to those things that must be done next, to those daily regularities that insist on the continuation and preservation of the world. Cows must be milked, and animals fed, and these are certainties on which even loneliness must found an alleviation.

We also discovered other things to do. Tried wine-making, one summer, without benefit of text. Our young scientist built a still, but most of us crushed grapes and mixed in what were probably fatal doses of yeast and stolen sugar. Charlie Frakes, our slow bully whom I made my friend, I came across one night in the workshop boiling dry field corn in a number-ten can. We boiled it together, for two hours, but it was hardly soft even then. Charlie took the stew and loaded it with sugar and hid the mess in the hayloft. Word finally reached our agriculture instructor, who lived at Drumm with his wife, and he declared amnesty on a full-mooned summer night and found his small back porch covered the next morning with Mason jars and tin cans filled with God knows what strange growths. We smoked grapevines, pungent as Gauloises, or crushed autumn leaves rolled in cornsilk. I spent whole Saturday afternoons with a truncheon of a magazine waging war on the wasps that occupied our dormitory's front porch, killing more than a hundred in one energetic day. Some of the boys, tired of the marauding cats which crowded around the milkhouse door at separating time, would corner the screeching beasts inside the building and hose them down. Charlie liked to toss the sixteen-pound shotput and watch a mongrel dog—we kept a pack of them around for love and scraps—attempt to retrieve it across the playing field. Or we would sled down the hill in the south pasture, jumping the creek bed at the risk of breaking our young necks. Or steal vitamin C tablets, tart as lemonade, from the canning house where they were stored in a plastic bag to be used in preserving fresh peaches. Or pocket apples, four winy Jonathans at a time, from the fruit cellar, while loading up a basket of potatoes for the kitchen.

Each year, as a reward for our summer's work of farming, we would pack up and take a long camping trip. Then we saw the land, out beyond the cities. Our bus had a governor and couldn't go more than forty miles an hour, but in it, and trailed by our carry-all, the superintendent's car, and our two-ton truck with a storehouse built onto its bed, we wandered the Middle West and the West for the last month of summer. We took our finest trip during my first summer at the home: through Kansas to New Mexico, across to Arizona to the Grand Canyon, to the Petrified Forest, to Carlsbad, to Santa Fe, through the Texas Panhandle and Oklahoma back to Independence. We followed the Santa Fe Trail, modern Forty-Niners, and every mile of our journey was glorious with freedom from chores and great quenching sights to see. Another year we drove to Yellowstone, which in those days was not as crowded as it has become today, and but for three straight days of rain it was also an extraordinary sight to us, because none of us had ever traveled so before, cooked our meals morning and night over open campfires, fished in clear lakes and streams, seen nature in her most fanciful forms.

A place and a time are all of a piece, coherent, and you may look anywhere and catch some glimpse of the whole. That is why the chapters that follow discuss such different subjects. Yet when you have read them they should come together to demonstrate something of this region, this place or these places, this inland ground.

# 2 / Some Forebears

## THOMAS JEFFERSON

What he did for us cannot be measured. As Washington was our first hero, so Jefferson was our first *mind*. There is a moment early in any enterprise when one man may give such shape to a region that later men may live and die only within his frame. Jefferson was that man, and lived at that moment. Because he understood the continent's extent, and coveted it all, it was his to do with as he would. Others, like Daniel Boone, might experience it, but they had no seats in the Star Chambers of power. Let a young and brilliant man, who knew what he wanted, sit down and write, and he could have his way. We were not a country yet, but only a commercial coast fronting a wilderness. If a young man wants to make an impression, then let him. England is the problem, not the wilderness at our back door. Even Franklin, that chattering, self-important journalist, must have missed the point, or he would certainly have written the Declaration himself, and by the time everyone had finished reading all its maxims and qualifications and asides they would have forgotten its purpose and gone about their business and we would be England's still.

And so Jefferson held sway. The young should never be awarded such exception. He was allowed to draft the Declaration. The language, lofted on Lockean clouds, so impressed those high-minded American tradesmen already intimidated by the Virginia accents of Jefferson's voice that they all but gave in, made a few emendations and let the thing go—reserving, thank God, the practicalities of constituting a nation to their own commercial regard. The most handsome face in American history, the perfect eighteenth century man.

Built Monticello, his little mountain, perfecting it only after his wife's death. Built an Apollonian house, a private, intimate, consciously serene extension of his own shapely body. With homely corners of invention, the weathercock inside, the clock's pendulum disappearing below the floor when it needed winding, the conveyor carrying the pot of nightsoil discreetly from beneath his bed as if the heavy indiscreet body might be tamed if only one were clever enough.

Not knowing what to do with itself, the nation called him back. He sent out Lewis and Clark, and later, in the other direction, Monroe. We might have established a viable coastal civilization and left the interior, as in Africa, to be wandered by explorers and feared by children late at night, but Jefferson would have none of it: he had to find everything out, rationalize it, explain it all and frame a plan for it, lest the wilds overcome his careful defenses. Monroe would not have spent that sixteen million dollars had he not thought President Jefferson would back him up; whatever Jefferson had officially told him, his spiritual commission was clear, an open hand and an open pocketbook. Monroe back with Livingston and the shocking news, Jefferson conveniently forgot his own deep Constitutional qualms and urged ratification of the Louisiana Purchase, knowing that he was taking severe chances with the still-tender sensibilities of a young nation to make such a recommendation, but arrogant enough, destructive enough, prescient enough to recommend it regardless: because *he* knew best, *his* was the cosmic American consciousness, *he* had invented the United States of America after all, damn Washington and all the others who merely made it work. And turned thereby a militant but straightforward English people who could do nicely, thank you, without George's taxes, into a forlorn people who would spend the next several millennia trying to recover from their expansion and figure out who they were, all because young Tom, young Squire Jefferson, thought he knew best.

He organized the American wilderness, before its details were even mapped, on a grid borrowed from Euclidian geometry: so laid it out despite the fact that he was a countryman who understood curving fields and wandering streams and the vagaries of plantings: laid it out to our eternal complication, his grid the woe of his fellow citizens ever afterward, impossible to find those damned cornerposts, impossible to track those inhuman squares. A Dionysian land, a Dionysian continent, plains and tortuous rivers and sharp mountains and wandering shores, and he overlaid upon it a Euclidian grid as if Apollo truly reigned and the Furies were forever banished.

He socketed his bed into the wall between his bedroom and his study: was that ambivalent, that torn. Our first Kennedy really, as handsome and as outwardly rational and as inwardly Greek: this man caused his stool to be removed by pulleys: this man caused a continent to be penetrated, then bluntly annexed, then measured out in squares. He embodied all the American contradictions: extended his fantasies and his fear of those fantasies out onto the land itself: loved it and hated it, and because of that love and hate saw it uncertainly. Without him we would not have the shame. Without him we would not have the glory. He shaped America. He shaped the inland ground.

JOSIAH GREGG

Josiah Gregg, frail, studious son of a Missouri farmer, left his home for the prairies of Kansas and the Southwest two months before his twenty-fifth birthday, in May of 1831. A semi-invalid, he suffered from what one of his biographers calls "chronic dyspepsia and consumption." It had confined him to his bedroom for most of the preceding year, until his doctors, all other treatment unavailing, suggested a prairie trip for his health. He signed on as a bookkeeper for a Santa Fe trader operating out of Independence, Missouri.

Two weeks into his first expedition, Gregg had recovered enough to exchange his carriage for a horse—a remarkable healing. In the next nine years Gregg traveled from Independence to Santa Fe and back four times, leading the last expedition and blazing a new trail.

In 1844 Gregg published a book of his travels, *Commerce on the Prairies*. It would go through fourteen printings and become a handbook for travelers and settlers in the regions he described. In 1845, pursuing an old interest, Gregg spent two semesters studying medicine at the University of Louisville, but itched to return to the wilds. The University agreeably awarded him an honorary degree and he again traveled to Santa Fe, had some part in the Mexican War of 1846, went east once more, then returned to Mexico to practice medicine. He could not stay put. After a year he gave over his practice for a botanical exploration through Mexico to California, accepted a commission there to find a bay north of San Francisco lost since early Spanish times, and on that expedition, at the age of forty-four, was killed in a fall from his horse.

Intensely shy, Gregg never married. His hypochondria, though its physical effects subsided, persisted throughout his life. He nagged his men, was impatient of details, was difficult to get along with, especially in his last year; one of his monumental arguments, on that final, fatal expedition, gave California's Mad River its name.

He achieved some scientific distinction: practiced tolerable medicine, drew an excellent map of the prairie regions, discovered new varieties of plants and birds in the Southwest and in Mexico. His most lasting monument is his book.

Since they gave him back his life, it should not surprise us that Gregg all but worshiped the prairies. He writes of them in *Commerce on the Prairies*:

> Those who have lived pent up in our large cities know but little of the broad, unembarrassed freedom of the Great Western Prairies. Viewing them from a snug fire side, they seem crowded with dangers, with labors and with sufferings; but once upon them, and these appear to vanish— they are soon forgotten.

Earlier in the same chapter he explains what he means by the "freedom" of the prairies:

> I have hardly known a man, who has ever become familiar with the kind of life which I have led for so many years, that has not relinquished it with regret.
>
> There is more than one way of explaining this apparent incongruity. In the first place—the wild, unsettled and independent life of the Prairie trader, makes perfect freedom from nearly every kind of social dependence an absolute necessity of his being. He is in daily, nay, hourly exposure of his life and property, and in the habit of relying upon his own arm and his own gun for protection and support. Is he wronged? No court or jury is called to adjudicate upon his disputes or his abuses, save his own conscience; and no powers are invoked to redress them, save those with which the God of Nature has endowed him. He knows no govern-

ment—no laws, save those of his own creation and adoption. He lives in no society which he must look up to or propitiate. The exchange of this untrammelled condition—this sovereign independence, for a life in civilization, where both his physical and moral freedom are invaded at every turn, by the complicated machinery of social institutions, is certainly likely to commend itself to but few,—not even to all those who have been educated to find their enjoyments in the arts and elegancies peculiar to civilized society;—as is evidenced by the frequent instances of men of letters, of refinement and of wealth, voluntarily abandoning society for a life upon the Prairies, or in the still more savage mountain wilds.

"That government is best which governs not at all," Henry David Thoreau would argue four years later before the Concord Lyceum. But Josiah Gregg was no Thoreau. His adoration of prairie life is sincere, but his reasons are personal, not philosophic, and whenever he attempts to explain himself philosophically his logic goes awry. That phrase "broad, unembarrassed freedom," for example. Later in his apologia Gregg says that prairie men prefer to stay on the unpopulated ranges because they cannot reconcile themselves to "the habits of civilized life":

A long absence from such society generally obliterates from their minds most of those common laws of social intercourse, which are so necessary to the man of the world. The awkwardness and the gaucheries which ignorance of their details so often involves, are very trying to all men of sensitive temperaments. Consequently, multitudes rush back to the Prairies, merely to escape those criticisms and that ridicule, which they know not how to disarm.

"Unembarrassed," then, is no metaphor: Gregg means it personally. Freedom from civilization is not, for Gregg, Thoreau's transcendental necessity. It is a loosened collar and muddy shoes, an ordinary country boy's distaste for the big city. Again: Gregg, says a biographer, "detested meeting people and was unduly modest in the presence of his intellectual superiors" (whoever those might be, considering Gregg's accomplishments—college graduates, presumably, as Gregg was not). Perhaps Gregg's discomfort explains his choice of "men of letters, of refinement and wealth" as his sole example of the type of men who refused to give up the freedom of prairie life. Who could he mean? Most of the "men of letters" who wrote books about their prairie experiences only passed through—Francis Parkman, Washington Irving, Richard Burton, John Frémont. The example must be defensive, as that exaggerated "multitudes rush back" is defensive, and more than a little wistful, since Gregg is writing at this point from a Philadelphia boardinghouse.

The man was obsessed with details, as we might expect of a hypochondriac. John Bigelow, the journalist who helped Gregg prepare *Commerce on the Prairies* for publication, complains of him:

> He had no notions of literary art and he knew it, but he was morbidly conscientious, and nothing would induce him to state anything that he did not positively know as if he did know it, or to overstate anything. . . . Then Gregg had about as little imagination as any man I ever knew . . . He would not allow his version of a fact to be expanded or contracted a hair's-breadth, no matter what the artistic temptation, nor however unimportant the incident; he always had the critics of the plains before his eyes, and would sooner have broken up the plates and reprinted the whole book than have permitted the most trifling error to creep into his description of the loading of his mules or the marshaling of one of his caravans.

Is this the same dyspeptic traveler who complains that ignorance of the "details" of "those common laws of social intercourse . . . so necessary to the man of the world" forces prairie
men back to the wilds? Gregg loved details, collected details,
broke down every experience into manageable details. An eye
for details distinguishes *Commerce on the Prairies*. It is the
very quality that has kept the book alive and in circulation for
more than a hundred years. Yet he capitulates before the details
of civilized life.

His anxiety must have been unbearable whenever he confronted civilization. It was, as we know. It sent him cowering
to bed, a fester of symptoms. No wonder he insists that freedom is a necessity of prairie life. Not a feature, not a privilege:
a necessity.

Civilization worried him even where his beloved prairie was
concerned. He takes pains to make the wilderness polite, pop-
ulating it with gentlemen, talking mysteriously of "the still
more savage mountain wilds." He cannot admit how much the
quite adequate wildness of the prairies means to him, though
obliquely he does so in another illogical paragraph:

> It will hardly be a matter of surprise then . . . that this pas-
> sion for Prairie life . . . will he very apt to lead me upon
> the plains again, to spread my bed with the mustang and
> the buffalo, under the broad canopy of heaven,—there to
> seek to maintain undisturbed my confidence in men, by
> fraternizing with the little prairie dogs and wild colts, and
> the still wilder Indians.

How does a man maintain his "confidence in men" by fraternizing with animals? Does Gregg mean he is more confident
of men when he can view them from a distance? But that is
not what he says. Does he mean that what little confidence he
has he prefers to leave undisturbed? But that also is not what
he says.

He says fraternizing with prairie dogs and colts and Indians maintains his confidence in men. Nature, as he would have conceived it, nature unrestrained, as his own nature was inhibited. The necessity of freedom: to he natural, muddy boots and all. Not by accident did Gregg consider the wild mustang the most noble of beasts.

He came as near as he could to freedom from his symptoms while traveling the prairies, but that was none too near. He followed a respectable trade. He kept the wilderness at a distance by objectifying it, by studying it as a collection of details rather than a complete experience. Yet he understood without ever quite admitting it to himself that life—his life—depended on the wilderness, that he must ride toward the squall line, the boiling thunderheads, not back toward the cities of men.

Gregg himself confirms these assertions. He is writing what amounts to a guidebook for prairie travelers, traders, settlers: extolling the beauty, the wealth, the healthfulness, the variety of the prairies. Anyone reading *Commerce on the Prairies* immediately itches to travel them himself, especially since Gregg insists one soon forgets the dangers. And there is the excellent map he included in the book, the careful mileages between landmarks. Yet, at the end of his book, Gregg declares that this land which he has praised to the skies for its salutary effects on man is "chiefly uninhabitable." Even though its "unequalled pasturage" might "afford a sufficiency to graze cattle for the supply of all the United States." Its choicest valleys and river bottoms, especially—where homesteaders traditionally settle first—are "too isolated and remote to become the abodes of civilized man." As if Gregg had never seen a railroad, as if all of America had not once also been too remote.

Josiah Gregg is a triumph, a neurasthenic who found a neurasthenic's paradise, a land where he could be miraculously healed from sickness, a land where he could even escape, for an hour or two on a warm afternoon, his obsession with details, and happily watch the prairie dogs play. Who wouldn't nail up a NO TRESPASSING sign on such a paradise?

The heartland as hideout: it is a theme that recurs.

HENRY CHATILLON

Henry Chatillon appears and disappears quickly enough. He represents a type of man who belongs to the midwestern past and should be noticed, the type represented also by Jim Bridger and Daniel Boone. Chatillon was Francis Parkman's guide during the expedition "of curiosity and amusement," as Parkman calls it, that resulted in Parkman's book *The Oregon Trail.*

Parkman and his Harvard classmate Quincy Adams Shaw have come out from Boston, both of them twenty-three years old and two years graduated, to make a tour of the prairie regions. They will follow Nebraska's Platte River to Fort Laramie, ride south along the eastern edge of the Black Hills to Pueblo, and follow the Arkansas River back to Westport Landing. They are both accomplished horsemen and fair shots, Parkman serious and sure of himself in any circumstance, Shaw lazier, with something like a sense of humor. Both are snobs, in a casual way, but the snobbery gives an edge to Parkman's characterizations that is entirely agreeable. Even in his first description of Henry Chatillon there is a touch of condescension, but thereafter, in *The Oregon Trail*, he never refers to Henry without the respect the man deserves. This is Henry Chatillon, a portrait in lavender and iron:

> On coming one afternoon to the [Fur Company office in St. Louis], we found there a tall and exceedingly well-dressed man, with a face so open and frank that it attracted our notice at once. We were surprised at being told that it was he who wished to guide us to the mountains. He was born in a little French town near St. Louis, and from the age of fifteen years had been constantly in the neighborhood of the Rocky Mountains, employed for the most part by the company, to supply their forts with buffalo meat. . . . He had arrived in St. Louis the day before, from the mountains, where he had been for four years; and he now asked only to go and spend a day with his mother,

before setting out on another expedition. His age was about thirty; he was six feet high, and very powerfully and gracefully moulded. The prairies had been his school; he could neither read nor write, but he had a natural refinement and delicacy of mind, such as is rare even in women. His manly face was a mirror of uprightness, simplicity, and kindness of heart; he had, moreover, a keen perception of character, and a tact that would preserve him from flagrant error in any society. Henry had not the restless energy of an Anglo-American. He was content to take things as he found them; and his chief fault arose from an excess of easy generosity, not conducive to thriving in the world. Yet it was commonly remarked of him, that whatever he might choose to do with what belonged to himself, the property of others was always safe in his hands. His bravery was as much celebrated in the mountains as his skill in hunting; but it is characteristic of him that in a country where the rifle is the chief arbiter between man and man, he was very seldom involved in quarrels. Once or twice, indeed, his quiet good nature had been mistaken and presumed upon, but the consequences of the error were such, that no one was ever known to repeat it. No better evidence of the intrepidity of his temper could be asked, than the common report he had killed more than thirty grizzly bears. He was proof of what unaided nature will sometimes do. I have never, in the city or in the wilderness, met a better man than my true-hearted friend, Henry Chatillon.

From St. Louis the party proceeds by steamboat on the Missouri River to Westport Landing (which is today part of Kansas City, Missouri) and from there west into Indian Territory across what is now eastern Kansas north to the Platte. The men meet Indians; hunt buffalo; explore the Black Hills; live in Indian camps, Parkman for a time alone. Parkman contracts malaria and suffers from the weakness of it for two months of the journey, but presses on regardless, though at times he is too weak to do much more than hold on to his saddle. The two stocks which are most obviously missing from the prairies today—the Indians and the buffalo—occupy much of Parkman's narrative, thronging, both stocks, with an excitement and confusion that seems a foreshadowing of their end, as if they were performing for this Brahmin white man their final performance, colored and heightened perhaps by Parkman's febrile vision of them.

Chatillon is distinguished, in Parkman's narrative, by his frequent absences from it, yet one always feels his presence in the background, directing and easing the journey. He knows the land, the tribes, how to hunt, when to lie low. And each time he appears, the appearance has a quality of tact and good sense and profound feeling that leaves no doubt of the man's distinction.

His first words in the text are plain enough. The sky has darkened; the party has left Fort Leavenworth forty miles behind to the south; they are encamping for the night: "'Drive down the tent-pickets hard,' said Henry Chatillon, 'it is going to blow.'" Blow it does, and rain with it, that night and for several afternoons thereafter, breaking up every morning to allow the tour to proceed.

Henry's next appearance is humorous, the kind of humor Gary Cooper embodied: "Henry Chatillon, before lying down, was looking about for signs of snakes, the only living things that he feared, and uttering various ejaculations of disgust at finding several suspicious-looking holes close to the cart." More Gary Cooper soon after: "Henry Chatillon still sat cross-legged, dallying with the remnant of his coffee, the beverage in universal use upon the prairie, and an especial favorite with him. He preferred it in its virgin flavor, unimpaired by sugar or cream; and on the present occasion it met his entire approval, being exceedingly strong, or, as he expressed it, 'right black.'"

These are most of the personal details we learn of the man in the entire book. They're enough: Henry is human after all, Parkman has shown us that, completely at home in the wilds.

The buffalo, Parkman says much later, are Chatillon's book, but Chatillon seems also to have been Parkman's book, to his great benefit. Giving Parkman all due credit for courage and resourcefulness and intelligence, he could nevertheless not possibly have enjoyed so safe and satisfying a tour unless Henry were behind much of what he did. He was too untutored in exploration, too green, to have done alone the things he did.

An aside: the major theme of *The Oregon Trail* is the journey itself, and Parkman's experiences in the course of it, but a powerful minor plays through the text, evidence of Parkman's deep feelings for the natural world he is traversing: of the wildness of the wilderness, a wildness now forever lost. Standing guard somewhere in northeastern Kansas with his cook, Deslauriers, Parkman wakes from a doze to find Deslauriers asleep. Henry and Shaw, their turn at guard yet to come, are also sleeping, and Parkman realizes his isolation. Consistently, his best writing will describe this sensation:

> Far off, beyond the black outline of the prairie, there was a ruddy light, gradually increasing, like the glow of a conflagration; until at length the broad disk of the moon, blood-red, and vastly magnified by the vapors, rose slowly upon the darkness, flecked by one or two little clouds, and as the light poured over the gloomy plain, a fierce and stern howl, close at hand, seemed to greet it as an unwelcome intruder. There was something impressive and awful in the place and the hour, for I and the beasts were all that had consciousness for many a league around.

That isolation hardly exists today anywhere in America; it was where Henry Chatillon made his home.

It's difficult to say how aware Henry was of his impression on Parkman. A few touches—his well-fitted dark suit in St.

Louis, the name he gives his horse, "Five Hundred Dollar," his personal neatness, his pride in his hunting skills—indicate that he was a more complex man than Parkman makes him seem, and undoubtedly he was, since Parkman's hero-worship must have softened his view of his guide. Yet Henry would have been curious about his wealthy Harvard boss too, and proud to be guiding him on so exceptional an expedition. It seems unlikely that the man would have left St. Louis two days after arriving there from four years in the Rockies for any less an assignment. So both men fared well from their bargain, and both seem to have come out the better for it.

Parkman went on to become a skilled and influential historian, especially of the French settlement of Canada and the influence of the Jesuits there; Chatillon drops out of sight, but we can assume his appearance in so widely read a book as *The Oregon Trail* did his reputation no harm.

We catch other glimpses of Henry's quality. At Fort Laramie he receives word that his squaw, "a woman with whom he had been connected for years by the strongest ties which in that country exist between the sexes," is dying at a village a few days away. Says Parkman:

> Henry was anxious to see the woman before she died, and provide for the safety and support of his children, of whom he was extremely fond. To have refused him would have been an inhumanity.

Parkman and Shaw resolve to ride with Henry to the Indian village, but the night before their departure Parkman is struck down again with malaria, and must stay behind. The other two men go, and return short days later:

> At noon of the following day they came back, their horses looking none the better for the journey. Henry seemed dejected. The woman was dead, and his children must

henceforward be exposed without a protector, to the hardships and vicissitudes of Indian life.

And then this quiet note:

> Even in the midst of his grief he had not forgotten his attachment to his *bourgeois* [meaning Parkman and Shaw], for he had procured among his Indian relatives two beautifully ornamented buffalo-robes, which he spread on the ground as a present to us. . . . It was some time before he entirely recovered from his dejection.

Parkman has a novelist's eye for significant details, and some skill at generalization, and Henry's intimate knowledge of prairie life to draw on, and his own country childhood as a guide. *The Oregon Trail* is entirely an American story, styled with a Boston accent. "No man is a philanthropist on the prairie," he writes in one place. Certainly, as his selfish account of Henry's Indian wife shows, Parkman was not. But who wasn't selfish at twenty-three?

Henry Chatillon as hunter: that is his finest role in Parkman's book. Here is his epiphany:

> When Shaw left me he had walked down for some distance under the river-bank to find another bull. At length he saw the plains covered with the host of buffalo, and soon after heard the crack of Henry's rifle. Ascending the bank, he crawled through the grass, which for a rod or two from the river was very high and rank. He had not crawled far before to his astonishment he saw Henry standing erect upon the prairie, almost surrounded by the buffalo. Henry was in his element. Quite unconscious that any one was looking at him, he stood at the full height of his tall figure, one hand resting upon his side, and the other arm leaning carelessly on the muzzle of his rifle. His eye was ranging over the singular assemblage around him. Now and then he would

select such a cow as suited him, level his rifle, and shoot her dead; then quietly reloading, he would resume his former position. The buffalo seemed no more to regard his presence than if he were one of themselves; the bulls were bellowing and butting at each other, or rolling about in the dust. A group of buffalo would gather about the carcass of a dead cow, sniffing at her wounds; and sometimes they would come behind those that had not yet fallen, and endeavor to push them from the spot. Now and then some old bull would face towards Henry with an air of stupid amazement, but none seemed inclined to attack or fly from him. For some time Shaw lay among the grass, looking in surprise at this extraordinary sight; at length he crawled cautiously forward, and spoke in a low voice to Henry, who told him to rise and come on. Still the buffalo showed no signs of fear; they remained gathered about their dead companions. . . .

Henry knew all their peculiarities; he had studied them as a scholar studies his books, and derived quite as much pleasure from the occupation. The buffalo were a kind of companion to him, and, as he said, he never felt alone when they were about him. . . . Henry always seemed to think that he had a sort of prescriptive right to the buffalo, and to look upon them as something belonging to himself. Nothing excited his indignation so much as any wanton destruction committed among the cows, and in his view shooting a calf was a cardinal sin.

Henry allowed Parkman and Shaw to shoot all the bulls they wanted, because the bulls far outnumbered the cows, but he was a natural conservationist, and must have looked with horror on the slaughter that extinguished the buffalo in the 1860's, if he lived to see it.

The hunting scene is Henry's last appearance in the book except for Parkman's heartfelt parting from him in St. Louis, but it is enough. Men are not separate from their experiences, and it is safe to say that no more Henry Chatillons exist in America: his most powerful quality is his oneness with the natural world from which we are now cut off. It is useless to regret the loss of nature; it is impossible not to admire a man who knew no separation from it.

Even Parkman seems to understand the loss that will take place. Midway through his book he predicts the destruction of the Indians, though he overestimates how long it will take, placing it a hundred years in the future when in fact it took only another fifty to confine the last of them to narrow reservations. But looking back on his own last campfire, somewhere in southern Kansas, he captures his sense of foreboding in images of blackness and death. They are appropriate to an abandoned hunting camp, but they are appropriate also to the abandonment of hunting as a way of life, the only way the prairies knew until the farmers came. It is as if the clearing away of the buffalo and the clearing away of the Indian were merely part of the clearing of the land out there where no trees grew, and with that clearing came the disappearance of the kind of man Henry Chatillon was, and history began in the Middle West:

When we had advanced about a mile, Shaw missed a valuable hunting-knife, and turned back in search of it, thinking that he had left it at the camp. The day was dark and gloomy. The ashes of the fires were still smoking by the river side; the grass around them was trampled down by men and horses, and strewn with all the litter of a camp. Our departure had been a gathering signal to the birds and beasts of prey. Scores of wolves were prowling about the smouldering fires, while the multitudes were roaming over the neighboring prairie; they all fled as Shaw approached, some running over the sand-beds and some over the grassy plains. The vultures in great clouds were soaring overhead, and the dead bull near the camp was completely blackened by the flock that had alighted upon it; they flapped their broad wings and stretched upwards their crested heads and long skinny necks, fearing to remain, yet reluctant to leave their disgusting feast. As he searched about the fires he saw the wolves seated on the hills waiting for his departure. Having looked in vain for his knife, he mounted again, and left the wolves and the vultures to banquet undisturbed.

WILLIAM HORNADAY'S WONDERS

*In the 1880s, the Smithsonian Institution woke up to discover that the vast herds of buffalo which had thronged the prairie West had disappeared. It sent out a man, William T. Hornaday, to attempt to locate any buffalo remaining alive. Excerpts from his report follow.*

The geographical center of the great southern herd [of buffalo] during the few years of its separate existence previous to its destruction was very near the present site of Garden City, Kansas. On the east, even as late as 1872, thousands of buffaloes ranged within ten miles of Wichita, which was then the headquarters of a great number of buffalo-hunters, who plied their occupation vigorously during the winter. On the north the herd ranged within 25 miles of the Union Pacific, until the swarm of hunters coming down from the north drove them farther and farther south. On the west, a few small bands ranged as far as Pike's Peak and the South Park, but the main body ranged east of the town of Pueblo, Colorado. In the southwest, buffaloes were abundant as far as the Pecos and the Staked Plains, while the southern limit of the herd was about on a line with the Southern boundary of New Mexico. . . .

During the years from 1866 to 1871, inclusive, the Atchison, Topeka and Santa Fe Railway, and what is now known as the Kansas Pacific, or Kansas division of the Union Pacific Railway, were constructed from the Missouri River westward across

Kansas, and through the heart of the southern buffalo range. The southern herd was literally cut to pieces by the railways, and every portion of its range rendered easily accessible. There had always been a market for buffalo robes at a fair price, and as soon as the railways crossed the buffalo country the slaughter began. The rush to the range was only surpassed by the rush to the gold mines of California in earlier years. The railroad builders, teamsters, fortune-seekers, "professional" hunters, trappers, guides, and every one out of a job turned out to hunt buffalo for hides and meat. The merchants who had already settled in all the little towns along the three great railways saw an opportunity to make money out of the buffalo product, and forthwith began to organize and supply hunting-parties with arms, ammunition, and provisions, and send them to the range. An immense business of this kind was done by the merchants of Dodge City, Wichita, and Leavenworth, and scores of smaller towns did a corresponding amount of business in the same line. During the years 1871 to 1874 but little else was done in that country except buffalo killing. Central depots were established in the best buffalo country, from whence hunting parties operated in all directions. Buildings were erected for the curing of meat, and corrals were built in which to heap up the immense piles of buffalo skins that accumulated. . . . At first the utmost wastefulness prevailed. Every one wanted to kill buffalo, and no one was willing to do the skinning and curing. Thousands upon thousands of buffalo were killed for their tongues alone, and never skinned. Thousands more were wounded by unskillful marksmen and wandered off to die and become a total loss. . . .

The slaughter which began in 1871 was prosecuted with great vigor and enterprise in 1872, and reached its height in 1873. By that time, the country fairly swarmed with hunters, each party putting forth its utmost efforts to destroy more buffaloes than its rivals. By that time experience had taught the value of thorough organization, and the butchering was done in a more business-like way. By a coincidence that proved fatal to the bison, it was just at the beginning of the slaughter that breech-loading, long-range rifles attained what was practically perfection. . . . Before the leaden hail of thousands of these deadly breech-loaders the buffaloes went down at the rate of several thousands daily during the hunting season. . . .

Of course the slaughter was greatest along the lines of the three great railways—the Kansas Pacific, the Atchison, Topeka and Santa Fe, and the Union Pacific, about in the order named. It reached its height in the season of 1873. During that year the Atchison, Topeka and Santa Fe Railroad carried out of the buffalo country 251,443 robes, 1,617,000 pounds of meat, and 2,743,100 pounds of bones. The end of the southern herd was then near at hand. Could the southern buffalo range have been roofed over at that time it would have made one vast charnelhouse. Putrefying carcasses, many of them with the hide still on, lay thickly scattered over thousands of square miles of the level prairie, poisoning the air and water and offending the sight. The remaining herds had become mere scattered bands, harried and driven hither and thither by the hunters, who now swarmed almost as thickly as the buffaloes. . . .

White hunters were not allowed to hunt the Indian Territory [defined at that time by the southern border of Kansas], and the southern boundary of the State of Kansas was picketed by them, and a herd no sooner crossed the line going north than it was destroyed. Every water-hole was guarded by a camp of hunters, and whenever a thirsty herd approached, it was promptly met by rifle-bullets.

During this entire period the slaughter of buffaloes was universal. The man who desired buffalo meat for food almost invariably killed five times as many animals as he could utilize, and after cutting from each victim its very choicest parts—the tongue alone, possibly, or perhaps the hump and hind quarters, one or the other, or both—fully four-fifths of the really edible portion of the carcass would be left to the wolves. It was no uncommon thing for a man to bring in two barrels of salted buffalo tongues, without another pound of meat or a solitary robe. The tongues were purchased at 25 cents each, and sold in the markets farther east at 50 cents. . . .

Judging from all accounts, it is making a safe estimate to say that probably no fewer than fifty thousand buffaloes have been killed for their tongues alone, and the most of these are undoubtedly chargeable against white men, who ought to have known better. . . .

As a general thing, . . . the professional sportsmen who went out to have a buffalo hunt for the excitement of the chase and the trophies it yielded, nearly always found the bison so easy a victim and one whose capture brought so little glory to the hunter, that the chase was voted very disappointing, and soon abandoned in favor of nobler game. In those days there was no more to boast of in killing a buffalo than in the assassination of a Texas steer.

It was, then, the hide-hunters, white and red, but especially white, who wiped out the great Southern herd in four short years. The prices received for hides varied considerably, according to circumstances, but for the green or undressed article it usually ranged from 50 cents for the skins of calves to $1.25 for those of adult animals in good condition. Such prices seem ridiculously small, but when it is remembered that, when buffaloes were plentiful, it was no uncommon thing for a hunter to kill from forty to sixty head in a day, it will readily be seen that the chance of making very handsome profits were sufficient to tempt hunters to make extraordinary exertions. Moreover, even when the buffaloes were nearly gone, the country was overrun with men who had nothing else to look to as a means of livelihood, and so, no matter whether the profits were great or small, so long as enough buffaloes remained to make it possible to get a living by their pursuit, they were hunted down with the most determined persistency and pertinacity. . . .

By the closing of the hunting season of 1875 the Great Southern herd had ceased to exist. As a body, it had been utterly annihilated. The main body of the survivors, numbering about ten thousand head, fled southwest, and dispersed through that great tract of wild, desolate, and inhospitable country stretching southward from the Cimarron country across the "Public Land Strip," the Pan-handle of Texas, and the Llano Estacado, or Staked Plain, to the Pecos River. A few small bands of stragglers maintained a precarious existence for a few years longer on the headwaters of the Republican River and in southwestern Nebraska near Ogalalla, where calves were caught alive as late as 1885. Wild buffaloes were seen in southwestern Kansas for the last time in 1886, and the two or three score of individuals still living in the Canadian River country of the Texas Pan-handle are the last wild survivors of the Great Southern herd.

The main body of the fugitives which survived the great slaughter of 1871–74 continued to attract hunters who were very "hard up," who pursued them, often at the risk of their own lives, even into the terrible Llano Estacado.

In 1880 buffalo hunting as a business ceased forever in the Southwest, and so far as can be ascertained, but one successful hunt for robes has been made in that region since that time. That occurred in the fall and winter of 1887, about 100 miles north of Tascosa, Texas. . . .

In 1886 about two hundred head survived, which number by the summer of 1887 had been reduced to one hundred, or less. In the hunting season of 1887–88 a ranchman named Lee Howard fitted out and led a strong party into the haunts of the survivors, and killed fifty-two of them. In May, 1888, Mr. C. J. Jones again visited this region for the purpose of capturing buffaloes alive. His party found, from first to last, thirty-seven buffaloes, of which they captured eighteen head, eleven adult cows and seven calves; the greatest feat ever accomplished in buffalo-hunting. It is highly probable that Mr. Jones and his men saw about all the buffaloes now living in the Pan-handle country, and it therefore seems quite certain that not over twenty-five individuals remain. These are so few, so remote, and so difficult to reach, it is to be hoped no one will consider them worth going after, and that they will be left to take care of themselves. . . .

Such was the end of the Great Southern herd. In 1871 it contained certainly no fewer than three million buffaloes; and by the beginning of 1875 its existence as a herd had utterly ceased, and nothing but scattered, fugitive bands remained.

*From William T. Hornaday, "The Extermination of the American Bison, with a Sketch of Its Discovery and Life History,"* Smithsonian Report, *1887 (Washington, 1889).*

MOLLIE

Mollie is one who settled the Middle West. She kept a journal. It begins in 1857, a week before she and her family, the Dorseys, leave Indianapolis for Nebraska Territory. It ends when she and her husband, "By" (for Byron) Sanford, settle permanently in a Denver suburb in 1866, after the Civil War.

She treated her journal with special care, believing it represented a vital period of her life. She preserved the little book for three decades after its close; in 1895 she recopied and edited it during a long convalescence, and willed it to her grandson. "While I do not *pose* as a heroine, I know that I have had peculiar trials and experiences, and perchance *something* I have said or done may be a help to my posterity, for trials and tribulations come to all." The University of Nebraska published Mollie's journal in 1959.

Only superficially does it chronicle Mollie's pioneering. Where Josiah Gregg looked, and looked, and recorded every remembered detail of his travels, Mollie listens: listens for the feelings within herself that might explain her own uniqueness. She senses the uniqueness, worries about it, hardly dares suggest even to her journal that it is there. Reading the journal, we know that it is.

"There is something fascinating in the thought of the opening up of a new life, a change so complete as this will be," Mollie writes while still in Indianapolis. The change is complete—the change in her way of life. Mollie changes hardly at all.

She was born to pioneer.

By train to St. Louis, by steamboat to Nebraska City. "We are called the 'happy family.' . . . Capt. Barrows said our family had made the trip more pleasant." Thus they disembark. While Mollie's father looks for a homestead the family makes do in a log house, "one small room and a three-cornered kitchen directly across the street." Mr. Dorsey secures the land, "160 acres . . . 30 miles from here, on the 'Little Nemaha.'" The Dorseys migrated early to Nebraska Territory; they will have a log cabin in "Hazel Dell," their homestead by the river. Later homesteaders will brave the open plains and learn to make houses of sod.

With the cabin built, the family settled in, Mr. Dorsey works in town, and much of the responsibility for the children and the home falls on Mollie, his oldest daughter. Mrs. Dorsey came too late to the frontier; she can barely cope. Sam, Mollie's brother, is bitten on the finger by a rattlesnake. Mollie and her mother successfully treat the poisoning and Sam improves. "Poor Mother was perfectly prostrated after the fright was over. She sometimes feels wicked to think she is so far away from all help with her family. But it cannot be helped now." Practical Mollie. "I am so thankful that I am endowed with nerve and strength of character to help take care of the family." She means it, without egotism. "Of course I suffer from excitement as much as any of the rest, but I seem to always know what to do, and have the nerve to do it."

The nerve to do it. Mollie's strength. It worries her. She associates it with a tendency to frivolity. Alone one evening, she is "full of good resolves tonight to *do* better and *be* better than ever before. . . .

I can sit here in the mellow evening's light, so still, so quiet, and commune with the angel spirits that sometimes come to me. They seem to tell me in soft, sweet whispers not to doubt, that this life, so full of cares and perplexities, is not all. There is a life beyond this vale of tears, and trials are but to prepare us for that life, where no sorrow comes.

I want to be *good*. I try to be, too, but some way, I fall into many grievous errors. Perhaps my light frivolous nature was given to me to help those differently constituted. I'll try to keep from going into any foolish excesses. May the sweet angels watch over me, and keep me in the memory of the vows I make tonight.

By "good," Mollie means "somber," serious, as she implies in this entry and in many others. She fears she laughs too much, finds humor in too many situations where others see none. A lawyer comes courting, his visit delayed by a brush with a rattlesnake. Describe it, Mollie asks—this is before Sam's accident, she has not seen a rattlesnake yet—and he falters before the word "tail." "'On the end of its tail, Mr. Mann,'" blurts Mollie. "'Yes!' he gasped, 'on the end of its t-a-i-l.'" "I might have said 'narrative,'" Mollie quips to her journal, "since he was too modest to use the more vulgar expression." But she was not.

One day the cow strays. The family "several days without milk," the boys having failed to locate the animal, Mollie decides to bring it home herself. "It occurred to me how much easier I could get through the tangled underbrush if I were a man! and without letting anyone know of my project, I slipped out into the back shed, and donned an old suit of Father's clothes, pulled on an old cap over my head and started on my pilgrimage."

She stumbles into a camp of men. "I could not scream nor faint as that feminine resource would certainly betray me, but thought 'discretion the better part of valor' and that 'he who runs away will live to fight another day,' and the way I travelled through those woods to the house was a caution."

Of her whirlwind entrance into the house: "It was very funny to all but Mother, who fears I am losing all the dignity I ever possessed."

Mollie contends with the ideal of somberness that her religion would impose upon her. She worries that she is not fragile, as ladies are supposed to be. She wonders at her nerve. But there is more yet to her, the source of all her best qualities. A passion, a sensuality? The words are too blunt, yet something of both, a warmth, a deep openness to others and especially to her men.

One suspects it early in the journal, when Mollie has not yet met By, when she is settling with her family at Hazel Dell. She senses presences others do not:

I have had a queer experience that I must relate. I had gone to bed one night, but could not sleep. My father was constantly in my mind. I seemed to feel that he was coming home, altho he had only left two days before, and his visits home only occur every two or three weeks, as it is so far, and he generally walks, as it is too expensive to hire a conveyance. So the idea of his coming directly back was too absurd for anything, but still the impression that he was coming, and would be with me soon was so strong that I finally got up and started a fire. It was not so cold, but I was shivering for some cause. Mother awakened and asked what on earth I was doing, and when I told her I was looking for Father, she thought I was losing my senses. Hardly aware of what I was doing, I ground and made some coffee. Mother was about to get up and shake me, when we heard the dogs bark, then voices, and soon Father was at the door. He was accompanied by Mr. Sanford and a Mr. Holden, whom they had brought out to get land.

"Mr. Holden is a spiritualist," Mollie concludes, "and readily accounted for it all by saying I was a 'medium.'" She is not ready for so glib an accounting. "I hope if I am to be controlled by any spirit, it will be for good"—that dutiful word again— "but I don't believe in spiritualism as I have heard it"—and in this disbelief the steady girl, the girl who almost always knows her own mind.

And the deeper Mollie, where is she? "Only I know I have strong impressions sometimes, something I hardly under-stand."

With these qualities Mollie contends, helping her family, working in town, being courted by Mr. Sanford for two years before she marries him (she refuses to marry until she is twenty-one). Only once in the entire journal does she have dif-ficulty with her steadiness, though she and By cross western Nebraska at a bad season, though they struggle at mining in the gold regions around Denver, and By goes to war, and they lose their firstborn son, and a flood destroys their house, and grasshoppers drive them off their homestead.

Only once, on the occasion of their overland journey to Den-ver. Mollie and By will travel with Mr. and Mrs. Clark. Mrs. Clark, "Minnie," proves almost more than Mollie can handle.

Trouble begins before the trip:

Mrs. Clark, who all along has been almost angelic, took a "tantrum" (her husband calls it). If this is a sample, I fear repetition of it. Then when we came home we invited her to stop at the house, but she preferred to stay in her tent, and said so many unkind things and made me feel so de-pendent, that we held a "council of war" and almost gave up going at all.

Minnie apologizes. The trip begins. *Friday, 17th:* "Minnie, Mrs. C., is improving." *Sunday, 26th:* "'Minnie' has not spoken to me today. We were alone in the tent all this afternoon, so I have had plenty of time for meditation." *Friday, June 1st:* "I walked 3 miles today and helped By drive the cattle, as 'Minnie' wanted Mr. Clark to ride with her. I wish I could walk all the way." *Monday week:* "Mr. Clark and Minnie had a quarrel. She threw herself into my arms and had hysterics. . . . I kept amiable, and succeeded in restoring peace, and tonight Clark is holding Minnie in his arms."

So it goes, to the end of the journey, when Mollie comments on it:

> This is my first experience at not getting along with anyone but I have heard that a trip like this would try one's friendship. Of course Mrs. Clark was only an acquaintance. I have always prided myself that I could adapt myself to *anyone,* but I have made a miserable failure. So many of the Nebraska people we have met have said, "I could have told you all about her disagreeableness," but I know she is not well. She makes me feel our dependence.

"She makes me feel our dependence"—it is Mollie's only insecurity.

We expect Mollie's journal to reveal the typical experience of women on the frontier. Instead it reveals—Mollie. She may have been unique among the women of her time, or she may not. She would be extraordinary today, or any day.

She was probably better educated and more intelligent than many of her contemporaries. She lived to a better standard; she and By's prospects were better. She stands out from the other women in her journal and in other journals; she exhibits a modern alertness and independence, joined, comfortably somehow, with the old deference to and dependence on men.

Her passion remained in her, its object removed from her father to her husband. It is her most outstanding quality, the one she depends on for her mysterious strength.

During the Civil War, after By has been in battle and she has waited tense days, with the other wives, to hear who has survived, the word comes back that only single men were lost. Soon after, some of the volunteers decide to return home:

> Today we have had news that a number of the 1st Regiment had resigned and were coming home, Col. Slough and Capt. Sanborn of our company. Now if our Capt. *has* resigned I fear By will not, and I am all used up. I have cried all day, and do not feel like writing. I feel like "one deserted."
>
> . . . Last night while brooding over my troubles I had one of my impressions that By was coming home. As the names of Sanborn and Sanford often get mixed, I hoped it had this time, and sure enough! this morning the advance guard arrived, and as Col. Slough shook hands with me he said, "Let me congratulate you, Madam. You will soon see your husband." And so my dream came true, and I am happy in the anticipation of meeting him tonight.

By is late, Mollie has gone to bed. She hears his footsteps:

> And now our life begins again, and if we have but little of this world's goods, I feel rich!! so rich!!

# 3 / The Farther Continent
of James Clyman

*IN MEDIAS RES:* FORT LARAMIE ON THE OREGON-California Trail, June 27, 1846, a day of reckoning. Francis Parkman was there that day, beginning the tour that he would chronicle in *The Oregon Trail*, the Harvard man come out west for health and curiosity, nobiliary, disdaining the common emigrants who halted at the Fort to tighten their iron tires and recruit their oxen, effusively admiring the stylish Sioux. The Sioux were there in the thousands, camped round Laramie at the invitation of the American Fur Company to trade, at truce with the emigrants, preparing war against the Crows. Lilburn Boggs was there, former governor of Missouri who had driven the Mormons from his state the previous year and thus indirectly set them on their exodus to Utah. Boggs had just been elected captain of a large party of emigrants. Wiliam H. "Owl" Russell, Kentucky colonel, had resigned the post the week before in a dispute over campsites, and drunk now, he cornered fastidious Parkman and belched indignation. The Boggs or Russell Party included businessmen and farmers from Illinois, emigrants from Germany and Ireland: George and Jacob Donner, James Frazier Reed, Lewis Keseberg, Patrick Breen. Soon George Donner would captain it. The Donner Party, it would come to be called.

Another traveler was there as well. He had just returned from California. For convenience he had accompanied a promoter and erstwhile author named Lansford W. Hastings along the way. Hastings had published a book popular among the emigrants—one of the Donners had a copy in his saddlebags—*The Emigrant's Guide to Oregon and California.* The traveler knew the quality of the book and the quality of the man, and meant to condemn them both. He passed Francis Parkman, this traveler, on the trail beyond Laramie, but laconically chose not to record the event in his journal. Parkman made the note, not much impressed: another greasy, trail-worn mountain man.

The traveler, James Clyman, camped among friends at Laramie. He enjoyed "a cup of excellent coffee . . . the first I had tasted since the early part of last winter." He talked with his friends "untill a late hour." Near the end of his life he reported the substance of that conversation. One of his friends at Laramie was James Frazier Reed. Reed and Clyman and Abraham Lincoln had fought together in Jacob Early's company in the Black Hawk War. Now Reed and the Donners were hot for California, Clyman cold. Reed at least was hot for Hastings' new Cut-Off, which the promoter had grandly sketched in *The Emigrant's Guide*:

The most direct route for the California emigrants, would be to leave the Oregon route, about two hundred miles east from Fort Hall; thence bearing west southwest, to the Salt lake; and thence continuing down to the bay of St. Francisco.

But Clyman had just endured that route in reverse, and so had Hastings, for the first time. Reed and Clyman argued. "Mr. Reed, while we were encamped at Laramie was enquiring about the route. I told him to 'take the regular wagon track, and never leave it—it is barely possible to get through if you follow it—and it may be impossible if you don't.' Reed replied, 'There is a nigher route, and it is of no use to take so much of a roundabout course.' I admitted the fact, but told him about the great desert and the roughness of the Sierras, and that a straight route might turn out to be impracticable."

It did, as we know, and led the Donner Party to disaster. To twenty days wasted cutting forty miles through the untracked Wasatch Mountains. To four days and five nights crossing the Great Salt Desert without water, the oxen scattered, the wagons abandoned, the cattle lost. To early Sierra snow, and snow-burial, and poor beef and boiled hides and finally, in extremity, the flesh of the dead. If Reed and the Donners had listened to Clyman they would have achieved California in mid-September, as the other emigrants did, roundabout course or not. Governor Boggs listened, and left the Party for Oregon the next day.

James Clyman has not been given his due. He was farmer's son, surveyor, mountain man, soldier, businessman, wanderer, captain of emigrants and finally farmer again; he saw much of the opening of the West, and contributed his considerable skills to it; he was present at the inception of more than one great event; but he was not celebrated nationally in his own lifetime, as Daniel Boone and Jim Bridger were, nor has he been accorded much more than passing references and footnotes since. He deserves better. His life was varied and dramatic: he was himself the westward-moving frontier. His journals are important historical documents. Most of all, his quality as a human being—Clyman's exceptional character—can enlarge our understanding of the intellectual and emotional range of the American pioneer. A nation at its best is at least a composite of its best men. Clyman was one of them.

James Clyman was born in Fauquier County, Virginia, on a farm his father leased from George Washington, in 1792. The retired first president often rode the boundaries of his lands, and Clyman may have met him on one of those rides. Clyman's father wanted more than a life-lease, even on Washington land. He wanted land of his own. He moved the family to Pennsylvania and then to Ohio when Clyman was fifteen.

Clyman himself struck out early. After a young manhood spent wandering the Middle West as a farmhand, woodchopper and provisioner, he hired on with a government surveyor in Indiana. In 1821, having learned the trade, he contracted with William S. Hamilton, Alexander Hamilton's son, to finish a course of surveying Hamilton had begun along the Vermilion River in Illinois. More surveying, along the Sangamon, led him to St. Louis early in 1823 to collect his pay. "My curiosity now being satisfied St Louis being a fine place for Spending money I did not leave immediately   not having spent all my funds I loitered about without employment." That is a foretaste of Clyman's humor, dry and ironic. He would need it in the years to come.

In St. Louis he caught the eye of Lieutenant-Governor William H. Ashley, who was preparing to make his fortune in the fur trade and "was engageing men for a Trip to the mouth of the Yellow Stone river." Ashley hired Clyman to assist in recruiting, searching out likely candidates "in grog Shops and other sinks of degredation." When the keel boats sailed from St. Louis up the Missouri, the Ashley Expedition was seventy strong. Jedediah Smith, the calm, devout mountain man, would meet it along the way. "A discription of our crew I cann<sup>t</sup> give," Clyman wrote later, "but Fallstafs Batallion was genteel in comparison." I am looking for mind here: Clyman had only "a smattering" of education, but its texts were the best of the day. His journals allude to Byron, Milton, Shakespeare and also to the Bible; the wryness was his own.

The expedition met setbacks up the Missouri, fighting off two villages of Arikaras—eleven wounded, fifteen dead. "The worst disaster in the history of the Western fur trade," Dale L. Morgan calls it in his *Jedediah Smith*. "Fallstafs Battallion" hastily retreated from the sandbar below the villages under the withering fire from the Arikara fusils, but Smith held his ground, Clyman fighting beside him. Forced at last to swim the river to escape, Clyman let go the rifle and pistols that weighed him down. Three Arikaras swam after him and chased him more than a mile across the prairie beyond the river before he found a hole to hide in on the other side of a hill. He made his way back to a point of land below the battle site and the boats, retreating downriver, luckily picked him up.

Ashley sent a party of men westward then on horseback, Clyman among them and William Sublette, captained by Jedediah Smith. In the Black Hills they surprised a grizzly and Clyman learned another trade. The grizzly attacked Smith, badly chewing his head and almost tearing off one ear. "None of us having any sugical Knowledge what was to be done one Said come take hold and he wuld say why not you so it went around I asked the Cap^t what was best he said . . . if you have a needle and thread git it out and sew up my wounds . . . I got a pair of scissors and cut off his hair and then began my first Job of dressing wounds . . . after stitching all the other wounds in the best way I was capabl and according to the captains directions the ear being the last I told him I could do nothing for his Eare O you must try to stich up some way or other said he then I put in my needle stiching it through and through and over and over laying the lacerated parts togather as nice as I could with my hands . . . this gave us a lisson on the charcter of the grissly Baare which we did not forget."

Smith survived the ordeal and the men rode on west, through "a grove of Petrifid timber," across shale and waste and prairie to the Powder River, among the Crows to trade horses, to the

Wind River Valley to winter in. Their rations were short. When they could find them they shot mountain sheep and antelope and buffalo. Caught out one night in a blizzard, Clyman and Sublette nearly froze. Clyman saved them; Sublette was too stiff with cold to move.

The party went without meat for four hungry days before the provisioning team of Clyman and Sublette tracked a buffalo and brought it down, "many of the men eating large slices raw." Their bellies full, they rode west for water across a high, cold plain at the southern terminus of the Wind River chain. The water they found—the men hacked away at it with tomahawks and pronounced it frozen to the bottom, but Clyman pulled a pistol and fired through the ice and "up came the water plentifull for man & horse"—flowed west. It was Pacific water: they had crossed the Continental Divide and rediscovered the South Pass, the broad road through the Rockies that would open the western continent to wagons, and thus to family emigration, and thus eventually to annexation to the United States. Jedediah Smith is properly awarded the credit for the find, since he was the party's captain. But Clyman earned it equally: he was there to see it, and his buffalo led the way.

He trapped beaver on the Green River that winter and spring, detached from Smith, and the next June, waiting at the Sweetwater to rendezvous, had to hide out from Indians for eleven days and lost contact with the other men and lost his horses too. He "began to get lonesome." With "plenty of Powder but only eleven bullets" he struck out for civilization—on foot, a distance of 600 miles over landscape he'd never seen before that he walked in eighty days. He lost most of his powder and bullets in another encounter with Indians. Down to one bullet, he retrieved the ball from the occasional buffalo he shot and chewed it round again. "I could not sleep and it got so damp I could not obtain fire and I had to swim several rivers." He realized he was wandering in circles and jerked himself straight. "I went on for some time with my head down when raising my eyes with great surprize I saw the stars & stripe waving over

Fort [Atkinson] I swoned emmediately . . . certainly no man ever enjoyed the sight of our flag better than I did." Thus Clyman's initiation into the wilderness. He would never again find himself at so great a loss.

As soon as he recovered, he turned around with Ashley and headed back west. His story for the next three years is a story of trapping and hunting and exploring, living out on his own a thousand miles from store and home. The year 1826 was a high point. Smith was looking for new beaver country, breaking trail on the north shore of the Great Salt Lake. The party could go no farther on horseback—there was nothing for the horses to eat. Clyman, Moses "Black" Harris, and probably Louis Vasquez and a man named Henry G. Fraeb, built bullboats—hide canoes—and paddled south along the lakeshore, riding high in that dead, bitter water. Its circumnavigation took them twenty-four days. They knew thirst and probably hunger. They might have seen dead trout and catfish floating, washed in from mountain streams. They may have seined for the brine shrimp that even today are harvested from the lake. Significantly, they found no outlet. Fanciful geographers had imagined that the salt lake was an arm of the Pacific—they had consistently underestimated the continent since Columbus's day—Clyman's circumnavigation proved that it was not. "This wide spread Sterility," Clyman called the lake and the land beyond it when he saw it again in a later year. He did not return to St. Louis until the fall of 1827, and not all was sterile on his four-year tour. He sold his last year's catch of beaver skins for $1,251, wealth enough to buy a substantial farm.

He bought the farm, in Illinois, and set up his two brothers to manage it. Farming was not yet to his taste. He fought in the Black Hawk War. "Abe Lincoln served in the same company with me," he told a biographer later with a wink. "We didn't think much then about his ever being President of the United States." He went into partnership with a man named Hiram Ross and laid claim to government land in wilderness Wisconsin, land on which Milwaukee was later founded. Too many people came on; he moved out. In November, 1835, traveling with a man named Burdett, looking for wilder land, he bought a canoe from an Indian woman whose son and husband weren't at home, intending to float a river. A mile-and-a-half float brought him to sundown, and he and Burdett stopped at a deserted cabin to camp. Clyman went out to collect wood while Burdett started a fire. The Indians, father and son, trailed them to retrieve the canoe and, says an old chronicle, "to avenge the death of a brother of the squaw, who was killed by a soldier at Fort Winnebago, two years before."

The son shot Burdett; Clyman came running back; the father raised his gun; Clyman took off dodging through the woods. Not all his luck was with him: one bullet broke his left arm below the elbow, and the son, taking up Clyman's own shotgun, managed to hit him in the thigh. "This last shot was not very effective," the chronicle goes on, "on account of the distance Clyman was from them by that time, for he could run like a deer; and the principal effect was to make him as he expressed it, 'as mad as hell' to be peppered in that way with his own gun, and he would have liked to return the compliment very much, but as *sauve qui peut* was the order of the day just then, he kept on, until the voices of his pursuers . . . were lost in the distance, when he hid under a fallen tree." At one point the Indians actually stood on the tree wondering where Clyman had gone.

He made his way at night, then, carrying his broken left arm in his right, on foot, through rain and unbroken wilderness, and continued the next day and the next night and part of one day more, to Milwaukee, a distance of fifty miles. For a time, in and around Milwaukee, no Indian felt safe in Clyman's presence. The chronicler: "And it might truthfully be said that the fear of him was upon every Indian then here, for not one of them would remain in the town twenty minutes after they got sight of him. A whole regiment of soldiers could not have inspired them with a greater desire for the soltitude of the wilderness, than did the presence of this one man."

An interlude then to wandering: Clyman settled down. He built a sawmill in Wisconsin in 1836 with Hiram Ross, near what is now Wauwatosa, and he remained in business there until at least 1841. This is the man at 48, in 1840: look at him now: he has yet to make, twice more, the great emigration: "He was nearly or quite six feet tall," remembered an acquaintance, "erect and straight of rather sparse build though well formed and firm in person with a firm elastic tread, deliberate in all his movements, of a sandy complexion, high and very slightly receding forehead neither very broad nor very narrow, rather a thin elongated face, rather a small mouth slightly inclined to pucker, good teeth but like his person rather long and narrow." Another acquaintance thought he looked like Washington, the Washington of "Lot Trumbull's portrait at Yale College."

"A hoosier gentleman," another said. And another—men didn't forget him—"His manner very quiet, modest, voice pleasant and low very amiable and agreeable person." Hiram Ross, his sawmill partner: "Clyman was over six feet high rather slender his personal appearance was very pleasant his trait of character was good he was a styraight forward and up right man." In 1835, when his old friend Dan Beckwith died, "armed with pick and shovel," Clyman "wended down to the Old Williams Burying Ground and dug a grave in the frozen soil. There were other willing hands to help, but Jim, with the soul of a poet, wanted in this way to pay last tribute to his friend."

He had endurance, and patience, and a mind. Running the sawmill, whiling away his time, Ross outside on a cold winter afternoon building a sleigh, he filled the margins of a ledger with philosophical musings and wry observations:

Two things Infinite Time and space   Two things more appear to be attached to the above infinity (wiz) Matter and number   Matter appears to prevade the infinity of space and number attempts to define quantity of matter as well as to give bounds to space—which continually Expands before matter and number—and all human speculation is here bounden in matter and number leaving space at least almost completely untouched

About the year 650 from the fowning of Rome the difficulties commenced between Marius and Sylla from which I date the commencement of the decline of the Roman commonwealth.

of all People it seems to me those are the most tiresome who never convers on any subject but their misfortunes.

= Put on a damp night cap & then relapse
He thought he would have died he was so bad
His Peevish Hearers allmost wish he had

[Winter] appears to be the night the time of sleep and rest for the vegetable kingdom   leafless and frozen they are now taking their rest and matureing the subsistance thy recieved during the last summer   it appears as if the revolution of the earth around the sun was the day & night for the vegetable as is the earth's revolution on its own axis [for the animal]

We may comprehend the globe we inhabit pretty fully and even the sollar System but a million of such systems becomes incomprehensible although even a million such Systems may fall verry short of the quantity of matter in existance throughout the universal Kingdom

More in the ledger on hibernation and the extirpation of animals by man and the velocity of light and the possibility of a finite universe, the only such speculations Clyman found time to record; hereafter he turns his attention to the land, and to his countrymen.

In the spring of 1844, troubled by a lingering cough, he journeyed down into Arkansas and up to Independence. There he remembered his wilderness health, like many another prairie traveler. The trains were forming. He signed on, for Oregon, and resolved to keep a journal day by day.

Fifty-two, he noticed the ladies now: "I took my rifle and walked out in the deep ravin to guard a Beautifull covey of young Ladies & misses while they gathered wild currants & choke chirries which grow in great perfusion in this region and of the finerst kind." He noticed the constriction of the buffalo from their former range: "this vally [Bear River Valley above the Great Salt Lake] is the early Rendevous of the mountain Trappers & hunters But in the last 7 or 8 years the Buffaloe have entirely left this country & are now seldom seen west of the Sweet water." When travelers caught up with the train with news from civilization he exercised his ironic humor: "As it appears there has been a great Troubling & Striving of the eliments the mountain having at last brot forth J.K. Polk Capᵗ Tyler & the invincible Henry Clay as candidates for the Presidency. go it Clay. Just whigs enough in camp to take the curse off." Humor in camp as well when emigrants following the trail for the first time disagreed with his old friend Black Harris: "our pilot Mr Harrisˢ 22 years experiance and advice is perfectly useless in this age of improvement when human intelect not only strides but actually Jumps & flies into conclusions." And somewhere along the way, for his own amusement or Harris's, he penned the old mountain man's epitaph:

> Here lies the bones of old Black Harris
> who often traveled beyond the far west
> and for the freedom of Equal rights
> he crossed the snowy mountin Hights

was free and easy kind of soul
Especially with a Belly full.

Without serious incident the train trudged on to Oregon.
Clyman, as so rarely in his life, was bored. "Our selves & animals are becomeing tired of travel," he noted somewhere west
of Fort Boise. He hadn't even bothered to visit the fort. He studied rock and flora and fauna, recorded his doubt of a "M^r. Es-
py^s" theory that the smoke from prairie fires, which had thick-
ened the air for days, could produce rain—it hadn't rained in a
month—and finally detached himself from the interminable
train with a small party of men and rode ahead to the valley of
the Willamette.

Oregon charmed him. The journal he kept of his time there
alternates between bursts of eloquent observation and long
weeks, busy weeks apparently, of fragmentary weather reports.
Here was something new, bountiful land and as yet few settlers. His journals elaborated into consciously composed accounts of the country and long letters home, as if he had determined to add authorship to his kit of skills. Waterfowl along
the Willamette, for example:

For miles the air seemed to be darkened with the emmenc
flights that arose as I proceeded up the vally the morning
being still thier nois was tumultuous and grand the hoarse
shrieks of the Heron intermingled with the Symphonic
Swan the fine treble of the Brant answered by the strong
Bass of the goose with ennumerable shreeking and Quack-
ing of the large and Smaller duck tribe filled every evenue
of Surrounding space with nois and reminded one of Some
aerial battle as discribed by Milton and all though I had
been on the grand pass of waterfowl on the Illinois River it
will not begin to bear a comparison with this thier being
probably Half a Million in sight at one time and all apparently Screaming & Screeching at once

Or this astute observation, in a letter to Hiram Ross, of his Oregon compatriots:

> I never saw a more discontented community, owing principally to natural disposition. Nearly all, like myself, having been of a roving discontented character before leaving their eastern homes. The long tiresome trip from the States, has taught them what they are capable of performing and enduring. They talk of removing to the Islands, California, Chili, and other parts of South America with as much composure as you in Wisconsin talk of removing to Indiana or Michigan.

But if he had been roving and discontented, he was now clearly thinking about marriage and a home, this wanderer of fifty-two. From Oregon on, his journals note landscape not as geology or cartography but for the lie of it, its probable fertility and its prospects. And the ladies turn up frequently, as before this emigration they have never done:

> And I must say that female beauty is not exclusively confined to any particular region or country for here too may be seen the fairy form the dark Eye and drk hair so beautifully described by Byron displayed in the person [of] Miss Smith.

Clyman remained in Oregon until late May, 1845, when he packed up with a party of men planning to work their way down the coast to California. He was entrusted with a constabular duty, to carry letters from Elijah White, the United States' Indian subagent in Oregon, to Thomas Larkin, the U.S. Consul in California, inquiring about the murder of a Wallawalla chieftain's son in a dispute at Sutter's Fort. It was another of Clyman's brushes with history. As Charles L. Camp, the editor of Clyman's journals, explains: "White requested that [the murderer], if guilty, should be brought to trial, but nothing came of the investigation which followed. The unavenged murder is said to have been one of the causes of the Whitman massacre and disastrous Indian wars in the Northwest." The reason why the murder of an Indian, even a chieftain's son, went un-avenged is obvious from Clyman's record of the journey down from Oregon City. Some of the men in his party, he noted with disgust, routinely shot Indians along the way. Clyman was not himself a bigot or a hater, and kept his peace except when per-sonally wronged. Not surprisingly, then, Sutter's method of feeding his Indian workers appalled him:

> The Cap$^t$ keeps 600 or 800 Indians in a complete state of Slavery and as I had the mortification of seeing them dine I may give a short description 10 or 15 Troughs 3 or 4 feet long were brought out of the cook room and seated in the Broiling sun all the Labourers grate and small ran to the troughs like so many pigs and feed themselves with their hands as long as the troughs contain even a moisture

He encountered a California similar in some ways to California today, remarking on the general nakedness of its natives in the mild climate, recording an earthquake, praising the "Beautifull and picturesque" land. Something was stirring in him, some-thing that made him judge California's occupants—the Span-ish from Mexico, the Indians, his fellow foreigners from the States—more harshly than had been his wont when he was only a rover passing through. "The Callifornians are a proud Lazy indolent people doing nothing but ride after herds or from place to place without any apparent object The Indians or aboriginees do all the drudgery and labour and are kept in a state of Slavery. . . . The californian Plough is a curiosity in agra-culture. . . . Harrow no such thing known. . . . Several kinds of red pepper are grown in greate abundance and enter largely into the californian cookery so much so as to nearly strangle a for-igner. . . . The forigners which have found their way to this country are mostly a poor discontented set of inhabitants and but little education hunting for a place as they [want] to live easy only a few of them have obtained land and commenced farming."

In this discontented mood—perhaps discontented with himself—Clyman finished up his business, which included a visit to Monterey and San Francisco and a bear hunt, and wrote to Captain John Charles Frémont proposing to assemble an armed party for a return to the States. Frémont, the Pathfinder, would have none of it. Ostensibly in California to explore, he intended to stay on and stir up revolution; California would join itself to the States in the space of one more year.

If not Frémont, then Lansford Hastings, a promoter who seems to have dreamed of establishing a republic in California with himself at its head and who was returning to the vicinity of Fort Laramie with 150 horses and a whirlwind of bad advice. Clyman joined Hastings at his camp on Bear Creek, above Johnson's Ranch in the foothills of the Sierra, on April 16, 1846, the same day the Donners and the Reeds left Springfield, Illinois, for Independence.

Crossing the Sierra Nevada eastward in early spring was hard. It would be deadly to the Donners going the other way. Clyman recorded the descent from what would be called the Donner Pass with grim attention:

here we commenced the desent over step Pricipices rough granite Rock covered in many places through the chasms with snow 15 or 20 feet deep and luckily for us we lost no horses allthough we had to force them down several perpendicular cliffs afer about 3 hours unpacking and repacking we succeeded in clearing the steepest pitches of the whole length of which is not one mile

you may imagine that we felt a happy relief to find ourselves on bear ground onc more which we found at the head of truckys [later Donner] lake a small sheet of water about two miles in length and half a mile wide the N hill

sides being intirely clear of snow but verry little green vegitation   made six miles and encamped at the foot of the
Lake

That camp would become the major Donner camp; here un-
knowingly Clyman sets the stage.

Beyond Truckee Meadows, now Reno, Clyman lost his dog
to a boiling spring—the thirsty dog, a water spaniel that had
been with him since Wisconsin, jumped into the pool and
"scalded himself allmost insantly to death"—and the loss further depressed him. He rode on through barrenness to the
north fork of the Humboldt River, where wisdom decreed the
party turn north but Hastings insisted they head east toward
the Great Salt Lake. They did, to Pilot Peak, and looking eastward saw the terrible desert of salt that they would have to
cross. "This is the [most] desolate country perhaps on the
whole globe there not being one spear of vegitation and of
course no kind of animal can subsist and it is not yet asser-
tained to what extent this immince salt and sand plain can be
south of where we [are]." That day they traveled forty miles,
the next day fourteen, the next day twenty. They succeeded in
the crossing because they had horses. The Donner Party was
slowed by oxen and wagons, and nearly failed. Clyman's advice
to Reed had teeth. Onward to Laramie, where he delivered it,
and we are back where we began.

Clyman's mood by now, after Laramie, is almost melancholy.
His temperament was as equitable across the length of his life
as any man who ever kept a journal, but what he saw on his
long odyssey to Oregon and California and back again has left
him wondering: wondering about his countrymen, wondering
implicitly about himself. The West is no longer wilderness,
and he is no longer young.

So, on the 4th of July, having crossed the south fork of the
Platte River the day before, approaching Pawnee territory, he
swings ambivalently between joy and depression and expresses
a rare insecurity:

4 The sun arose in his usual majestic splendor  no firing of cannon was heard  no flags waving to the early morning Breeze  Nothing no nothing heard but the occasional howl of the wolf or the hoarse croak of the raven  nothing seen But the green wide spread Prarie and the shallow wide spread river roling its turbed muddy waters far to the East the only relief is the on rising ground occasionally doted with a few stragling male Buffaloe and one Lonely Junt of a cotton wood Tree some miles down the stream the only occupant of a small low Island (not much variety)  O my country and my Country men  the rich smiling surface of one and the gladsome Shouts of the other  Here we are 8 men 2 women and one boy this day entering into an enimies country who if posible will Butcher every individual or at least strip us of evey means of comfort or convenience and leave us to make our tiresome way to relief and this immediatly on your frontier and under the eye of a strong Militay post

Or is he remembering that long sore stumble from the Sweetwater two decades before? Or is he now, finally, after all his wandering, in the fullness of his years, experiencing a loneliness that in wandering he never felt?

His journal is almost ended. He gives us two more clues. On the 15th, on the east bank of the Blue River in what is now north central Kansas, he encounters the grave of James Reed's mother-in-law and probes to the bone the meaning of the inexorable western advance. It is Clyman at his finest:

This stream affords some rich vallies of cultivateable land and the Bluffs are made of a fine lime rock with some good timber and numerous springs of clear cool water  here I observed the grave of Mrs. Sarak Keys ageagd 70 yares who had departed this life in may last  at her feet stands the stone that gives us this information  This stone shews us that all ages and all sects are found to undertake this long

tedious and even dangerous Journy for some unknown
object never to be realized even by those the most fortu-
nate and why because the human mind can never be
satisfied never at rest allways on the strech for something
new some strange novelty

Not climate or land, not patriotism or destiny but a hunger for
knowledge never satisfied, knowledge even of strange novelty,
the insatiable human mind always on the stretch: Clyman's
autobiography compressed into a narrow roiling space and the
biography of his compatriots and his countrymen. His distinction was to perceive, to perceive calmly and with great thor-
oughness, and to come back and guide. Exploring an unex-
plored land is an act of creation, more rarely given and more
interior, more profound, than all the artistic creations of the
world. By exploration the land is made human, fit for habita-
tion, its alienage drained. The explorer records its contours
with an intimate stylus of muscle and nerve. He walks calmly
through terror—for the unknown object is terrifying—and al-
leviates it, and families follow after to settle. His is an ecstasy—first knowledge—Clyman's was an ecstasy kept at ge-
nial peace.

If he was melancholy at Sarah Keyes's grave, he was melancholy because he knew the continent was bridged and his years
of exploration were over. That is the second clue. He has found
his object, and in the next to the last entry in his journal, back
in Independence, perhaps not yet aware of the decision himself,
he notes it down: "the [weather] was verry warm and suffocating and in this particular you find a greate difference in the heat
of the summer   in California you find it cool and pleasant in
the shade while here you find [it] hot and suffocating in [the]
coolest place you can find." He is ready for cool and pleasant
California now, ready at fifty-four to settle down.

The following year, Clyman closed out his land and business
interests in Wisconsin and Illinois, and in 1848 he moved to
California. He guided a large family there, the McCombs of

Indiana. He may have panned some gold. He didn't linger at the mines. He bought land in the Napa Valley and took up farming near the sea and married, after due courtship, a small, pert woman of twenty-seven years, Hannah McCombs.

His later years were peaceful, sweet and serene despite the loss of four of his five children to scarlet fever. In hours free of farming—he nurtured a trim and prosperous farm—he wrote verse, homely verse that could soar to sudden strength. More than once he celebrated the virtue of simplicity:

> Now while hot roles surround you[r] plate
> Dont envy either wealth or state. . . .

He celebrated his home, his neighbor's garden, the seasons and their burden of death and renewal:

> But I mourn not for the flowers
> I mourn not for the grain
> I mourn not for the birds for they will come again
> The spring and the summer again will return
> Therefor for these I seace to mourn
> I have seen manhood both active and strong
> In the midst of ambition to death they were drawn . . .
> For the strength and the beauty of manhood I mourn. . . .

He kept his humor, even in "Hard Times":

> Live while you live This is my text
> Then feast to day, then *starve* the next . . .
> And if we live on bread alone
> We'll take the world without a groan
> But if our bread should chance to fail
> We'll Turn out Tramps or go to Jail.

He preserved a lyricism and a love of life that was, I think, the deep current of his years:

Decoration Day 1881

Strew flowers oer the heros head
Who for your country fought & bled
He fought for eaqul rights for all
Let raining flowers oer him fall
He died your countrys life to save
Strew flowers oer the heroes grave

He died that year, 1881, peacefully. His wife and daughter survived him, but only by repute his name. His journals were finally edited, brilliantly, by Charles L. Camp and published in a limited edition in 1928, 330 copies, and 1,450 copies in a second limited edition in 1960.

"Not that he settled Kentucky or made a path to the west," writes William Carlos Williams of Daniel Boone in *In the American Grain*, ". . . but because of a descent to the ground of his desire was Boone's life important and does it remain still loaded with power—power to strengthen every form of energy that would be voluptuous, passionate, possessive in that place which he opened. . . . Filled with the wild beauty of the New World to overbrimming so long as he had what he desired, to bathe in, to explore always more deeply, to see, to feel, to touch—his instincts were contented." James Clyman explored a farther continent, "the rich smiling surface," as voluptuously as Boone a nearer. It grew up into him; he fitted it; with others he gave it to us; sensuously contented he gave it back himself. *Strew flowers oer the heroes grave.*

# 4 / Fulton, Missouri: Signs and Wonders

EVERY PEOPLE DESERVES ITS GODS, AND EVERY COMMU-
nity deserves its achievements of fame and notoriety. The central Missouri town of Fulton, with a state mental hospital to
the east, a Presbyterian men's college to the west, a defunct
railroad terminal north and an A&W Root Beer stand south,
has achieved much. It is the "capital" of the Kingdom of Callaway, a sovereign state created momentarily during the Civil
War in the blundered truce agreement of a Union general. It
served as the Gothic source of Henry Bellamann's 1940 best-
selling novel *Kings Row*, a book subsequently converted into a
successful Hollywood movie starring Ronald Reagan. In 1946

59

Winston Churchill delivered at Fulton's Westminster College his speech "Sinews of Peace," in which he authorized, *ex cathedra* as it were, recognition of the "Iron Curtain." More recently, Westminster memorialized Churchill's visit by reconstructing on its campus an honest-to-Goshen eighteenth-century Christopher Wren chapel transported over stone by stone from London. It is a beautiful building, but, gods being gods, it looks totally out of place in Fulton.

Far from least in Fulton's Hall of Fame is Jesse Ernest "Outlaw" Howard, a spry octogenarian living out his final years among the ragweed and thorn trees up on Old Jeff City Hill, in the southwest corner of town.

Howard paints signs. The signs have messages on them which he composed himself, with narrow means that include a sixth-grade education, an old Webster's Dictionary, two daily newspapers, and a King James Bible. The messages are often cantankerous, usually argumentative, sometimes witty, occasionally wide with awe. They have not endeared Howard to Fulton. His seemingly pleasant retirement hobby has forced him to confront, painfully, the aesthetic, psychological, technical, and social realities of print culture. The price of that confrontation has been loneliness and some fear, but triumph too. Howard is behind the times by urban standards—we city folks are all postliterate, after a fashion—but he is a pioneer among his country neighbors.

He is, in fact, the Grandma Moses of print culture. Up on Hell's 20 Acres and the Suburbs of Hell, his two spreads on either side of Old Jeff City Road, you can see where it all began, all that daring, single-minded reduction of the rich evanescence of speech to the hard discrete permanence of print which made modern civilization and which now burdens it to distraction. And down in Fulton, so slowly do values change there, asking people about Jesse Howard means finding out what our forebears thought of print culture in the American heartland a hundred years ago. Howard is Fulton's pariah, a condition which charges his signs with an understandable bitterness:

SOME OF THESE FULTONITES
HAD BETTER TAKE A COURSE IN CIVILATION

Civilization, that is, or perhaps civilization and revelation together, an appropriate slip of the brush for a religious man.

HE NO LONGER POSTS HIS BEST SIGNS AT ROADSIDE. A spacious display of older signs can still be seen there, but his best work is stored away in thirteen handmade, locked sheds scattered around the acreage. Howard stopped posting signs because country crackers and Westminster fraternity pledges stole them as fast as he could nail them up. Someone threw a cherry bomb against the screen of his bedroom window one night when he was spying out a raid, making him fear for his eyes. A group of local purists even circulated a petition to have him committed to the state mental hospital, a place some Fultonians, Howard included, still call the State Lunatic Asylum, and fear accordingly. The petition failed, because his neighbors refused to sign it, but it made Jesse skittish and got him off on a quest by Greyhound to Washington, D.C., to see his representative and ask for protection, a quest that ended shamefully when the Secret Service picked him up in the Capitol Building, put him in a wheelchair, delivered him back to the bus station and told him to go home. He did, and despite numerous incidents of theft and harassment, has continued the work that sets Washington and Fulton and even his own family against him.

"I ain't never got anywhere with any of this," he says with a sweep of a thick hand. "They just keep a-going right on by. Right on by. I don't understand it. Never got anywhere. Got no cooperation a-tall."

It is a reasonable lament, but it expects too much of his community. The surprise of Outlaw Howard is that he got as far as he got in so short a time. Born in 1885, he didn't begin making signs until about 1953, after a long life as an itinerant worker, farmhand, and odd-job man. Since 1953 he has conceived and constructed hundreds of signs, painted several primitive paintings, invented his own version of manuscript illumination, drafted a long, entertaining chapter of nostalgic autobiography, and written fragments of a tragicomic epic about an eleven-year-old boy named Little Joe Cooper who hauls out his shotgun to defend his dog Tippie from the legalisms of a school principal and the dog pound. Howard may have accomplished more than this. He mentions a manuscript about John F. Kennedy, and other notebooks he has kept, but even in a week of visits to what he calls Sorehead Hill you can't see all his works.

"Jesse is only interested in making some money," a local official told me from the depths of a dark office, a Great Dane snoring at his feet. Of course a man who must live on his wife's Social Security check is interested in money. Howard has little idea of its value. He still talks about plush times when he was making a dollar and a half a day. "I have a reputation that I am proud of," he wrote me several years ago. "I never sassed my father, or mother in my whole lifetime. I never was drunk. I never shot dice. I never played a gambling card for money. Don't know one card from another. Did use tobacco. But quit." Of what use is money to a man with no vices?

Jesse Howard hasn't, to Fulton's way of thinking, the credentials to be an artist. He must therefore be a promoter, or simply a madman. His "registry books" are full of the signatures of people from out of town who have stopped by to see his work. Their interest is something Fulton doesn't understand, and assumes to be patronizing. Thus Howard is a victim of culture shock. Locals know he emerged from the same rural past as they, a way of life founded on a reserved, indirect verbal tradition. The public candor of his signs violates that reserve.

Howard's signs are a medium of their own, combining the functions of newspaper headline, billboard, and town crier's ban. They link him with the literate world he discovers in newspapers and books, and because he is a primitive on the edge of that world, he believes the linkage magical. Speech requires feedback; so must print, goes Howard's logic. If public figures speak to him through the St. Louis *Post-Dispatch* and the Fulton *Sun-Gazette*, then he can speak to them in turn through his signs:

---

MR. HARRY TRUEMAN YOU AND YOUR FRIEND MR. ADLAI STEVENSON ARE GREAT GLOBE TROTTERS. NOW I SUGGEST THAT YOU RACE HORSERS GET YOUR TROTTING HARNESS ON: AND TROTT TO EGYPT. AND MEET A MAN OVER THERE BY THE NAME OF NASSER. GO TO NEW YORK AND PICK UP MR. CELLER. MAYBE THE EGYPTIANS WILL GIVE A GOOD PRICE FOR

---

"Wonder what ole Harry Truman would say if he could see that sign," Howard said to me when he brought it out of a storage shed. Truman, a country boy himself, would probably be pleased. Deep down we are all equal. Most of the people whose names turn up on Howard's signs are pleased when they see one.

With few exceptions, Howard confines his sign-writing to public discussion. He reserves his private life for his notebooks unless a personal incident illustrates a public event:

---

A MAN STOPPED AND WAS READING MY SIGNS. I ASKED HIM IN AND TO SIGN MY REGESTRY BOOK, WHICH HE DID, AND MAKE SOME REMARK ABOUT MY WORK, WHICH HE DID: HE SAID KEEP ON GIVEING THEM HELL" THEY = HAVE = IT = COMING.

---

> LAW, AND COURT SHOULD BE CHOSEN FROM BOTH MEN AND WOMEN, WHO ARE HONEST. TRUTHFUL. HONOURABLE. AND LAST, BUT NOT LEAST, LOYALTY. YES, LOYAL TO YOUR FELLOW-MEN. BOTH, WHITE AND BLACK. YES, AND WHAT ABOUT BEING LOYAL TO OUR COUNTRY? AMERICA, THE NOBLE FREE AND AT ONE TIME THE GREATEST NATION IN THE WORLD.
> BY JESSE HOWARD.

> I MIGHT BE A TOUGH OLD GUY. I NEVER PUT ON A UNIFORM, GUN AND A STAR, AND THEN GO OUT & BEAT A WOMAN UNTIL SHE LOST HER BABY. I NEVER PAID OUT $500 TO BE THROWN IN JAIL FOR. YET THEY THROWED ME IN ANY WAY. IF THEY CANNOT GET ANYTHING ON YOU THEY WILL FRAME IT. YOU DON'T KNOW THESE CROOKS LIKE I DO. I NEVER HAVE BEEN SUED FOR $30,000 HOMEBREKING. I NEVER MURDERED ANYBODY FOR MONEY OR DOPE. NEVER BURNED A NEGRO.

Yet among the jeremiads, occasional signs reveal his natural wit and lyricism:

> WHAT EVER BECAME OF JOHN THE BAPTIST'S HEAD?

> IN GOD WE TRUST
> GOD BLESS THE OWL THAT PICKED THE FOWL
> AND LEFT THE BONES FOR OLD MAN HOWARD.

> SOME PEOPLE SAY THERE IS NO GOD, ANSWER THIS ONE? THE COW, BLACK IN COLOR, THE FOOD SHE EATS IS GREEN GRASS, THE MILK SHE GIVES IS SNOW WHITE, THE MILK AFTER IT IS CHURNED INTO BUTTER IS AS YELLOW AS GOLD, AND WHEN EATEN AS A FOOD IT IS GREAT NOURISHMENT FOR THE BODY. AND SOUL. BY JESSE HOWARD. THE MAN WITH SIGNS AND WONDERS.

And something beyond lyricism informs this Christmas sign,
a heavy plank sawn in the shape of a star and wreathed with a
string of colored lights:

A GREAT
STAR FROM HEAVEN BURN-
ING AS IT WERE A LAMP,
AND THE NAME OF THE
STAR IS CALLED WORMWOOD.
MANY MEN HAVE DIED BECAUSE OF
THE BITTER WATERS OF WORMWOOD.
SEE REVELATIONS: A GREAT WON-
DER IN HEAVEN A WOMAN
AND UPON HER HEAD A
CROWN OF 12 STARS.

*Kings Row*, Henry Bellamann's 1940 novel, shocked Fulton
as Jesse Howard's signs shock it, but flattered the town as well.
Bellamann had credentials. "A lot of people talked about that
book," one of Fulton's older citizens told me. "They thought
they found themselves in it—they *hoped* they found themselves in it. Bellamann was a local boy, and a genius. Writing
wasn't his real field. He was a musician. Director at Juilliard,
professor at Vassar. His brother still lives here. He's a house
painter, though he's old and sick now."

Henry Bellamann published five novels during his lifetime;
his wife completed and published a sixth for him after his
death. Two were set in Fulton. "The present volume," writes
Mrs. Bellamann in her preface to the posthumous *Parris
Mitchell of Kings Row*, "departs somewhat from its original
purpose; it was to have been the psychoanalysis of the town as
viewed and understood by Dr. Mitchell." Dr. Mitchell is Bellamann's alter ego in both Fulton novels, a young genius who
grows up in turn-of-the-century Kings Row, leaves it for psy-
chiatric training in Vienna, and returns to do his part in saving

the town from itself. There is much that needs saving: a mad-scientist doctor who sleeps with his beautiful daughter, another doctor who is a sadistic religious fanatic and delights in practicing surgery without anesthesia on patients he believes have sinned, a latent-homosexual poet, a respected banker who absconds with half the town's savings, an evil politician, a prominent family with Negro blood. Bellamann divides good and evil as dogmatically as a Fulton preacher divides them on Sunday morning, and only his torrential, operatic sense of time and transformation saves him. A cracker chorus of feed-store loafers periodically sums up the action in *Kings Row*, after which noble young Parris Mitchell moves on to confront the next outrage. Hearty stuff, but tasting of pasteboard, like a store-bought pie.

*Kings Row* stimulated Jesse Howard's sign work. He owns a copy of Bellamann's novel, one of his few books. "*Kings Row*— that was wrote out in Fulton. We all know of this. You remember readin about a man got his leg cut off in a railroad accident? Well, the poor man's dead and gone now, but I have his peg leg."

THIS LEGG MADE OF WOOD IS THE REMAINS OF THE MAN WHO HELPED TO WRITE THE BOOK, KINGS ROE. AND THE MAN, WHO LOST HIS LEGG IN A RAILROAD ACCIDENT, POOR OLD DOLL, WAS KICKED FROM PILLAR TO POST. I HAVE HAD MANY CONVERSATIONS WITH THIS MAN. THE LAST TIME I HEARD, THEY HAD HAULED THE MAN TO THE S.L.A. AND HE DIED THERE.

S.L.A. means State Lunatic Asylum. The man's name, according to Howard, was Dahl Nevins—"Drake McHugh" in *Kings Row*.*

"He's got a brother here, livin here," says Jesse, referring

---

*Ronald Reagan's role, during which he wakes up to find his legs missing and shouts the line that serves as the title of his autobiography: *Whatever Became of the Rest of Me?*

again to Bellamann. "I didn't know of the book. That's one of the things that kinda started me with this"—gesturing toward his signs. "I didn't know there was such a book wrote. People begun to tell me that they'd read *Kings Row*—that was one reason why I started this thing out. Course you wouldn't recognize the places they speak of in *Kings Row*. And it's so true—it just hits em. Now, all these old kings, what lived on Kings Row at the time, they're dead. But there's another bunch already come on."

The American Middle West is still a region of small towns, towns permanently small. They do not grow; they only imperceptibly decline. "The town could lose more and more of its blood," Parris Mitchell muses in *Kings Row*, "until it became as empty and dry as a locust shell. So many things, people—individuals and organizations—retain their form long after life itself has withdrawn." Fulton is like that. It was a town of kings once, if proud and energetic and ambitious men are kings in America. Despite Howard's awe of the town's moneyed leaders, Fulton's kings are no more.

Daniel Boone, in 1802, camped on what would become the townsite of Fulton. The first railroad west of the Mississippi was built early in the 1800s through the county of which Fulton is the seat. Lewis and Clark trekked across the southern edge of the county, along the Missouri River. The region came alive in the second decade of the nineteenth century when settlers arrived in considerable numbers from Virginia and Kentucky:

> The site of Fulton was selected by James Moss and James McClellan of Boone County, and James Talbert of Montgomery County, who were appointed commissioners for that purpose by the [Missouri] General Assembly. They located the town July 29, 1825, and named it Volney after the French philosopher. The County Court on the first day of August following changed the name to Fulton in honor of Robert Fulton, inventor of the steamboat. . . .

The original town contained 147 lots, many of which sold for $1.00 apiece. The highest price paid was $56.00, and the proceeds from the sale of the lots all together amounted to $1,946.18. The first lots were sold September 5, 1825. Edward G. Berry, who died in 1905 at the age of 97 years, carried a chain for the surveyor who laid out the town of Fulton. Mr. Berry was a son of Richard Berry of Kentucky who signed the bond of Thomas Lincoln when he was married to Nancy Hanks, mother of Abraham Lincoln.

This from a pamphlet, *The Kingdom of Callaway*, by local judge and sometime historian Hugh P. Williamson.

Callaway County sympathized with the South during the Civil War. After one long battle, Union General John B. Henderson negotiated a treaty with Confederate Colonel Jefferson F. Jones of Callaway, "the terms of which," says Williamson, "were that General Henderson, purporting to speak for the United States of America, agreed not to invade Callaway County, and Colonel Jones, acting for Callaway County, agreed not to invade the United States of America. After this treaty, General Henderson retired with his troops. Callaway County, having thus dealt as an absolute equal with a sovereign power, became known as the Kingdom of Callaway, a designation which it has proudly borne and doubtless will for all time to come."

Jefferson Davis visited a county fair in Fulton in 1875, drawing large crowds. "Fulton has the warm friendliness of the Southern people who founded it," writes Williamson. That has not been the experience of all who live there, nor is it Howard's experience.

Bellamann decries the passing of Fulton's early leaders midway through *Kings Row*. Aging Colonel Skeffington, town lawyer and skeptic, whose family had traveled out from Virginia to settle the new region, sits in his office in the late afternoon and wonders what Missouri will become:

The Colonel's old face sagged a little. He was disappointed in the whole damned state. They had lost sight of the thing that brought the best here in the first place. The unimportant people seemed to be conquering through sheer numbers. But even that might have aspects of hope if one saw anywhere among the young anything of those earlier qualities. They were little, they were downright picayune, they talked about money as if there were nothing else under God's heaven worth while. Their language was undignified and mean. They were not gentlemen. . . .

Well—he shifted in his chair, settling himself deeper— he mustn't be too pessimistic. The poor qualities of the human race were always in evidence. One might as well believe in the enduring persistence of a few good qualities, too. These problems were no longer his. Others would have to cope with them—but that was just the trouble— no one was coping. A new cheapness—a shoddy, sleazy social fabric was being accepted.

But . . . a shy feeling came from deep hiding in the heart of the old man . . . he loved this part of the country. He felt that it had been his country. He had helped it to grow. He wanted to see it do well.

At which point the Colonel dies quietly of heart failure.

Jesse Howard remembers another past, not of the small town but of the country around it. Memory makes heroes. A narrative of details is a narrative of magnification, and by it the flesh is made word, with all language's enlarging mystery and power. In a fragment of autobiography buried among the wandering events of the *Little Joe Cooper* notebooks, Howard recalls his parents and their way of life:

"Now I will go back to the time when we used to have neighbours and friends. And when people lived in houses built with logs. And some of them, only dirt for a floor. And only a clapboard roof to shed the snow and the rain. And the boards were split out with a mallet and froe, and when they made stick and clay chimleys to carry out the smoke. And when Father and Mother were sitting in peace and quietness smoking their pipes, and they were made of clay. And, O yes, Father owned a small herd of sheep, and when we only had brush fences to turn our sheep and our cattle.

"And when a sheep would die, and especially in hot weather, Father would say, Jesse, that sheep has been dead for a couple of nights and days, and it is good and mellow by this time, go get a sack to put the wool in, and this sheep lay dead and didn't even move a foot whyle I picked the wool off of it's dead body, and one thing that I needed verry much, and that I didn't have. And that was a bottle of camphor. And that sheep lay dead, by the side of a big shed that used to house an old mill, and of, where people for miles around would shell turns of corn, throw it on a horse, and sometimes only a sheeps hide for a saddle. And off to the mill they would go, and as the miller only took out his toll, and that was a fifth for grinding, they would start out with a sack plum full of shelled corn, and come back with a sack plum full of meal. And, O my, O my, that good, good old crackling cornbread, sorghum lasses, ham meat and striped gravy.

"And now I will go back to where I was pulling wool off of the dead sheep, and as I have said the sheep died by the side of the old mill shed, and of course the boiler required a lot of wood and water, and there was a large pond near by. And I use to stand on the old pond dam, and watch the old mother fish swimming around with her little brood of fish, and the man that owned the mill, his name was Gilbert, and a fine man was he, and he always kept poles, and fishhooks, near by and whyle the people waited for their turn of corn to be ground into meal, the men and boys would grab a pole and line, and if they had good luck catching them, why they would take home a nice string of fish for supper or breakfast, and a plenty of good fresh corn meal, to fry their fish in too, yes what about those good old grayham muffins, with lots of butter and sorghum lasses.

"Well maybe you can stand another verse of Scripture, and here it is—quote. Now David was the son of that Ephrathite of Bethlehem Judeah. = whose name was Jesse: = and he Jesse, had eight sons. = And the man went among men for an old man in the days of Saul. = First Samuel. Chapter, 17. and verse 12. page. 343 =

"And now back to the sheep and the wool, and I had to help pick that wool over, and I will tell you how it happened, and why. There was no well at the house, our drinking water came from a spring, away down under a big hill, and as there was a plenty of water in the old mill pond, and it took a lot of water to wash that wool, we washed and washed it through some three or four times, and after it was washed, it was spred out in the sun to dry, and after it was dry, we would sit and pick and pick, until we got all the sticks and fine trash out of that wool. And at that time most every family had old time hand cards, which had little fine teeth, made of wire, and made, what they call rools, and they were only about a foot long, although there was a carding machine at that time, in Mexico, Mo. about the year 1890, that made rools about two feet in length, and Mexico, Mo. is some thirty miles away.

"And at that time Father had a spring wagon, and something like 200 head of sheep, and Father said to me, Jesse, I have a trip that we will have to make, and that is to Mexico, Mo., with some of our sheep, and we will have to drive them. So Father picked a moonlight night, and it was in the time of summer, and pretty hot, Father hitched his team to the spring wagon and said, Jesse, go get the wool that we washed, and picked, and put it in the wagon, and we will take it to Mexico and have it carded into rools, and about three oclock in the afternoon, and after it begun to get cool in the evening we drove the sheep out into the road, and started on the way to Mexico, and it was quite a long journey for a little boy and the sheep, at about two o'clock in the morning and we reached our destination at about five o'clock in the morning, we had breakfast with a man by the name of Brown, and at his place, is where we left the sheep.

## "BILL OF FARE AT THE HESKET BROWN HOUSE

"Pretty soon Mrs. Brown had breakfast ready, and a fine one at that, the bill of fare, was, ham meat and striped gravy, eggs, hot biscuit's with a plenty of butter, sorghum lasses, honey, and an assortment of jellys, and preserves, cream of wheat, ground with the old french burrs, and an assortment of all kinds of fruit, and their drink was, hot cofee, or tea, milk or water, and while we were in the house eating our fill, the horses were at the barn, filling theirselves with corn, oats, and hay, yes, Mr. and Mrs. Brown really possessed all of the good things that all good people should possess. And Mr. and Mrs. Brown's treatment was just the reverse, or opposite from the way that the scribes and the Phariseese and the Sadduseese, and the hypocrites, treated Jesus Christ, just before they drove nails through his hand's and nailed him to the cross of Calvaree, yes, Jesus was thirsty and when he asked for a drink of water, they gave him vinegar, to drink. And when he, Jesus, ask for some meat, they went out to, maybe a dead dog, and cut off a piece of liver, and was shure that they got the gall, and gave it to Jesus for meat. . . .

"And even after giving, Jesus, vinegar to drink, and gall for his meat, they were not satisfied at that, and so they thought of even a more bitter dose than that, and so they add wormwood to the vinegar, and liver gall, the word wormwood, is what we call tobacco, and as I never went to high school or any kind of college, and I do not know whother it is a Greek word, or Latin. And here is a verse out of the Bible, in the book of Lamentations that uses the word wormwood. Quote, Remembering mine affliction and my misery. The wormwood and the gall. Lamentations. Chapter. 3 and verse. 19. page. 848.

"And now since Mr. and Mrs. Brown had treated us so courteous and fine, both men and horses, got a good feed, and some rest, we hitched up the team, and over to the wool carding mill we went, and like all other mills, Father waited his turn at the carding mill, and my best recollection they had the wool carded into rools, at about two p.m. that day, and as Mr. and Mrs. Brown, lived just a little way's out of the town of Mexico, Mo. we stopped at their place to bid them good day. And on our journey toward home, which is near that great city of Calwood, Mo., in the city of Peth where one lives well, and the other two half starves to death, in other words they just barely exist, and as we drew near our place we called home, of which is four miles southeast of Calwood, and my best memory, it was about ten o'clock that night, and there was a woman, looking, yes, standing in the door, and looking, for Father and I. And that woman that was standing in the door, and looking, yes, looking, was my dear loving Mother, and I am the fruit of her womb, and as I am writing this, with tears in my eyes, that I can hardly write, yes, I can see her dear loving face, as though it were only yesterday, yes, Mother, dear Mother, was full of fond affection, kindhearted, and true, with grace, mercy, love, and peace wrote all over her dear face, and never one cross and vulgar word did I ever hear, either, Father, or Mother, utter from their lips. . . .

"And, Father, yes, Father was a man that was small in statue, and always wore a beard, and I never seen Father without that beard. Father's name was Lawson Thomas, and he makes me think of the picture of Thomas, you know that old familiar picture that we see hanging on the wall of Christian homes. . . .

"Mothers name was Martha Elizabeth, and the mother of ten children. Four boys, and six girls, and five of us living yet today. Yes, Ettie, and Jesse, we are twins, and the youngest of them all and think of the task that father and mother stepped into when they both said I will. They were not like the two old katy dids sitting in a tree, one said to the other, Katy did, Katy didn't, Katy did, Katy didn't. Sleep all day long, go to bed early, and sing the same old sing song all night long. Man and wife cannot do this and expect to get along. Now I will go back to the sheep and the wool. The meat of the sheep is mighty good to eat, and is better than vinegar and gall. And the wool off of the sheep makes good warm clotheing, and it beats mosquieto bar, like some people wear today.

"Mother would say, Jesse go out to the barn and bring me some nice clean shucks off of the corn, that she wanted to do some spinning today, and of course I never said no I won't go, for I always did as Father and Mother commanded me to do, and there was no sassing back, no, no, I knew better than that. I have seen Mother dampen the shucks, something like the women dampen their clothes before they iron. Mother would pick up a piece of the corn shuck, that I brought in, and then she would give the big wheel a turn with her right hand, and you aught to see how fast that little spindle would go, and then with her left hand, she would read out and pick up a card of pretty white wool, and then she would use the tip of her fingers to hold the card of wool to the shuck and in the spindle, of which was making hundreds of revolutions in a minuet, and the point of this little spindle is something like the point of a pitchfork tine, and by the side of the old spinning wheel, Mother would walk, to and fro, and the point of this little spindle, would twist the card of wool into yarn, and after Mother had spun the card of wool into yarn, then she wound it on, what they called a broach, and the broach, was the same length of the little spindle, of which is about eight inches long, can you not see that the yarn, as it was spun was rapped around the cornshuck, just like the thread is wound on a spool, and all of this was done at the same operation, and at the end of the day, Mother would have a big basket full of broaches. And it is hard to tell how far that mother had walked that day by the side of the old spinning wheel. And the next operation, was to pick up the broaches and wind the yarn into small ball's. And the next thing was the knitting needles, when Mother would sit up late at night and knit, and knit, until she had knitted two pairs of stockings for each one of the family. And the stockings that the women folks knitted in that day and age came away above their knees, now there is gloves to be knitted, and o, a dozen other things to do, babys crying, the geese to be picked, and I have seen the old gander reach around and almost bite a piece out of Mothers side, and there are the turkeys, Father and Mother would take them to Wellsville just a few days B.4 Xmas, and do their shopping, they would start early in the morning, and be late getting home that night, we children would go outside and look, and listen, yes, look and listen, and when we heard them coming, the older ones would go and meet them at the gate, for it was a long hard trip on them and the team, and in a day or two, Xmas would come, and there were nine stockings hanging on the wall, and gosh, they were big long ones too, we each one got something, some hard candy and a few nuts, or a harp, or a whistling bird, that would only cost a dime. No fussing, no grumbling, we each one got up early and with the biggest glee, and with that true Christ like spirit, and not only among our own household, that true Christ like spirit, at that time was with our friends and our neighbors, far and near, and how well I remember them running to greet each other with a merry Christmas, and a verry verry happy new year, and they would ask of each other's welfare, and how is everybody getting along, and this same Christ like spirit did not last only through the week of Christmas, why, it lasted the whole year through. And, O, that vow, which is only a three letter word, yes, that solom vow, that I myself took, when I took the wife to wed, and on new years morning, most every body would make a vow that they would live better lives and change their way of living, and some of them break that vow before the end of the week or month, and it would have been much better that they had never took that vow. Broken vows means broken homes, yes, broken homes.

### "GOOD NEIGHBOURS, DAYS PASSED AND GONE

"Yes, we use to go to our neighbor and see about their welfare, and if that neighbor needed help, we would see that that neighbour got the help that he needed, I remember that there was a man in our old neighbourhood by the name of Hall, this man was sick and was in destitute circumstances, when Father went over there to see of their need's, Father came back home and hitched to the old spring-wagon, yes, the old spring-wagon that we used when we went to Mexico with the sheep, Father would tell each neighbour, of Mr. Hall's circumstances, and ask them to help this poor man out. Well you auto have seen the old wagon loaded down with every good thing to eat, there were all kinds of canned fruit, sorghum mollases, meat, and potatoes, apples and pears, pumpkin, and squarsh, cabbage, and beans, well I do not know how much money that load of groceries would cost Mr. Hall today, and your guess would be as good as mine.

"And now it is getting time for some more scripture out of the Bible. And how many people are going out of their way to see about the welfare of their neighbour? And true fellowship and love, in Genesis. chapter.43 and verse. 27. page 68. Quote. And he asked them of their welfare. And said. Is your father well. The old man of whom ye speak? Is he yet alive?

"And in that neighbourhood the family spent manny years of their life, I was only a boy of about eight years of age, when Father moved to the old mill site, and there is nothing left today, only the old pond dam, and O, my, talk about good neighbors. And what fine times we use to have, and when the threshing machine would move in, there would be a plenty of help with their pitchforks and everything else that was needed to get the job done, they all worked, and worked with a will. And whyle the menfolks were out in the field, there would be all of the women in the whole neighbourhood, there helping to get a square meal, and talk about, ham meat and striped gravy, yellow legged chicken with dumplings, or dressing, beef roast, or mutton, O my, those hot biscuit, with all kind of jellies and preserves, and those fine cakes and pies, pass them around and say, which kind do you want, they always had a variety of manny kind. And their drinks were pretty much of the same variety, and that was not all that was gained at these big fine dinners and social workings. The young men had a chance to pick out a good cook. For what good would a wife be to a man if she could not even boil water without scorching it?

"And the young girls had a chance to pick out a good working man for a husband, they had the opportunity to look out in the field, and if they seen a young man using the pitchfork for a prop, and maybe a bottle in his pocket, that young girl had better let that young man alone. Yes, these kind of people will bring gray hairs with sorrow to their grave. . . .

"Yes, fifteen and 20 years ago we had some neighbours. They were mighty fine men and women, and when we went to butcher our hogs, the neighbors were there just like the threshing of the grain. We sharpened our butcher knives to butcher hogs. And not butcher men. And it was a pleasure to work with these men, and these were neighbours that lived near the old mill pond, and talk about honour, manhood, and diety, these men and women had it. If a man's word is no good, neither is he, well there is always work to be done at a butchering, first thing to do is to put the kettles on some rock or in their frames with leggs, and next thing fill kettles with water and the next, build fire under the kettles, or vat, and then there is the platform to scald and scrape the hair off, and then there is the forks and pole to hang the hogs on after they are scalded and scraped, and the man most usually has all of this work done before his help arrives.

"Well I have the scalding barrel all set and the water it begins to boil, pretty soon the men will be popping up over the hill, and when they come, they most always bring their wives. And there is always a lot of work for the women folks to do, well here comes John Gray and Frona, John was always an early riser and he most always got there first, then comes Charley Noble, he married my sister Lena, and he was always an early riser too. Then here comes James Linton. We always called him Jim for short, well he was just the opposite for he was about 6 ft. 2, he was my fatherenlaw. For I finally married his daughter, and was a man that made friends anywhere he went, always jolly, always had a pleasant word to say, we lived neighbors for over 50 years and never a hard word between us. . . . Now here comes brother Dolph, and I do not see how that brother Dolph stood up and carried the burden that he did carry. It seemed as though he and his wife, Anna, and one daughter Gertrude, that their lives were all misfortion. Always jolly and jovil, their spirit with which they lived, is all that carried them through. They had no riches in silver and gold, all three are passed and gone, these people were rich in the eyes of God."

Good neighbors, days passed and gone . . . Kings today visit Fulton, but they do not claim its Kingdom. Winston Churchill arrived there on a windy March 5, 1946, to find 25,000 people waiting for him in a town where wags say the population numbers 10,000 souls only if you count the inmates at the state hospital. Churchill came to Fulton to deliver a message to the Western world, at Harry Truman's invitation.

The British statesman delivered "Sinews of Peace" at Westminster College. "It was one of the greatest speeches I ever listened to . . . and part of the policy of the Free World ever since," Truman said later. Churchill withheld his most important lines from the advance text, hoping the surprise of them would add emphasis. He knew how to coin a phrase. The cameramen, unfortunately, chose that moment to change film magazines. No motion picture of the scene survives. Only a recorder registered the key paragraph:

From Stettin in the Baltic to Trieste in the Adriatic, an iron curtain has descended across the continent. Behind that line lie all the capitals of the ancient states of Central and Eastern Europe. Warsaw, Berlin, Prague, Vienna, Budapest, Belgrade, Bucharest and Sofia, all those famous cities and the populations around them, lie in what I must call the Soviet sphere and all are subject in one form or another, not only to Soviet influence but to a very high and increasing measure of control from Moscow.

| | |
|---|---|
| UNITED WE STAND LIKE THE SOLID ROCK GEBRAL- TA. ONE OF THE BEST FORTIFIED ROCK IN THE WORLD. | YES SEPARATED WE FALL APART. LIKE AN OLD WOODEN STAVE BARREL IN HOT DRY WEATHER. |

"Mr. Churchill does not contemplate any other public engagements in the United States at the present time," a press release said. He came from England to Fulton and returned home.

In Churchill's place, in the mid-1960s, as if his iron words had been planted and had sprouted Portland stone, grew St. Mary Aldermanbury, a London church burned out in World War II and subsequently scheduled for demolition. *Pravda*, perhaps alerted to the existence of Fulton by Churchill's visit two decades earlier, disdainfully acknowledged the transfer, cementing for Fulton yet another connection with the entire known universe:

> What attracted the Fultonians in St. Mary? Maybe the fact that within its walls some time ago the great poet John Milton was married. But maybe something else: here is buried Judge George Jeffreys, who sent hundreds of people to prison. Or finally perhaps because in the Court of the Church are buried the friends and associates of Shakespeare—the actors Heminge and Condell, the editors of the famous first editions of Shakespearean plays—"The First Folio." The only copy of this Folio was sold long ago to the United States. One way or another, cash on the barrelhead, and the stones are going to Fulton. Now it is up to you to figure out if the Chicago slaughterhouse kings take a fancy to St. Paul's—and yet you say this cannot be.

Shippers mixed up the numbered stones on the way over from London, leaving the master mason, a man from Columbia, Missouri, a gigantic puzzle to work, but the chapel went up in good time. St. Mary sits on an ugly base of modern stone like the base of a monumental paperweight, but that is its only fault. Christopher Wren, the English architect and mathematician, designed it among fifty-three churches he planned, between 1667 and 1711, to replace those destroyed in London's Great Fire of 1666. The steps in its bell tower date from the eleventh century. St. Mary Aldermanbury is symmetrical, spare, a pleasantly subdued structure supported inside by twelve Corinthian columns, lighted through large circular windows, decorated outside with stone carving and pediment-surmounted entrances. Elaborately carved lyres frame its large east window. The chapel contrasts painfully with the Steamboat Gothic town: despite its age, Fulton no more than the rest of America was built to last.

The paperweight base of the chapel is a museum filled with oddities of Churchilliana. Admission was free when it first opened, but vandals broke out expensive handmade window-panes in the chapel upstairs, stuffed paper down the public toilets, and stained the museum's white interior walls. Now there's a charge for admission, which pays for daily upkeep but is an irritation to Fultonians, who expected to come and go freely through a chapel they already think of as their own.

Patrick Horsbrugh, professor of architecture at Notre Dame and one of the Churchill Memorial Foundation's original consultants, described in a 1964 speech the connections he saw between Fulton, Missouri, and the rest of the world: "I ask you to consider, ladies and gentlemen, this extraordinary phenomenon of unrelated ideas and events that are now so directly linked together; a thriving college, a century old; a spirited man, mighty at the moment of distraction; a near-prophetic speech, derided at the time; the foresight to compound these factors; a memorial to needle-eye the past towards the future; a church by Wren, transported; the old made new to serve again its ancient purpose, now to stand rededicated, chipped and scarred as a constant declaration that, under God, human tyranny shall be defied." That reads like a worthy Shakespearean epilogue, and perhaps, as history comes to a close in the Kingdom of Callaway, it is.

Jesse Howard has built too, not in the high style of Christopher Wren but in the vernacular tradition of the frontier. He is a surviving example of one who works with what John A. Kouwenhoven has called, in *Made in America,* "the frequently crude but vigorous forms in which the natural creative instinct sought to pattern the new environment." Howard uses discarded materials, because his sensibility was shaped at a time when scarcity decreed that nothing be junk until it fell apart, and sometimes not even then. What others in Fulton throw out, Howard collects and puts to new use.

He has mounted the sturdy, simple door handles of old automobiles on the doors of his many weathered sheds. The front of an ancient Bendix automatic washing machine, freshened with aluminum paint, becomes the window of a new shed he has built, admitting light through its round porthole. A model airplane the size of a small tricycle, nailed together out of slats and turnings of broken furniture, decorates a mount of signs a car's length off the road amid green pasture. An entrance improbably located at the corner of a shed solves the corner with a gothic arch framed around the pointed door. Another shed is windowed with the flat, thick glass of an old Ford windshield, and the bottom edge of the windshield, a graceful convex curve shaped to fit the rounded hood of the old car, meets planking Howard has shaped with equal grace. The chromed front of a car radio, knobs intact, hangs nailed to the wall outside one shed. Green glass insulators from a telephone pole hang on another, and ceramic red roses on another, pure decoration. Commissioned by a neighbor to paint a dedicatory message on the wooden door of the neighbor's new doghouse, Howard responds with a selection of doggie biblical quotations:

—DOG. CHILDRENS BREAD CAST TO DOG'S. ST. MAT-
THEW, 15 = 26. PAGE. 997.
—DOG. CAST TO DOG'S. ST. MARK. 7 = 27. PAGE. 1026.
—DOG. DOG'S, UNDER TABLE. ST. MARK. 7 = 28. PAGE. 1026.
—DOG. THE POWER OF DOG'S. PSALMS. 22 = 20. PAGE. 620.
—DOG. THE DOG'S COMPASSED ME. PSALMS. 22 = 16.
PAGE. 620.

Serendipity is the essence of the vernacular. In Howard's hands an icebox becomes a rat-proof filing cabinet for his newspaper clippings and notebooks. Planking from razed houses becomes canvas for his signs and raw material for his storage sheds. A sheet of masonite and two buckets he converts to a bench under a comfortable shade tree. He uses fragments of colored glass to make clerestory windows over the door of a shed.

His paintings have the comic freshness of vernacular art. Most depict animals, burlesques of human virtue and vice: owls, fish, skunks. As at Lascaux, the fish appear in X-ray views, fish inside of fish watching fish eating fish, a witty commentary on the natural world. The skunks appropriately illustrate a sign comparing their qualities to those of judges and lawyers. Other fish, with silver dimes glued to their mouths, are painted on raw shoe soles, Howard's own combination of sight gag, biblical incident and Christian symbol.

In his notebooks he has revived manuscript illumination, spelling out words in block capitals with red and blue pencil alternating. An early page in the *Little Joe Cooper* notebooks shows a gourd vine, the vine in green, the gourds worked in gold paint, with this text:

THIS GOURD VINE REPRESENTS THE SHADOW
OVER JONAH'S HEAD. QUOTE, AND THE LORD GOD
PREPARED A GOURD. AND MADE IT TO COME UP
OVER JONAH, THAT IT MIGHT BE A SHADOW OVER

HIS HEAD. TO DELIVER HIM FROM HIS GRIEF. SO JO-
NAH WAS EXCEEDINGLY GLAD OF THE GOURD. JO-
NAH. 4TH CHAPTER, AND VERSE 6, PAGE 949.

On the same page, below, the vine is painted gold, its gourds
missing. A green worm with seven legs, twin horns and a bale-
ful green eye gnaws at its roots:

THIS REPRESENTS THE WITHERED GOURD VINE,
QUOTE, BUT GOD PREPARED A WORM, WHEN THE
MORNING ROSE THE NEXT DAY, AND IT SMOTE
THE GOURD THAT IT WITHERED. JONAH. 4TH
CHAPTER AND VERSE. 7. PAGE 949.

Following Howard around Sorehead Hill on a summer day to
see his constructions and writings, I sweat in the heat and
swelter in the sheds. He sweats not at all. Liver spots mark his
temples, temples high beneath gray hair cut back at the sides
like a soldier's, a spread of white stubble on his cheeks. He is a
short man, with a ski-jump nose, eyes blue but clouded with
cataracts, thick workman thumbs and fingers, hands that can
wonder over individual kernels of the strawberry popcorn he
raises, surprisingly dexterous in their care for small things. He
wears ancient bib overalls, a rawhide watch fob looped through
its special buttonhole on the top edge of the bib, blue work
shirt open at the collar but with sleeves rolled down and buttoned even in the heat. His skin is weathered, leathery, his
laughter surprisingly youthful, with an edge of shyness to it.

Once he traveled the western United States, a tour that
ended in 1905 which he remembers so well today that in tell-
ing his life story he spends more than an hour on the working
tour and passes over fifty years of marriage and parenthood in
a few sentences.

It is a narrative of jobs, mostly farm work: shucking corn,
threshing wheat, milking cows, digging potatoes, putting up
hay. Only a few events stand out, and those are the "wonders"

he means by the phrase he repeats again and again about his work and the world, "signs and wonders."

One wonder was an ocean-going ship in Cosmopolis, Washington:

"Great big old ship standin there on the docks. They'd been loading that old ship a week or ten days, with lumber. I was always the dickins of a man to get out and look around, see what I could see. Loading that old ship, every way, putting it on there with derricks, horse carts 'n everything. Finally got the old ship loaded. I got up there on that old ship, you know, I didn't know anything about it. Had an old tugboat down the river, swiftest river I ever seen. Purty soon I seen that old tugboat had a rope up to that big ship, course the biggest part of it was clear under the water, purty soon I noticed the old big ship leaving the dock. I run as hard as I could run, and just made a daggone bee from there, off on the old dock. Three minutes, y'know, I'da been out there on that old big ship."

Where was it going ?

"Australia! All that kept me from goin was that I didn't like those foreign languages. Lots of foreigners on the ship. The only thing that saved me was my legs. My legs has saved me several times from pickles."

The wonder of the ship, the mingled fear and delight at the idea of shipping out to distant ports, the anxiety over foreign languages—all these emotions are part of Howard's work today. In San Francisco he visited Chinatown and was told by his guide that some of the Chinese there ate tiger meat in the belief that it made them strong. It was a tale of horror he never forgot. It reappears on several of his signs, sixty years later:

FULTON, MO. MARCH 5. 1967. QUOTE. AN EAST GERMAN
DOCTOR WHO SPENT 30 YEARS IN RED CHINA SUS-
PECTS MAO TSE-TUNG IS SUFFERING FROM HARDEN-
ING OF ARTERIES OF THE BRAIN. DR. ERIC BONDE-
LEE, SAID, THIS WOULD EXPLAIN WHAT HE CALLS
MAO'S UNCONTROLLED BEHAVIOR. YES, AND EATING
TIGER MEAT. AND DRINKING THEIR BLOOD TO MAKE
THEM VISCIOUS. YES, THESE PEOPLE ARE FOOLS, FOR
WANT OF WISDOM. PROV. 10=21. YES, MAO TSE-TUNG
HAS SUFFERED ALL HIS LIFE. FOR

Jesse Howard is an enthusiast. Except for the harassment
that follows from Fulton's disapproval, he has no trouble enjoying life. Fulton is another matter—not thriving, not dying, sus-
pended between. As with many country towns in the Middle
West, its coherence failed at the end of the First World War. Its
older citizens look back to that coherence with nostalgia, and
find little in modern life that they can value. Its young people
leave town, by the day or forever. A life of sorts goes on at drive-
ins and taverns, as it always has, but it is a life that appalls. The
few institutions in Fulton that prosper—the college, the hospital—look beyond the town. Only its merchants talk Fulton
up, and they confine their expressions of allegiance to billboards out on highway 54, to garish new trash containers
posted on street corners, to new store fronts faced with dusty
plate glass.

Whatever Fulton's sources might be, old or new—and Jesse
Howard is one of them as surely as is St. Mary Aldermanbury—they have not been tapped, despite the fact that small-
town life is more intimate than city life and more permeable,
and offers great potential for beauty. It is as if the entire town
were waiting for the modern age to end. Meanwhile, the population slowly drains from the heartland's rural counties. The
churches settle on their lots like ancient tombs, patient for
Sunday morning. Variety stores sell Ouija boards. Cards in the
windows of doctors' offices and drugstores announce county-

wide revival meetings and promise healing by faith alone. Old men roam the town squares.

"It is just like this," writes Howard in one of his *Little Joe Cooper* digressions, "I ask a man 85 years old, I will only use his initials, and they are C.C. and I have known him most all of my life, we were standing on the street corner, and the thought came to me to ask him, this question, I said to C.C., if you had your life to live over, would you make any changes? And his answer was this, I would not want to live my life over. And the conversation stopped at that. And I see this man on the street most every day. And I asked an elderly lady, the same question, her age was 92, and her answer was this, yes I would. Now you might think that this is a verry inquisitive old man, well, well, that is where I get a lot of wisdom and knowledge, of which, we never get too old to learn."

Jesse Howard, reinventing the past up there among the ragweed and thorn trees on Sorehead Hill, is not too old to learn, but Fulton may be. Why else would a town so veined with the sources of the world beyond its walk continue to turn only inward?

---

IS THERE ANY LOVE IN THIS TOWN TODAY? GRACE. HOPE. FAITH. LOYALTY. DEITY. MANHOOD. CONFIDENCE. WHO CAN YOU PUT CONFIDENCE IN TODAY? I HAVE HAD A GREAT NUMBER OF PEOPLE TO GO AWAY FROM THIS PLACE WITH DECEIT & LIES WROTE ALL OVER THEIR FACE. 4 OF THESE ARE WOLVES & IS IT POSSIBLE TO FALL FROM GRACE LIKE THAT. GOD SAYS HE WILL STRIP US NAKED AND UNCOVER OUR SHAME.

## 5 / How I Rode with Harold Lewis on a Diesel Freight Train Down to Gridley, Kansas, and Back

It should be well-known fact that, all over the world, the engine-driver is the finest type of man that is grown. He is the pick of the earth. He is altogether more worthy than the soldier, and better than the men who move on the sea in ships. He is not paid too much; nor do his glories weight his brow; but for outright performance, carried on constantly, coolly, and without elation by a temperate, honest, clear-minded man, he is the further point. And so the lone human at his station in a cab, guarding *money, lives, and the honor of the road, is a beautiful sight. The whole thing is aesthetic.*

—Stephen Crane, "The Scotch Express"

WHETHER HIS TRAIN BE MERELY TWO ENGINES AND three cars, as Harold Lewis's was when I rode back with him from Gridley, Kansas, or whether it be a monster of fourteen hundred tons, a locomotive engineer has only two controls: a throttle and a brake. Three, if you count the sander. Harold's throttle had six notches, each equivalent to approximately ten miles an hour. The brake comes in two parts, a smaller handle that controls the engine brake, a larger handle that controls the brakes on every car simultaneously. Not quite simultaneously: the air pressure feeds back from the engine a car at a time, so that each succeeding car's brake is set automatically in sequence, a matter of nice timing for the engineer as all his train work is and must be.

The sander is an anachronism. In the proud noses of railroad trains, trains run these modern days by efficient diesel engines connected directly to huge generators that convert the mechanical power of the diesels into electricity to feed electric traction motors mounted on each of the diesel's four sets of wheels, in the proud noses of such trains can be found a dusty toilet for the engineer and a fifty-gallon tank of dry sand. With a small handle next to his cab window the engineer can force sand onto the track directly in front of each of his engine wheels, increasing with homely sand the friction of the steel wheel against the steel track. Each wheel makes contact with that track across an area the size of a dime. The sand improves the wheels' purchase enough to allow the train to accelerate even uphill. The whole point of railroading is that little dime of area, because so little contact means very little friction, which means the train can carry unbelievably heavy loads and carry them fast and hard in almost any weather. The fourteen-hundred-ton train, Harold said, was pulled by only two engines.

We had four—or three, if you discount the one that didn't work—to pull thirty-one cars on our outbound run and two to pull three cars on our side trip to Gridley. The needle on his amperage gauge rarely lifted above its first quadrant.

Harold Lewis is a man, a gentleman, of transportation. Tall, lean, with a weathered face and trim blond hair. My next-door neighbor in country Kansas when I lived there. He plays the electric guitar. A Reorganized Latter Day Saint. A paratrooper in World War II, then a ranger. He flashed motorcycles all over Scotland, landed early on Normandy. After the war he raced motorcycles for a precarious wild living, restlessly leaving jobs when he discovered he didn't like them. His father had wanted to be a locomotive engineer and finally convinced Harold to start down that road, working in the yards, becoming a brakeman, then a fireman, finally an engineer. Working doggedly, with grit, because that is how you become an engineer, exchanging your restlessness for plain, daily, concentrated determination.* You learn, as Crane would have it, to be constant, cool, and without elation. Except that to be an engineer is the essence of elation, because the conductor may keep track of your cars for you and the brakemen may throw your switches, but one man, you and you alone, makes everything go on that train even if the cars stretch behind you for half a mile. With two hands and two, perhaps three controls you make it go and make it stop, ring the bell and blow the horn, calculate when to brake and when to accelerate, figure exactly where to halt before a switch, how much slack to hold between the cars, where to back up to leave a car precisely opposite the door of a shed on a siding, how much power to feed the wheels to hold

---

*With the exception, in Harold's case, of a continuing interest in the farther shores of transportation that led him, some years ago, to build and fly his own experimental airplane, a single-engine one-place construction of wood and tubular steel and fiberglass which he put together on a friend's farm near Emporia, Kansas, while waiting between trains and successfully flew until he pranged one day into a tree; and a ten-speed derailleur racing bike on which he occasionally takes one-hundred-mile rides.

the train at the many different speed limits that towns and suburbs and curves and hills and the conditions of the track require. If you are good, and Harold is very good, you spend your life learning and never do learn everything you would like to. "I try to remember what I saw the good ones do and forget what I saw the bad ones do," Harold told me as we drove to the yards.

The size, the weight, the sheer mass of the engines. Sixteen cylinders the diameter of dinner plates. An engine block long as an automobile but cast iron, not sheet metal. Two generators big as kitchen stoves, one to feed the wheels, one to supply low-amperage electricity to light the lights and power the controls and, very occasionally, to start the engine. The wheels themselves half as tall as a man and milled steel, shiny as silver when they're new, their rims slightly angled so that they can slide across the rails around curves, one sliding to a smaller and therefore faster circumference, one to a larger and therefore slower circumference to compensate for the lesser and greater distances on the inside and outside rails. A flange, a lip, to hold them on. The Atchison, Topeka and Santa Fe freight engines are deep blue and yellow. In their massiveness they might seem malevolent, but every American boy over thirty and perhaps under thirty too grew up at railroad crossings, watching the engines toot by, two long blasts on the whistle (that is now the horn), one short, one long modulated by the Doppler effect of the train's speed so that your ears knew the instant the engine had stopped coming toward you and begun going away, counting then the cars, always losing count because you were nudged, then attracted, then compelled, awed by the names, Erie, Boston & Maine, Chesapeake & Ohio, MKT, New York Central, Wabash, Rock Island and Pennsylvania and Southern Pacific and Union Pacific and Great Western, a map of America and a history of America and American railroading flashing before you like giant cue cards for some ultimate final examination that loomed much larger in the mind of every country boy than any city recounting of baseball scores. And so from the age of perhaps four on if you are now over thirty and maybe if you are under thirty your secret, your cherished ambition in life, to hell with doctors and lawyers and merchant chiefs, was to be a locomotive engineer or, failing that, to ride with one.

And somehow, even then, you knew why that ambition was so important to you: because the railroads put this continent that once was wilderness together, opened it up, made it accessible to the loving and plundering human beings who laid down the tracks and then rode over them into every nook and cranny of the land, and without the railroads we would still be clinging to the continent's ocean rims and looking fearfully over our shoulders at its jungle interiors. For you and for most Americans the very towns you live in were founded because the railroad went by, were usually named by railroad men, and grow and prosper or shrivel and die because the railroad goes there more often now or has stopped going there at all. Or did, before the automobile mocked the reluctance of railroad owners to carry passengers and the truck their reluctance to compete for freight. The Santa Fe's passenger service, I should add, is a little better than the others. You can still ride a clean and pleasant Amtrak Super Chief from Kansas City to Los Angeles, but only if you are willing to board it in the middle of the night.

We board Harold's engines at five in the afternoon at the Santa Fe's Argentine yards in the river bottoms west of Kansas City, and Harold checks out the four diesels as a pilot might check out his plane. The diesels are never shut off except for repairs. Sitting idle in the yards or moving down the track, they run on day and night, because they last longer that way. They even can't be shut down, because the cooling jacket around the manifold is designed to operate at high temperatures and would leak if its temperature dropped below 120 degrees and would then have to be drained, heated and refilled. Harold pulls the oil sticks and reads the water gauges on all four engines. He removes the control handles on the back three, sets the two engines that face backward into reverse, and snaps the handles into place on the front engine. Two engines are the required minimum for a working freight train, because there is no place along the way where the engines can turn around. Instead of running backward, then, the engineer shifts over to whichever engine is facing in the direction he wants to go.

Snapping open a panel on the wall behind his chair, Harold turns on the power for his radio, a telephone handset mounted to his left on the side of a row of gauges that indicate his power and speed, a receiver horn painted neutral gray, like the interior of the cab, mounted at the top center front of the cab. Seated in his chair, he has these controls at hand, from left to right in a semicircle: the lever that controls the air pressure to the train brakes, mounted on a standard the size and heft of a fire plug; the smaller lever that controls the engine brakes, mounted on a smaller but similar standard; behind the engine brake lever a row of recessed switches that control various lights; directly in front of Harold the throttle, accessible to his right hand; mounted on the right wall of the cab a small lever like the handle of a Colonial table knife that controls the sander; and under his left foot, to circle back now and down, a flat steel pedal from which he may never while the train is in motion remove his foot for more than ten seconds without actuating an alarm and for more than twenty seconds without throwing the train violently to a halt: the deadman.

The deadman is a chilling reminder that behind Harold ride tens or hundreds or thousands of tons of careening metal and whatever clever or commonplace or lethal materials American ingenuity can think of to pack inside, and one man is controlling it all, watching out for cars and people at numberless crossings along the way, making sure its speed on curves by highways and on overpasses over streets and houses doesn't lean it past its center of gravity. The theory is simple: if a man dies suddenly he will probably lose his foothold on the deadman; the pedal will come up; the train will automatically stop. Today some engines have a different deadman, based on an even more likely theory, an electric field between the cushion of the engineer's chair and the controls. The engineer must make and break some connection every ten seconds, touch the throttle, touch the brakes, tap the window-sill at his side, or hear the warning buzzer or stop the train. The engine is studded with emergency devices, with levers to pull and switches to throw, but the deadman is the ultimate emergency device, because it depends, like everything else on the train, on the engineer.

We hook up our cars and ease out of the yard, moving over to one of the two main tracks that head southwest from Kansas City to Wichita. For a few miles the tracks parallel the Kansas River, brown and swollen from recent rains, then they swing south and leave all big towns behind. We pass Olathe, sere county seat of prosperous Johnson County, and quiet Gardner, and now it is night, the huge headlight in the nose of the engine making daylight before us except when Harold courteously dims it for cars passing on the highway alongside the tracks, catching then the glowing eyes of prowling possums and cats; Harold speeding up to sixty on the long open stretches, watching the speed-limit signs posted along the roadbed, one speed for passenger trains, a slower speed for freight, watching the W signs that alert him to a crossing where he must blow his horn, watching most importantly the signals—trainmen call them "boards"—that by night with lights and by day with arms announce whether or not the track ahead is clear. An earlier freight precedes us down the track, so that every other board turns up yellow and once even red: we stop for the red. "You never know what might be on the other side of a red board," Harold says. "Might be a mile away or one foot on the other side." Then speed up to sixty, the wind blowing cool into the big square windows on each side of the cab, the brakeman in front of me swinging out the windscreen to moderate the gale, calling back to Harold his response to Harold's call of the boards, the clicking rails rushing by below. At 10:30 we have parked in Ottawa and the engines purr in the yard and in the back of an electrician's pickup we ride to our hotel in town. Nothing is open in Ottawa on an autumn Sunday night;

the brakeman and the conductor make their suppers on candy bars and Cokes, but Harold has prudently brought lunch, as at his instruction have I, and we eat in the quiet of our rooms and sleep to the whine of semis gearing down a hill outside. Railroad men keep no regular hours. As they are assigned different runs they are called; they may leave the yards immediately upon arriving or three hours later, depending on the traffic; they only know that they will not be required to work more than sixteen hours at a time and that between any two runs they will have eight hours off. Our run to Ottawa took five and a half hours and now we are off, to be called again at seven in the morning so that we can board our train at eight.

And then, that next morning, we go free, two mighty engines pulling what you and I call a caboose and what trainmen call a waycar. We are scheduled to run to Gridley, Kansas, to pick up a flatcar, an empty boxcar and a boxcar full of hay. It's not my dream of a train ride: I would have preferred a two-hundred-car behemoth. But as we switch off the main line onto an ancient trunk for a run the Santa Fe makes only once a week, I realize that this small side trip has virtues no two-hundred-car train could compass, that Harold by chance will take us on a run into the antique past of American railroading, complete with ghosts of towns that existed when Harold last made this run, twelve years before, and exist no more. Twelve years before, but Harold remembers every hill and curve and real and ghost town too.

The brakeman switches us onto the trunk and Harold slows his train to twenty miles an hour, a speed we will not exceed and will often decrease during the fifty-eight-mile journey, because the rails are old and poor. I leave the cab to sit on the catwalk in front of the engine, perhaps three feet above the rails as they roll by under us. They are rusted, light in weight compared to the heavy rails of the main line and only precariously fixed to weathered ties sunken in their age to ground level. They seem to plead for the weekly cleaning the engine's wheels bring them; they click by with a sound out of my childhood that takes some miles to place: the sound, first, of the miniature steam train at a Kansas City park to which my father, in some gentle version of a busman's holiday—he was a railroad man too—sometimes took my brother and me on one of his few days off. And the sound, second, of a means of transportation that once linked the cities and suburbs of America in comfort and quiet, the electric trolley. With Harold's diesels muted by the mild demands of our light train and slow speed, the sound that drifts forward to the catwalk where I sit is the hum of electric motors accelerating and decelerating as the governors adjust our speed, and that sound was the sound of the trolleys.

We rode them as children. They gave way, as the railroads gave way, to the absurdities of the automobile, but in their time they worked magic on children, their conductors running them with a simple handle and brake pedal, their brakes long electromagnets that clamped down on their rails to slow and stop them. My father rode one to work every day for forty years. He called it the Dinky because it was smaller than the usual trolleys; it had controls at each end so that it needed no turn-around, and as the conductor moved from one control station to the other he flipped one by one the wicker seats to face the direction in which he would now drive. Another trolley, an excursion car, was open to the air and sported a fringed top, like the surrey of the song, which for years I thought it was. It ran through town on gay summer nights, crowds of revelers aboard. You could travel out to grandmother's farm in those trolleys of long ago, traverse the city, go to the park, for a nickel or a dime. Perhaps, when the automobile has entirely failed us, we will publish some modern edition of the trolley. Heart-attack rates would go down, children give up Barbie Dolls for lollipops and elderly ladies smile again.

Harold's train flushes fat coveys of quail from the brush beside the track, four, eight, once even sixteen birds taking off in their short whirring flight, a burst like a feathered shotgun blast that forecasts their probable end. Black-eyed Susans wink yellow in the tall grass; pink Scotch thistles sway; blue chicory flowers glow like sample lakes reflecting the sky. Only the blast of Harold's horn at little-used dirt crossings reminds of the business of the ride; I might be on a handcar running back to the rural we have so precariously forsaken. There is irony, too, in that, because the railroad did its major share of creating cities. At the terminus of several different railroads our cities grew: at those points and near them the railroads were forced to charge competitive rates for moving freight and people, but in regions where only one line ran they could and did jack up their prices, and the effect of their robbery was to force factories and people into the terminal towns. Then the automobile and the truck replaced the railroad, and the old trunk lines withered like severed vines. This quiet trunk to Gridley must be one of them: Harold says it once moved three passenger trains a day, and now it is visited by a freightless freight train once a week, banally to move a boxcar full of hay.

Inside the cab, sitting easily at his station, his foot tirelessly on the deadman, Harold clicks the throttle up one notch, down one notch, small adjustments to hold our speed exactly at twenty, entertainment for the long run. He times himself between the mile markers to check the accuracy of his speedometer. With his horn at a crossing he gives the regulation blasts, then allows the final blast to drop to a moan. "These things are either all on or all off," he remarks. "You could really make the old whistles sit up and talk." We pass Homewood and Williamsburg, Waverly and Halls Summit, small towns and old, most with deserted stations. We pass a ghost town that once sheltered a utopia: Silkville, where an eccentric entrepreneur brought mulberry trees that still grow on the cattle ranch that has taken its place, and when the trees had matured set out trays of silkworms to feed on their leaves, hoping to start an industry in industryless Kansas in the days before the Russian Mennonites brought their modest Turkey Red wheat over and endured the scoffing of locals to put Kansas on the map. Free love, free money and silkworms would make the earth fruitful, but the scheme failed and Silkville disappeared, leaving behind an ancient schoolhouse of heavy limestone rock.

Somewhere along the way, riding through tall brush now that whips against the cab and throws a leaf or two onto the cab's floor, we ascend the highest grade on the line, then down a steep hill and around a sharp curve that would be trouble for a longer or faster train but only brings squeals of stripping rust to the wheels of ours. Harold doesn't even need the sander: the rust serves for traction. Below us the roadbed has recently been worked where over the years it had filled in, brown dirt now turned over with a plow as if a farmer planted sticks and nails that grew up ties and track, new ties too tucked in along the way where old ties had rotted. Twice we stop for road crews repairing and leveling the track who ride yellow handcars powered with engines the size of lawnmowers and precede us like couriers to sidings where they can switch out of the way.

Children wave from the crossings of small towns as they have always waved at trains, and Harold waves back, this one of the engineer's prerogatives and obvious pleasures, the man dreaming of having been a boy, the boys dreaming of being men, the girls perhaps dreaming of the men the boys will be. He is everyone's father, the engineer, and he plays his role well, confirming the camaraderie with a wave toward a schoolyard, recalling again as this country ride recalls that sense of small towns, good and ill, where everyone knew everyone and spoke easily from porches and sidewalks. At lunch, in Burlington, the largest town on our line, the pert woman who brought our leathery roast beef and heavy mashed potatoes charmed from Harold the explanation that he was making the Gridley run for another engineer who was on vacation and then requested that Harold, like the man he replaced, sound his horn at a town up the way that appears on no maps: that was where she lived, she said, and the other man always tooted as he went by. On our return trip Harold casually complied.

Finally, after lunch, we reached Gridley, a five-hour run over fifty-eight miles, and then began the process of switching. The brakeman pulled the pin on the waycar and set the brakes and we left it on the main track. Harold removed the control handles from the forward engines and we walked to the rear engine, which now became our forward engine for the trip home. We backed up to a switch. The brakeman unlocked it and moved its weighted lever from the ground to its right to the ground to its left, shifting the siding rail against the main track. Harold eased backward and the engines turned into the siding, and a hundred yards down slowly closed on the flatcar, a two-dimensional model of a docking in space, bumping the car at less than four miles an hour and throwing the couplings together like two clasping hands. Then the brakeman dropped in the pin and hooked up the air brake and we returned to the main track and on other sidings picked up the other cars. Then we backed up across open switches to retrieve the waycar and began our trip home. Lulled by the afternoon heat and the heavy lunch I fell briefly asleep; Harold drove on at an unvarying twenty miles an hour, the pitch of the engines a little higher now with the weight of three cars behind us, drove past the furrowed earth, past the flowers fading with the afternoon, past the quail bursting up and flying off the other way: *déjà vu*.

It was six in the evening by the time we reached the signal board near our turnoff outside Ottawa. The board showed red, and we stopped to watch a long freight roar by from another trunk line to our left. The men's spirits were up now; they'd worked ten hours and would work three more to return to the yards; they might be required to work out their full sixteen hours, but Harold thought he had heard that train crews got to go directly to the yards after making the Gridley run, especially since another crew on another local was in the area and had started work half an hour later than he. The call came over the radio to come on in to Ottawa, and at the modern station there Harold stopped to pick up new orders and heard the dispatcher direct the other crew to some local work in Olathe. Back aboard, everyone was grinning. We took off on the right-hand side of the double tracks and the sixty-mile-an-hour speed limit added to our exhilaration. A few miles outside Ottawa, we shifted over to the left track to make room for a crack freight train bound for the Gulf Coast; it roared by us on its thirty-three-hour run loaded with piggyback trailers that would be peeled off at its destination and trucked to factories and stores—one belated way the railroads have learned to survive even though stubborn railroad men still believe it gives aid and comfort to the enemy. We are moving now, with instructions to beat the nightly passenger train, late out of Kansas City, to Gardner, where we can shunt back to the right-hand track to allow the passenger train to breeze by us on the left. We make it easily and soon roll along beside the Kansas River again.

Now it is night, the yards aglow with switches, high boards and low pots red and yellow and green, and our rails spread out from four to a dozen or more like tributaries of a silver river. Jets wink by above us; towers and overpasses shine in the moonlight; lightning cracks in the northern sky; and as Harold carefully shifts the engines across rows of rails to the siding where they will park for the night I recall another night in railroad yards, a night as a boy of four or five when my father brought me to see the roundhouse where he worked as a boilermaker on the old steam engines, a grueling job that required him to clamber into the boilers before they were cool to replace tubes and firebrick that had leaked or cracked. We rode the wicker trolley to the top of a bluff overlooking the yards—these of the Missouri Pacific—and walked down hundreds of wooden steps and across blocks of rundown houses and across rows of shining rails to the brick roundhouse, and inside from forges that towered to the top of the tall building fires flared as if in some workshop of mountain-makers, as if here were lathed and shaped and welded the landscapes of the world, the great trees and bluffs and rivers assembled, the plains worked smooth, the valleys hogged out by the massive hammers that in the night dropped shrieking to shape the iron and steel of steam engines worn out pulling the goods of America from farm and factory and town. The place stank of sulfur and hot oil and I held tight to my father's strong hand when he showed me the hammer where one night, working it, he felt his glove wet and pulled it off and discovered that he had pulled off the first two joints of the little finger of his left hand with it, a small tribute exacted by the giant hammer that might have exacted an entire hand or an arm instead.

There is that about railroading too: the fragility of the human body amid so much weight of iron and steel: for years after the invention of the air brake and the automatic coupling, the men who made their millions by watering stock and neglecting repairs allowed brakemen to be crushed between cars because brakemen were cheaper than air brakes: and men die today on the railroad as they died before, though more often now it is ordinary citizens in automobiles at crossings who die because they don't realize or don't care that a long and loaded freight train requires well over a mile to screech to a halt even with all its emergencies on: but all men die: the beauty and the glory of men like Harold Lewis, the lone human at his station in a cab, is that while they are working their engines so seemingly easily and so well, you forget the danger and forget the dying, caught up in the mystery of massive weight moved through space by the simple force of burning oil and the skilled ministrations of two human hands.

# 6 / Harry's Last Hurrah

INDEPENDENCE, MISSOURI, ON A SUNDAY MORNING IN
late spring, breathes the quiet of a country town, birds twittering resentfully at church bells, the people, at eleven o'clock,
gathered together for worship, and only an occasional car, rusting at its fenders, passing on the streets, aprowl for a Seven-
Eleven store that might offer up its blessings of eggs and Alka-
Selzer. The Baptist Book Store is closed; the courthouse on the
square that Harry Truman rebuilt is deserted; Denton Drug
Store is dark except for its dusty windows, where apothecary
jars glow with colored waters of no medicinal virtue; the offices of the *Independence Examiner* are locked tight against
any news of the outside world.

Dr. Billy G. Hurt will preach at the First Baptist Church, a block north of the Independence Memorial Hall, where, as a teenager, I danced folk dances with dirndled girls. Where I later registered for the draft. The First Baptist Church service has begun when I arrive, and an usher with graying, close-cropped hair points me to a row of dark plywood seats tucked back under the balcony. After a suitably discreet pause, the elderly lady next to me passes me a hymnal in time for me to turn to hymn number 487, "My Country, 'Tis of Thee." It's Memorial Day.

Dr. Billy G. Hurt wears the dark suit, white shirt, and white tie made familiar by another Baptist, Billy Graham. A pride of Billys in that denomination. Dr. Billy's delivery—his subject is "The Christian's Memorial Day"—borders on elegance. He's been to school, but he knows how to use his intellectual weapons without snobbery. "There is a demonic force loose in the world," he says, "call it the Devil or call it what you will." It rolled itself up to overwhelm the world at Christ's crucifixion, he says. "Our young men have died in numberless wars in numberless places, and where is that better day their sacrifice was to bring?" Dr. Billy's jowl is heavier on his right side than on his left, and he juts his head to the right as he speaks to protect that heavy jowl from scorn, his hands white at the knuckles twisting the pulpit as if he would wrench it from the floor to dramatize his point. "In these perilous times there are not many evidences that God's love is stronger than man's hatred"—surprising sentiment from a Baptist preacher in Independence, Missouri. "The Christian's Memorial Day"—does he mean Easter?—"is better." It's a somber sermon, a surprising conversion of the Baptists' traditional hellfire and damnation into a modern idiom. Dr. Billy G. Hurt hurts, and his congregation, composed of the very young and the very old, listens, or seems to, the members of the choir in their glossy purple robes lined up behind the preacher especially intent since they are on public display, their faces fixed and stern. A Wollensak tape recorder, looking like a small air conditioner, wheels silently atop a filing cabinet tucked into a corner of the wall next to me, preserving Dr. Billy for future generations of Baptists. The sermon sounds antiwar, the last thing I would have expected to hear in Independence, but the antiwar tone turns martial at the end when Dr. Billy proves unable to resist a metaphoric moral: "Christ's message to us is—keep up the fight!"

After the sermon, Dr. Billy welcomes a family recently moved to Independence from Kansas City, "Brother and Mrs. Calvin Strange," and we sing "Pass Me By" in ambivalent welcome—"I hope the Savior won't pass me by." As the postlude plays its response to Dr. Billy's benediction, the lady next to me does her duty and satisfies her curiosity, welcomes me to her church, asks me who I am. Did President Truman ever worship here? I ask her in return. No, he was a Baptist, but he always went out to Grandview, where his family lived, to the Baptist church there. When he was in Independence he worshipped with Bess at the Episcopal Church. Her church. Where, I discover later, Clifton Daniel of the *New York Times* and Margaret Truman, only child of Harry and Bess Truman, were wed. The lady introduces me to my usher, who looks at me noncommittally and shakes my hand. The line passing Dr. Billy is long; I leave by a side door.

Independence knows its age, as few American towns can. Founded in 1827, chartered in 1849, it settles today rotting in its history. Its very name praises the victory of that earlier Revolution. It was the watering hole of the westward movement well before Kansas City clambered up the Missouri River bluffs. Here rested pioneers heading for Oregon and California: Joseph Smith and his fanatic Mormon band; traders outfitting for Santa Fe; and later, petty criminals that we celebrate as outlaws of the West.

Independence had little enough to recommend it: no adjacent river, no prominent grove of trees, no dramatic elevation above the surrounding land. But it had a spring, pouring blue water into the big brick standpipe the town's founders caused to be built around it. The standpipe remains; above the wet mud at its bottom now is posted a sign: WATER UNSAFE TO DRINK. That is what has become of Independence. Kansas City, cleverly snaking out annexation lines around the older town, has completely surrounded it. The young people have moved out to their little 50'-by-50' imitation farms in the suburbs to fight crabgrass and sod webworms as their forefathers fought locusts and Indians, driving their camper trucks off into what is left of God's country on Sunday morning when they ought to be in church listening to Dr. Billy G. Hurt keep up the fight. Except to the very old, Independence is no longer a town at all but a crossover point between shopping centers. Wild Woody's Bargain Barn looms up just down the road. Wild Woody may be more in the spirit of the old Independence than the camper-trucked young who pasture around it: he is fervently Early American, his full-page newspaper ads with a banner titled WILD WOODY SEZ and below that a new pamphleteering slogan each week in krazily-spelled dialect.

Independence was different when I lived there, on a farm at the town's edge—the city limits divided one of our pastures—during the years of Truman's presidency. The town could not then have been more midwestern as my adolescence meant the word, rural and shaded and slow, withdrawn behind closed windows and cautious minds. Preacher Bob, at the Watson Memorial Methodist Church (which is gone now, torn down to make way for the Stake of Calvary Center of the Reorganized Church of the Latter-Day Saints), delivered more than twenty sermons on the books of the Old Testament, each sermon more boring than the last. Preacher Bob affected clerical robes, too, an ecclesiastical elegance that brought murmurings from some who preferred their Wesleyism plain. Another Woody—Preacher Woody—replaced him, a country man at heart, who met his name—it was really Woodruff—by carving a heavy cross for Watson Memorial's chancel and rebuilding the interior of the parsonage. One summer a Methodist preacher in a nearby town was called up for enticing boys, and I shuddered to hear of it because he and I had talked late and lonely by a campfire once of my onanistic sins and my profound desire for Christian comfort, and I think he had his hand on my leg for Christ's sake. Next to the Memorial Hall in Independence rose another Methodist church, more fashionable, I learned from an Independence girl who attended it and later attended Radcliffe and ended up in Ethiopia. The two Methodist congregations had divided during the Civil War, Watson Memorial going Northern, the other church Southern. Independence was that sort of town, too, though Preacher Bob made attempts at Christian charity. One Sunday he invited the pastor of the African Methodist Episcopal Church over—more murmurings—and once white missionaries recently returned from the Dark Continent told us of the horror with which their charges greeted a package of Aunt Jemima Pancake Mix, because the natives had become accustomed to finding inside America's packages whatever was illustrated on the cover. Or so I remember, but that may be a joke I read in *Reader's Digest*. It catches the missionary spirit, however. And down the street from the Watson Memorial Methodist Church, a short block away, where I now walked after leaving the Reverend Hurt's establishment, sat Truman's high, elderly house. Not really Truman's but Bess's, given to the couple on their wedding day, because the grandmother of the bride wasn't at all sure that the new son-in-law would make good, though he was fresh from a captaincy in World War I and had $15,000 in assets in his pocket. Independence people still call it the Wallace house; it bequeaths a silence to the spaces around it stiller even than Independence on a Sunday morning, a silence forced partly by the stature of the house itself—a quaint elegance of white Gothic curtained against the poisonous sun—partly by the stature of its inhabitant. Mr. Truman was President Truman during most of the years I attended Watson Memorial. I used to walk down the block in the half-hour between Sunday school and church to look at the president's house. Inside the wrought-iron fence that surrounded the house's large lot, reflected from tree to tree by clever mirrors mounted in black boxes nailed to the trees themselves, a protective beam of light circled the house like Ariel circling Prospero. I could not imagine that any occupant of that house, any native or long-time resident of that town, could possibly be president of the United States. My hero of the time, because I hoped to be a missionary myself one day, was Albert Schweitzer, a man with doctorates at heavy German universities in music and theology and medicine, and with all that learning off in Africa treating natives. How could a mere Independence man who wore loud Hawaiian shirts be president? I would stand across the street from the Wallace house in hopes that he would emerge, and watch tourists take their pictures smiling out from in front of the wrought-iron gate. Truman never appeared. Even when he was in town, he apparently stayed indoors except in the cool of the early morning, when I was out on the farm doing chores.

His vigor, as Dean Acheson reports it in *Present at the Creation*, would have surprised me. Independence moved slowly, as one moves when very old. Old men sat on the white benches young Judge Harry Truman caused to be built around the town square; the few restaurants served the same heavy, ponderously eaten fried chicken and mashed potatoes and buttered peas and cream gravy for Sunday dinner that we were served at home. You drove slowly through Independence; the few stoplights barely turned. At the summer meetings of the Independence 4-H Club the discussion of dues might run on through the entire evening. A president of vigor and sprightliness? But listen to him:

That summer of 1954 was abnormally hot in Kansas City [it was—the only time I can remember that we stopped haying at noon] and the thermometer outside the hospital windows [where Truman was recovering from surgery following a gall-bladder attack] ranged between 110 and 114 by midafternoon. Mrs. Truman was at my side constantly, and she read the newspapers to me, as well as current magazines and many of the letters and messages that came in.

I did not realize how punishing the heat was to the other patients and visitors to the hospital, which was without air conditioning. I do not mind the heat, and I have never cared for air conditioning for myself, preferring fresh air no matter how hot or cold.

When the director of the Research Hospital wanted to put in an air conditioner in my room I declined. . . . I felt that, despite the good intention of the hospital to provide me with every comfort, I should not be given special privileges, since no one else in the hospital was provided with air conditioning. . . .

But several days later an old friend of mine . . . said, "It may be all right for you without air conditioning, but what about Mrs. Truman sitting here day after day in this insufferable heat? Why are you being so stubborn, and why don't you let the hospital put air conditioning in?"

I sent for the hospital superintendent . . . and within the hour, an air conditioning unit was installed.

That is vigor, of a midwestern kind. And pride, and a courtliness that he made much of in his public life, though it has always been difficult to visualize Bess as the cute, blond-haired, blue-eyed girl of his dreams whom Harry often described. She was a champion shot-putter, his blue-eyed girl.

So many of Truman's qualities came directly from his midwestern past. His decisiveness. "He slept, so he told us," says Acheson, "as soon as his head touched the pillow, never worrying, because he could not stay awake long enough to do so." "With the President a decision made was done with and he went on to another"—Acheson again. Truman was called stubborn often enough. "Stubborn" is the pejorative of "decisive," and a physically small man, especially one so astigmatic as Harry, would learn stubbornness early in a small town if he had any gumption, and Harry did. He would be forever defending his stature, his weak eyes, his endless books, his rights in a knitted family that didn't always know the best of times, though it never knew the worst.

"My mother was partial to the boys," writes Truman in his *Memoirs*, "both in the family and in the neighborhood. I used to watch my father and mother closely to learn what I could do to please them, just as I did with my schoolteachers and playmates. Because of my efforts to get along with my associates I usually was able to get what I wanted. It was successful on the farm, in school, in the Army, and particularly in the Senate." It is the way the physically weaker but mentally more alert boy or man converts the stronger.

Imagine, then, Harry bantying around a battlefield, elated with his power to command for perhaps the first time in his life without subterfuge, yet learning awful lessons of the cost of his command in the lives of men he knew not only in battle but also back home. More than one historian has said Harry Truman was shaped there, in France, running a profitable commissary in his spare time with Eddie Jacobson (the same who would later help him near to bankruptcy and take that pledge himself) but facing, in the flaring darkness of battle, the cost of every decision he made.

And probably shrinking at first from such consequences, drawing the old stubbornness about himself for solace, yet gradually giving up the elation, clearing away the decision-making process until only the fact of the decision was left, until he knew that, whatever else it might cost him, a decision would not cost him his sanity or his self-respect; it would be made to the best of his knowledge and ability and he would then forget it: "He done his damndest," Harry's favorite epitaph.

One gives up squeamishness too in such a circumstance, as one gives it up on the farm, where after the war Harry spent twelve working years of his long life. Plowing makes way for sowing, and sowing for a solid field of wheat and tall corn, but the day comes when those sweated and nurtured crops must be cut and stored, or cut and sold, the grain to be fed to animals which in their turn will be slaughtered; and that is the way of the natural world, and you give up squeamishness or you subside. Truman then, and Truman as president, had no intention of subsiding.

Instead he became enamored of the process of making decisions, juvenated by the continual rediscovery that it was possible to make things happen, to move the world, to go from A to B to C and even all the way to Z by so simple and logical a procedure as making a decision. It became most of what he talked about and wrote about, and read about as well. He ranks presidents by their ability to make important decisions, and he will himself be ranked high because he made some of the most important decisions of the century. My God, no wonder the man is stubborn. Though he has read as many books as any man alive, he never went to college; to discover that among the Achesons and the Cliffords, fair gentlemen from Yale and St. Louis, he needed only listen to each man's information and opinion, test them against his encyclopedic knowledge of American history and his own good horse sense, and come up with the right decision more than half the time: that prided him beyond belief. Acheson ascribes Truman's perpetual cheerfulness to his healthy genealogy, but it came instead from his joy at being the man who gets to make more important decisions every day than any other on the face of the earth. He never doubted who he was, plain Harry Truman, a "great little man" as Acheson rather condescendingly puts it; but he never doubted, either, that he was possessed of a Jovian gift.

And for years after he left office, the people at the Truman Library say, political scientists came round asking Truman about his "decision-making process," and Truman laughed and scoffed and looked the other way. As far as he was concerned, it's the simplest thing in the world once you get the hang of it. "What was your most difficult decision?" the kids used to ask Harry when he spoke to them in the auditorium of the Library. "Korea. Korea," he'd say. "That was the most difficult decision, because that involved the whole free world. That was the most difficult decision to be made. And it saved Korea as a free government which had been set up by the United Nations, and the Republic of Korea was saved. But that was the hardest decision that had to be made because it involved the whole free world."

And the others? Dropping the atomic bomb? Joining the United Nations? Fighting John L. Lewis? The Marshall Plan? The Cold War? The campaign of 1948? The Berlin Airlift? Firing MacArthur? What on earth would the man have done with Vietnam?

After decisiveness, loyalty. Queer loyalty when it involved defending people like Harry Vaughan or showing up as president of the United States for Kansas City Boss Tom Pendergast's funeral. But remember also his loyalty to people like Acheson and Marshall. What else but loyalty from a battle commander, a 33rd-degree Mason, a man helped into office by Missouri's unregenerately partisan Democratic party? But what else also from a man who remembered, as a boy, a happy childhood full of pigeon-raising, wood-cutting, gardening and small-town gangs? "At the corner of Delaware and Waldo, east of us [in Independence], were the Sawyers, the Wallaces, and the Thomases. Lock Sawyer was older than we were, and the Wallaces were a year or two younger: Bess, Frank, and George Wallace all belonged to the Waldo Avenue gang. Across the street at Woodland College were Paul and Helen Bryant. Paul and Vivian [Truman's brother] were great friends and raised pigeons and game chickens in partnership. We had wonderful times in that neighborhood from 1896 to 1902. Our house soon became headquarters for all the boys and girls around." What else for Truman but intense loyalties? It was how he grew up, how he lived his life. Acheson, who used to return to Yale to visit his old secret society, Scroll and Key, understood well enough, and so did Clark Clifford, that handsome, brilliant, discreet mother of presidents. Truman's men began calling themselves "the old contemptibles"; Truman they called "the Chief"; and whatever their understanding of their group, for

Truman it must have seemed some nationally convened neighborhood gang. He conducted the affairs of state—we have Acheson's word for this, though what follows is not his patrician image—as if they were discussions of what activities, what mischief or good deeds, should issue forth from the treehouse today, and Truman chief of the Treehouse Association.

Writes Acheson: "[Truman's was] a truly hospitable and generous mind, that is, a mind warm and welcoming in its reception of other people's ideas. Not in any sense self-deprecating, his approach was sturdy and self-confident, but without any trace of pretentiousness. He held his own ideas in abeyance until he had heard and weighed the ideas of others, alert and eager to gain additional knowledge and new insights. He was not afraid of the competition of others' ideas; he welcomed it." It is not entirely fanciful to imagine the mature Truman remembering, amid the affairs of state, the old gangs and how they worked. Truman is fond of saying he is a cross between two of Missouri's other famous residents, Mark Twain and Jesse James. He may well be.

He was proud of the Marshall Plan, and it was his and Acheson's and Clark Clifford's more than General Marshall's; he was delighted with Point Four, the Peace Corps' predecessor, promising—as it did not fulfill—a sort of midwestern chiropractic of international healing; he regretted Korea with a fierce unyielding regret born of his own experience of battle; he was scared as hell of MacArthur, and immensely relieved when he removed that addled bully from his Japanese throne; he found Potsdam trying, but did his level best, and the odds were not favorable: "In a physical sense I found the [Potsdam] conference to be exacting. Churchill and Stalin were given to late hours, while I was an early riser. This made my days extra long. . . . I was glad to be on my way home." No country boy could hope to keep up with those two advanced alcoholics on their own terms. Truman moans the odd hour of their formal meetings—5:30 in the afternoon—but he stuck them out. He had known odd hours before.

Greatness as a president is not necessarily good, and it may very well be evil, depending on how you like what that greatness accomplished. Remember that this snappy dresser from Independence, this plain, practical man, helped to construct the national and global politics of our present age. He invented the Cold War; he desegregated the Armed Forces and the civil service; he laid the groundwork, in his Korean "police action," for Vietnam; he backed NATO and the United Nations; he confiscated the coal mines and would have confiscated the railroads to force the federal will; he took power from the other branches of government, as all strong presidents do. And he did it all in the name of sweet reason, a name he believes. The irrational has no place in his canon, though even his neighbor Dr. Billy G. Hurt insists that the diabolic was loosed into the world long ago. And soon enough we will have to dismantle this age Truman created with the clever Dean and the subtle Clark at his side; it has grown beyond its once rational limits, swollen in a kind of world-destroying acromegaly, gone knobby and awkward and bizarre, gone self-destructive, gone more than a little mad.

None of this can be what Truman intended; but what has happened is the result of the groundwork he laid. Present at the creation indeed: present now in the days before the flood, or perhaps the apocalyptic fire, blunt phallic ICBMs raining genetic death on a race that murders to create.

What does a president do when he leaves office? How can he bear the loss of power and authority? In this regard at least, John Kennedy was lucky; he died and passed over immediately into myth. Eisenhower was a myth before he even took office: no sweat. Hoover's Quakerism saved him, and his training as an engineer; he lived on to become the nation's most efficient vacuum cleaner, Hoovering up the starving refugees of World War II, Hoovering up the administrative mess of the war-swollen federal government, passing everything through his ample bag and leaving the rug of state decently clean. Lyndon

Johnson will bear the loss the worst of them all; presently he broods in the cavern of his guarded top-floor offices, spewing forth memoirs like a stricken whale gushing blood.

Truman solved the problem as only he could. He became a high-school teacher. First he wrote his memoirs, then he buried himself in the details of building and establishing a presidential library, then he taught school. His Library, on I-70 north of Independence, is laid out like a study unit for a civics course, with curios thrown in to hold the kids' attention. A major exhibit is devoted to the six jobs of the president as Truman defines them: chief executive, ceremonial chief of state, legislative planner, head of his political party, commander in chief of the armed forces, and director of foreign policy.

In one wing, plunked down on the bare limestone floor, sits Harry's prewar Chrysler, the car in which he conducted his senatorial reelection campaign in 1940, drove as senator and then as vice president, and turned over to his sister when he became president. She drove it from 1945 to 1951, frugal as he. The Chrysler Corporation later had it restored; pale green, with those impossibly large balloon tires cars used to wear, it still shows the hammered-out remains of fender dents earned careening down Missouri back roads and in the maze of Washington, D.C., traffic.

Thomas Hart Benton's mural, "Independence and the Opening of the West," three years in the making and painted with bravura right onto the wall by crafty old Tom, glows across from the Library's main entrance, a swollen montage of settlers and Indians rising to a peak over a large double doorway, an orgy of aniline in the plain limestone-and-marble hall.

Truman's White House office is preserved more or less intact in one wing, and by pressing a button you may hear the president himself explain to you the details of the room, the hidden doors, the furnishings. In such a setting one wishes Walt Disney's Imagineers would construct an audio-animatronic Truman to deliver the lecture in person, banging his plastic fist on the desk to drive each point home. The single black telephone on the presidential desk appears deficient and antique compared to the supercommunication systems of later presidents.

Visitors, says the museum's curator, like best the 12′-by-17′ Persian rug that hangs opposite the stairwell in the museum, all 29 million knots of it, a gift to Truman from the shah of Iran. They also like the ornamental swords encased near the main entrance, heavy with jewels. The White House floor beam that sagged under the weight of Margaret Truman's piano, cracked and dusty and ensconced in a glass case as if it were the Declaration of Independence, amuses visitors, as it must amuse Harry.

He himself no longer visits the Library. He used to be there every day at 7:45 sharp after a brisk one-mile walk from the Wallace house, due north to the Library through an old and quiet Independence neighborhood. His constituency in those days, the late fifties and early sixties, was children, bussed out by the hundreds from area schools to see a live president turned civics instructor. One May the museum curator kept count of the groups Harry spoke to: one hundred in one month. He would take on four or five bunches a day, cracking out sharp answers to their questions about tough decisions, about how to be good citizens. "Korea, Korea," he would tell them, still brooding on the deaths of that undeclared war, and "Read, read," he would tell them, knowing how far reading had gotten him over the years, what a good citizen it had made of him. He would autograph someone's cast and drag along visiting dignitaries to answer the kids' questions and to show the visitors that the Chief still had a constituency of sorts, albeit sans body hair. He would steadfastly refuse to discuss foreign policy, disclaiming knowledge of the facts but really remembering how damned difficult such partisan discussions had made his own presidential years. Ah, they were star turns, his appearances before those uncritical awed audiences, and they did him a world of good. Grownups came too, tourists from all over the country. It was a quick stop right there on the Interstate like a

Howard Johnson's halfway between New York and California and maybe we'll catch a glimpse of old Harry himself. Admissions fell off at the Library when Harry began staying home; people would drive by the Wallace house instead, hoping to see the old man on his side porch or out walking.

The real riches of the Library no one sees except the hundreds of scholars and journalists who have signed in over the years at the back door. In the stacks, boxes upon boxes of presidential papers stand in neat rows like massed troops, a total of six million sheets of paper. The juiciest are unavailable for reading, and will remain so until the people about whom they were written are dead and gone and no feelings left to be hurt. Each box is fumigated as it arrives, as if to fix it in a permanent present. Digging through a few of the boxes, you sense the enormity of the American presidency better than you can by talking to a president or pressing buttons in the Oval Room: letters of pride and heartbreak from ordinary citizens, numberless memos, drafts of speeches, handwritten notes, the minutely detailed history of an era.

But writing memoirs, building a library and giving civics instruction were never enough, could never be enough for a man who ran the world for seven years. "I hope you will remember what I have been," he told an audience at the New York World's Fair in 1964, "and not what I am today." He walked into the Jackson County Courthouse in Kansas City one day—he built that courthouse when he was presiding judge of the court, an administrative position. The three judges who run the county's business greeted him warmly enough, and he told them, "I just happened to be downtown and heard you were meeting and came over to see if an old man out of a job could get work."

He felt the deprivation keenly. He had no hobbies; he had no sports; when reporters tried to characterize him after his nomination from obscurity as vice president in 1944, he told them simply, "I'm a workhorse." Out to pasture, the workhorse cast about for something to do. One of the curious results of Truman's retirement was *Mr. Citizen*, a book as bare of substance as his two-volume *Memoirs* was crammed. In *Mr. Citizen* he discusses his friends, his operations, his grandchildren, his travels, and then makes a panicky plea for something to do:

> Congress should pass enabling legislation designating former Presidents of the United States as *Free Members of Congress.*
>
> These Free Members would have the right to sit on the floor of the Senate and of the House on all occasions.
>
> They would have the right to take part in debate, subject, of course, to the parliamentary procedures in each house.
>
> The Free Members *would not have the right to vote.*
>
> *They would* have the right to sit in on any meetings of any committee, subcommittee, or joint committee of both houses and take part in discussions. Here, too, they would not have the right to vote.
>
> Free Members would be assigned suitable office space in the Congressional buildings.

But without the right to vote, without a constituency behind them except for such national goodwill as remains after a president leaves office, what possible authority would Truman's Free Members possess? Or think of it this way: can you imagine Lyndon Johnson a Free Member?

(Notice that in the midst of this momentous proposal the ever-practical Truman provides for office space. He alone among twentieth-century presidents actually saved money out of his presidential salary—saved as much as a quarter of a million dollars, by one estimate.)

The pastured workhorse wrote a newspaper column for a while in 1964 but inexplicably stopped. When they laid the foundations for the Churchill Memorial Chapel in Fulton, Missouri, in 1964, Harry was on hand to turn a golden shovelful of dirt. Westminster College announced at that time an

$80,000 gift to establish the Harry S. Truman Chair of American History, and said that Truman himself would deliver the first eight lectures. He never did. That same year, augur of decline, Vergne Dixon of Dixon's Chili Parlor in Kansas City, where President Truman was wont to dine, died of a heart attack.

By 1966 Truman was reported at home suffering dizzy spells, and one reporter claimed the former president had Parkinson's disease. Truman's family physician, Dr. Wallace Graham, denied the claim, although Graham was quoted in a letter to the director of the National Parkinson Foundation as referring to a "Parkinson-like syndrome." What Truman did have was a tendency to vertigo whenever he stood on his feet very long; that more than anything else was responsible for his discontinuing his daily visits to the Library and his regular daily walks.

The traditionally Republican Citizens Party officials of Kansas City, Missouri, had never liked Truman. In 1967, when the city council was ready to name the new international airport under construction north of Kansas City, the councilmen hurriedly approved the name "Kansas City International" to avoid discussion of the name "Harry S. Truman International," discussion which might offend the former president. "What has Harry ever done for Kansas City?" was the tone of the meeting, a *Kansas City Star* reporter thought.

By 1969 Truman had visited the hospital again to recover from a bout of flu. Influenza was epidemic across the United States that winter. He went to Key West to recover, a successful trip. The same year, a Kansas City businessman named Alex Barket spent $80,850 on a railroad car claimed by its San Francisco owner to be the *Ferdinand Magellan*, the car on which Harry conducted his Give-Em-Hell whistle-stop campaign of 1948. Barket proposed to make the car available for static display, and spent a good deal of money refurbishing it, but the car's lineage soon came into question: it may have been a car in which Truman once rode, but it was probably not the car used in the campaign. Chagrined, Barket claimed he still believed his car was the *Ferdinand Magellan*, and anyway he could get his money back if it was not an authentic relic.

Harry S. Truman was eighty-five in 1969. He had pledged at eighty that he would live to be ninety. Once or twice each year, rumors fly around Kansas City that he is dead or dying at Research Hospital, his favorite, now a brand-new building and air-conditioned throughout. The rumors suggest that the people of the area are through with the living man and anxious to get on with the business of honoring his death—keeping up with Abilene, as it were.

And today Independence seems a town dispossessed, as if, Truman declining, it was being dismantled and carried away. It labored mightily to bring forth a great city, but brought forth something more valuable: a great man. It hardly recognizes him as such, knowing as it does the ground from which he came, but he is its finest issue. Behind Memorial Hall sits a cupola, white wooden dome over a brick foundation. For years it housed a replica of the Liberty Bell given to Independence by the town of Annecy le Vieux, France. Walking back from the Wallace house, I discover that the cupola is empty, the bell gone, the bronze plaque rudely torn out of its brick moorings. I wonder where the bell has gone (to the lawn of the Truman Library, as it turns out), as I wonder where the Watson Memorial Methodist Church has gone that no mark of its presence is left. On the square the courthouse is dilapidated, the windows dirty and spattered with paint, the sidewalk broken and faulted and bristling with aging parking meters. The equestrian statue of Andrew Jackson, the county's namesake, rides like a late commuter toward the bus stop on the southeastern corner of the square, and across the street discount stores and empty storefronts bleat urban decay. Somewhere along the way, breeding pioneers and gunmen and one mighty president, Independence lost its soul.

What is it, then, to be very old and to have been president of the United States in the sixth decade of the second century of their federation? It is to live in a body musted like old books, a shrunken body that no longer fills the clothes you wear, the shirt collars hanging from the neck, the pants baggy at the seat, the coat drooping over the ends of your contracted shoulders. Your body no longer responds; sluggish, cranky, it demands your attention, requires you to think about where next to place your foot for safety because the bones are brittle now and you can break your hip just stepping off a curb. It is to find your tongue sucking your front teeth like some lizard you have caught that fights to get away, lunging and lunging as you struggle to hold it still without pinching it into pain. It is to see a different face in the mirror every morning, a face shrunken at the cheeks, eyes looking out of deep cones created by the wasting away of subcutaneous fat, eyes with pupils constricted by your ever-present anger at being old, eyes that you have looked at too long and that now seem to look back at you with a despair you by now take for granted.

And to be old is to know that within this moldering shell which you once propelled proudly down miles of sidewalks at exactly 120 paces per minute, your brain is still alive and functioning, slower now, some of its nooks and crannies harder to reach, some of its cupboards bare that once opened onto home-canned riches of memory and logic and imagination, but still capable of so much more thought than your body can act upon that each sluggish response must make you mad. And so signals of anger flash back through the still-clear circuits, and you must recycle or unravel or suppress the anger or risk overloading the entire system and breaking down in simple rage—and you are someone who was never known for keeping your temper if you didn't want to.

Stored in that brain, stuck in that brain with no earthly value now (because the last thing anyone wants in America is an old man, especially an old man who once controlled vast power and thus can no longer be deferential to any man except perhaps another president, and probably not even one of those, since they don't make them the way they used to any more), stored in that brain is this enormous bank of data about the history of the world, American and British and French and German history and probably Tibetan and Angolese history as well. And nothing to do with it, no place to use it, no decisions to make out of this walking library loaded to the gunwales with good men and bad, good decisions and bad, sly Elizabethan ploys and hidden Napoleonic mistresses and stupid battle maneuvers and ships' cargo lists and gunpowder plots on all seven continents and the toilet habits of every American president and the exact number of bottles of wine that caused the downfall of the Roman Empire and all the words you had in secret and in public with the most powerful and the most brilliant men and women of your time.

And behind that synaptic bank of data another bank reserved for your long, quiet relationship with the woman you honored and respected and loved for half a century, and with a little girl grown to be an intelligent and pleasant matron.

And behind that bank another bank, loamier, misted, with farm animals and distant cousins and the names of country trees and the way it felt to ride a horse on an October morning in Grandview, Missouri, before anyone ever heard of horseless carriages, much less atomic bombs.

"I hope you will remember what I have been and not what I am today." All the depth of it is there, the chill and pinch of age, the sorrow and sadness and bitterness and anger. Once you cheered a staff of good and sturdy men who worshiped your power and respected your good sense; now your one secretary, aging too and prim, sits in the office you can no longer visit and keeps the light on through the day. Once presidents and prime ministers, emperors and kings, ambassadors ordinary and extraordinary, senators and representatives, heads of great departments of government, generals and admirals, captains of industry, poets and journalists, winners of Nobel Prizes and earnest brilliant scientists, ordinary citizens, young people, deferred to you, hung on your every word, nodded and blushed and smiled; now an occasional president stops by your door, often enough a man you detest on principle and for a fact, and you come to the door because you still feel the office deserves that obeisance despite riots and murderous undeclared wars (you had one yourself, but you won it and won it as clean as such wars can be won and probably think you could win in Vietnam too, but only God could do that). And other than presidents giving you the time of day because they want someone to give them the time of day when they also are old, you see only intimate visitors, and few enough of those.

You never gave a damn for the fussy protocols of office anyway, not for yourself as Independence boy, though you certainly gave a damn about them for yourself as chief executive officer. You learned that schizoid distinction as an officer in the war if not earlier as the elected head of the Independence Treehouse Association. But if you didn't care for protocol, you loved to see the people, like every politician and every decent statesman, loved to feel the massed weight of their bodies crowding around like ballots raised out of the valley of dry bones into flesh. You could govern so vast a country, so various a country, so fickle and coy and sometimes vicious a country, because you were a one-man cross section, small-town boy and country boy, soldier and dapper businessman, practical county judge and shrewd politician, self-taught historian and steel-rimmed facts-and-figures senator and snappy tough-minded president all rolled into one, with a whiff of the barnyard and a squirt of the church usher thrown in for good measure. You could dine with the Achesons and not eat your salad with your dinner fork and you could hunker down with a tough old farmer and bite off a hefty plug of Red Man and not choke. You were a countryman first and last and always, but you knew your way around.

And now he sits in his study, a small study, surrounded by books, reading books, reading a book a day (not some lighthearted novel or detective story, either, but a wordy historical study, the latest poop on the battle of Agincourt, the definitive printing of Abraham Lincoln's little-known early epic poems)—books and more books, so many books that Bess can't keep up with him despite the flood of new titles shipped out to Independence by unctuous New York publishers hoping for a quote, and must send out panic calls to friends like a little Dutch girl with her finger in the dike, *More books, more books, Harry wants more books.*

The memoirs are finished, the peculiar inhibited confession of ordinary citizenship is dry on the shelves of public libraries, not much checked out any more, the study of presidents never completed, the newspaper column abandoned, the lectures never given, the other books he wanted to write that he never told anyone about, books about the nature of the presidency and the nature of history and the nature of the universe never written; still he sits in that little study behind those thick glasses reading, reading, just as he did as a boy, reading, storing up even more facts, weighing each decision, playing president down all the corridors of history, no longer confined to that oval office with the plow on the desk and the secret secretarial doors and THE BUCKS STOPS HERE and the slicker mob of newsmen cooling their hot feet in the corridor waiting to catch him swearing again.

And all that reading useless now except to pass back and forth before his eyes for casual entertainment like a marathon Hollywood production, the events of history fading in and out of each other so that he can visit Waterloo with Caesar on the sidelines and confer with Napoleon about what he ought to do; visit Atlanta with MacArthur—no, not that son-of-a-bitch MacArthur—with Hannibal to advise Robert E. Lee about the advantages of elephants; walk down Pennsylvania Avenue with Lincoln at his side, Lincoln taking half as many steps to cover the same ground, Truman looking up at him but not deferring to him at all, Washington loping along behind, lost in ponderous Germanic thought, Truman snubbing the weakling Zachary Taylor as he passes, waving at Jackson and giving him a wink that says *We understand these city boys,* Truman's petite thin-soled rich-man's shoes clicking away the pavement under him; or he can mount his pony and go out and look for stretches of pasture beyond the windbreak where he can ride hell-for-leather just like Teddy's Rough Riders and no doting mother on hand to worry about his losing his glasses or breaking a leg.

And all the other flashing pictures, all of William James's wonderful stream of our consciousness that becomes paradoxically such a comfort and such a bitter burden now, the aching emptiness of the White House when Truman was alone at night and his wife and daughter were away; the warm Florida sun; the good bawdy jokes, all the thousands of them, that he told over the years to win the confidence of those seemingly manly, seemingly strong, big-jawed and big-chested men who were in fact little boys in need of Truman's strength, he more a man than any of them despite his small size and scratchy baritone, he tough as nails and stringy as a coyote on a cold day in March.

If he is very lucky, he doesn't know any more that he is merely sitting in his study in Independence. If he is very lucky, he believes he is sitting in the Athenian Senate holding a conference with Disraeli and Tom Jefferson and Jim Bridger and Attila the Hun. But probably he is aware; friends report he's as sharp as ever, though who believes friends? But probably he knows, knows his age now who never knew it before, who became senator in 1935 at the age of fifty-one and president in 1945 at the age of sixty-one. Probably he knows that he is dying.

But if he knows, as any man must finally know it, as every man feels his body sinking downward into death in a gradual descent that brings real fear because he never knows the day and hour it will happen (and even if he doesn't fear pain he still must fear that final cessation, though in those final moments if he has lived well he will cease to fear the rest); if he knows, if Harry S. Truman knows that he is dying, then why is he still preparing for the next great test of his ability to make big decisions and make them right by reading, reading, reading? But then again, why not? He prepared that way all his life, while the slick boys were out cutting a figure. He probably believes in an afterlife, and expects at very least to be one of Heaven's Free Members. And tough he always was, smart he always was, ready for the next challenge he always was, crude he sometimes was, but slick? Never. Harry Truman, Jesse James, Mark Twain: as Dr. Billy G. Hurt might say, Father, Son, and Holy Ghost. Amen.

# 7 / *Behold, How Good and How Pleasant It Is for Brethren to Dwell Together in Unity**

THE UNITY SCHOOL OF PRACTICAL CHRISTIANITY, IN Lee's Summit, Missouri, is a profoundly American institution. It was founded on prayer, and still lives by it. The School's department of Silent Unity shipped out more than 700,000 prayers to the world in one recent year, all of them in answer to personal requests. More than 6,000 letters, telegrams, and tele-

---

*Psalm 133:1.

phone calls reach the Silent Unity building each day. A second-story window in the building glows perpetually; inside is a telephone room where workers answer calls around the clock. Long before suicide centers, poison-control centers, and Dial-a-Priest, Unity waited patiently for your call, and waits at this moment.

"There were three connecting rooms," writes Dr. Marcus Bach in *The Unity Way of Life*, a Prentice-Hall book, "but the one I recalled this night was the one with the perpetually burning light, the votive light of prayer. There was a large round table in the center of that room, divided into arcs and equipped with telephones, and there were workers answering the calls in quiet tones, and I thought I heard them give thanks to those who called that every need is already fulfilled." That is Unity's sort of prayer, positive and affirmative and a little wacky, and it has its reward.

Prayer requests account for half of Unity's income; testimonials returned to Unity by those who believe themselves helped usually contain a gift of money—a "love offering," in Unity's term. The other half of Unity's income comes from subscriptions to its several periodicals, which are more or less self-supporting. *Daily Word*, a monthly calendar of scriptural meditations, is the best known.

"Silent Unity," says an officer of the School, "generates a great number of free-will offerings. Support for what I call our 'outreach' programs comes this way. These buildings were built that way. The property was acquired that way." But Unity does not disclose financial figures. "It's not that they're secret," the officer says. "We just can't see what good it would do." The Internal Revenue Service, he points out, reapproved their tax-exempt status some years back. The size of Unity's operations and the number of its employees suggest income of several millions a year.

"The prayer work is the thing that made Unity," according to James Dillet Freeman of Unity. Freeman is a handsome man of middle height and middle age. Iced with silver-gray hair, dressed in suede and corduroy, he looks the American poet whom he believes himself to be. Like many public lecturers, he speaks English when discussing the spirit, American when discussing the flesh. He believes in the Unity movement, and has given it his life. He is its historian, its permanent poet-in-residence, and a teacher at its School.

"Prayer attracted the people," he explains. "Healing is still a big item. The thing about this place—and this is true—is that it's always attracted people who very much believed in what they were doing—the people in charge are people who themselves are utterly convinced that they're serving—that their prayers are effective. Unity maintains a constant, round-the-clock prayer watch. They used to pass a picture of Jesus Christ from desk to desk. If the picture came on your desk, then you went into the prayer room and prayed until somebody else came in. There's no cynicism here.

"We have two things to give people," Freeman continues. "One is a feeling of faith—we are praying with you. You're not alone. Two, you're loved—here's somebody thinking of you, caring for you, interested in you and your welfare. Most human beings need these—pretty strongly. If we did nothing else than this, we'd do enough. These are the great things we've got to give people. Probably 650,000 people contact us every year. Most of it is word of mouth. Somebody is in trouble and someone tells them about us."

Unity maintains its perpetual prayer watch in a chapel down the hall from the telephone room. Workers drop prayer requests into baskets at the front of the chapel, where they absorb prayers for a month or so before being removed. "I think they stay there about sixty days now," Freeman says. That's a powerful dose of a sovereign remedy. Years ago, Unity printed a healing prayer on a red insert page in its monthly magazine; overzealous believers physically applied what they called the "red leaf" to their afflictions. Unity chided them for the practice, but gently, for who knows the ways of God? Prayer, tapping the free energies of the universe, may well work as a metaphysical unguent, a subtle and cosmic Ben-Gay.

Unity reaches out with many limbs. The School trains workers for Unity's churches (called "centers" to avoid any whiff of denomination) and publishes the organization's many books, periodicals, and leaflets in its own printing plant. Silent Unity handles prayer and healing requests. Silent 70, named from Luke 10:1 (*After these things the Lord appointed other seventy also, and sent them two and two before his face into every city and place, whither he himself would come*), supplies free Unity magazines, tracts, and books to the prisons of America. The braille department makes Unity materials available to the blind. The Department of World Unity spreads the Good Word across the world, and lately, according to Unity spokesmen, is making great inroads in England, where church attendance is down to a bare three percent of the population.

The past shadows the present, at Unity as throughout the Midwest. The traditional European forms of Christian worship—the cathedral and the priest, the solid stone church and the solid stone pastor—never were available in quantity on the frontier, and it could not have sat still for them if they were. Midwestern settlers wanted Higher Guidance; not finding it in traditional religion, which only reluctantly moved west, they devised their own. They injected religion into business and invented the Chamber of Commerce, into politics and invented Honest Government, into personal behavior and invented the Dale Carnegie Course. They didn't completely give up their Christianity, but they expected it, as William James did, to perform. The turn of the century was high tide for this new-time religion. It stirred more sentiment than passion. James Sheldon's *In His Steps*, written out of Topeka, Kansas, began its climb to all-time best-sellerdom in 1906, proposing that each of us literally follow Jesus' example, and many tried, including the founders of Unity, to the best of their understanding. When *In His Steps* came to town by lecture and lantern slide, grown women wept. New Thought steamed out of Boston and New York and Chicago on the 20th Century Limited; Mary Baker Eddy's pinched, Bostonian Christian Science began building its mock-Episcopal fortresses; healers roamed the countryside with magic incantations and bottomless pocketbooks, and the Midwest turned on.

A businessman and his wife founded Unity. Charles Fillmore was a real-estate salesman who dabbled in gold mining, popular science, and comparative religion at a time when all three were rich in undiscovered lodes. Fillmore might never have left real estate if his ingenious and attractive wife, Myrtle, hadn't become interested in faith healing. In her letters, published after Unity was well under way, she would gently insist that she had started the movement. She had, but her husband made it work.

Charles Fillmore was born in a log cabin on an Indian reservation in Minnesota in 1854. A Sioux medicine man carried him off for the day when he was only two years old. "Where they had taken him and what they had done with him, Charles could not remember," James Freeman writes in his history of Unity, "but he always had a feeling that they had used him in some mystical ceremony." When Charles was seven, his trader father moved to another cabin ten miles away, and after that the boy and his younger brother Norton divided their time between the cabins of their parents. They harvested wild rice, Indian-style; they wandered among the lodges, witnessing who knows what oddities of living; they got little schooling.

Norton ran away to the West at a tender age and never returned. Charles dislocated his hip one day in a skating accident. The leg failed to set properly and developed a bone infection. "I was bled, leeched, cupped, lanced, seasoned, blistered, and roweled," Fillmore later told Freeman. "Six running sores were artificially produced on my leg to draw out the diseased condition that was presumed to be within. Physicians of different schools were employed, and the last one always wondered how I ever pulled through alive under the treatment of the 'quack' that preceded him; and as I look back at it now it's a miracle to me how I ever got away from them all with the little bundle of bones and sinews that I found in my possession after they had finished their experiments."

The leg withered and grew no more. All his life, "Papa Charley," as Unity workers called Charles Fillmore, would pray the leg longer, though there is little evidence that it responded.

When he was old enough to leave home, Fillmore went to work as a printer's devil in St. Cloud, Minnesota. He worked in a grocery store and a bank. He befriended the son of an army officer, and the boy's college-educated mother—a rarity in those days—plied her son's bright friend with books—Shakespeare, Tennyson, Emerson, Lowell, Whittier. Much later, Charles would name one of his sons Waldo Rickert, another Lowell, in honor of his beloved transcendentalists, and there is much of New England mysticism in Unity, oddly blended, as it oddly blends, with Christianity.

In St. Cloud, Fillmore read about the West and found it challenging. He traveled to Denison, Texas, a town reputed to be as rough as they came in those days, but it was at a literary-society meeting in Denison that Charles met the red-headed schoolteacher, Myrtle Page, who would later become his wife. She had attended Oberlin College. She believed she had inherited tuberculosis. She had unusual religious ideas. When she returned to Clinton, Missouri, to teach school, Charles courted her with letters and books.

He lost his job in Denison and went north to Colorado, where he became a mule-team driver, studied assaying, and started to deal in real estate. He plucked Myrtle out of Missouri after marrying her there in 1881. In Pueblo, Colorado, Fillmore & Company, Realtors, temporarily prospered. "Charles's partner at that time was Charles Small, brother-in-law of Nona Brooks, who later founded Divine Science," remarks Freeman. The forces were gathering that early.

In 1884, the Fillmore family, now increased by two sons, moved to Kansas City, Missouri, then in the midst of a building boom. Charles Fillmore laid out a real-estate subdivision named Gladstone Heights, which still stands. It includes Myrtle Avenue, named for his wife, and Norton Avenue, named for his wandering brother. Charles packed the family one summer and went prospecting for silver in Colorado. He found a vein, but it quickly petered out. Back in Kansas City, the real-estate boom collapsed; simultaneously, Myrtle's tuberculosis flared up. "Her son Lowell," says Freeman, "recalls that the medicine cabinet was always full to overflowing with pills and nostrums with which she was continually dosing herself and all the other members of the family."

Ever restless, the Fillmores attended lectures. One they turned out for was delivered by a student of a woman who had worked with Mary Baker Eddy. The lecturer's main assertion buoyed Myrtle Fillmore's hope. She was in the right place at the right time. "I am a child of God," the lecturer announced, "and therefore I do not inherit sickness." Myrtle, believer in pills and nostrums, discovered a new faith: that statement founded Unity. "It flashed upon me," she wrote later, "that I might talk to the life in every part of my body and have it do just what I wanted. I began to teach my body and got marvelous results." "In just two years," writes Freeman, "Myrtle Fillmore was no longer an invalid. Through her prayers she was made absolutely whole."

Take that statement for what you will, Myrtle lived a long and healthy life.

People heard of Myrtle's miraculous healing and came to her for counsel. Charles was less easily convinced. "Although I was a chronic invalid and seldom free from pain," he wrote later, "the doctrine did not at first appeal to me." Two years later, finding the doctrine more appealing, Fillmore published the first issue of a little magazine called *Modern Thought*, "Devoted to the Spiritualization of Humanity from an Independent Standpoint." In the interim, his income had declined and a third child had been born.

*Modern Thought* received a small number of love offerings

and became *Christian Science Thought*, a more specific name. Papa Charley wrangled long with Mary Baker Eddy about his use of that then-generic term. Mrs. Eddy wanted to keep "Christian Science" for her exclusive use. Fillmore thought otherwise: "People of limited spiritual unfoldment," he wrote in his magazine, "are sticklers for names and creeds, and are thus worshippers of idols. . . . They quarrel over names, names, names, vapid, unmeaning names, that never were anything of themselves and do not even represent that which they allege to represent." But he gave in to Mrs. Eddy at last and rechristened his magazine *Thought*.

Quarrel over names who may, the Fillmore movement still lacked one—lacked what today we might call brand identity. Charles generated the missing name out of a prayer meeting one night, when he and Myrtle and a circle of students had "gone into the silence," as they called meditation. Freeman recaptures the excitement:

"That's it!" he cried out. "UNITY!" he told the others. "UNITY! that's the name for our work, the name we've been looking for."

Later he told friends the name came right out of the ether, just as the voice of Jesus was heard by Paul in the heavens. "No one else heard it, but it was as clear to me as though somebody had spoken to me."

Fillmore's revelation was fortuitous, even though it led to a persistent confusion of the Unity movement with Unitarianism, with which it was never associated and which it scarcely resembles. But Unity!—the merging of all religions, of all versions of New Thought, of science and faith, of theory and practice, of healing and help—was a name to conjure with.

Unity's religious virtues, or lack of them, the God of seasons and creeds must decide. Viewed secularly, Unity resembles the many family businesses that flourished in the Midwest from the late nineteenth century until after World War II, when most of them merged with large national corporations and lost their identity. The structure of a family business is the structure one would expect a midwestern businessman to give to a religious movement; it was the only mode of organization he knew. "This is not a business but a ministry," Charles Fillmore insisted, but he kept regular office hours, opened a vegetarian cafeteria in downtown Kansas City, and concerned himself mightily with the question of material prosperity, a question to which all forward-thinking Christians of the time gave heed. At the very beginning of the movement, Charles and Myrtle wrote out a covenant with God which reads like a contractual agreement; it was uncovered among some old papers in Unity's library in 1942:

*Dedication and Covenant*

We, Charles Fillmore and Myrtle Fillmore, husband and wife, hereby dedicate ourselves, our time, our money, all we have and all we expect to have, to the Spirit of Truth, and through it to the Society of Silent Unity.

It being understood and also agreed that the said Spirit of Truth shall render unto us an equivalent for this dedication in peace of mind, health of body, wisdom, understanding, love, life, and an abundant supply of all things necessary to meet every want without our making any of these things the object of our existence.

In the presence of the Conscious Mind of Christ Jesus, this 7th day of December A.D. 1892.

[signed] Charles Fillmore
Myrtle Fillmore

Unity's archives today celebrate the School's moves to successively larger quarters during the first decades of the twentieth century with the same proud and somewhat dusty nostalgia to be found in the gilded trophy rooms of midwestern corporations. The moves culminated in the piecemeal purchase of a 1,400 acre tract of land outside Lee's Summit, Missouri, which the Fillmores had the foresight to incorporate as a village, and so completely to control. Unity Village's mayor today is Charles Fillmore, grandson of the founder and the Unity School's chief executive officer.

Faith girded with business ability was the Midwest's peculiar institution in the early years of the century. Young, and usually dirt-poor, entrepreneurs did not merely found businesses in those days; they marched into prosperity with God and the people on their side. New Hampshire Baptist Russell Conwell bounced around the country to deliver his rousing lecture "Acres of Diamonds" more than six thousand times between 1877 and 1925, and founded Temple University on the proceeds:

> I say that you ought to get rich, and it is your duty to get rich.
>
> Many of my brethren say to me, "Do you, a Christian minister, spend your time going up and down the country advising young people to get rich, to get money?"
>
> Yes, of course I do.
>
> They say, "Isn't that awful! Why don't you preach the gospel instead of preaching about man making money?"
>
> *Because to make money honestly is to preach the gospel.* That is the reason. The men who get rich may be the most honest men you find in the community. . . . Money is power, and you should be reasonably ambitious to have it. You should because you can do more good with it than you could without it.

Horatio Alger got the message, and so did Jay Gatsby, and so did Henry Ford. Modified, made secular, it still informs Dale Carnegie's popular courses in personal success. For that matter, it still informs the American dream, and perhaps it is true. If faith can heal the body, then surely it can fill the pocket. And what else but faith has a poor boy to go on?

With the striving for prosperity usually came a striving for gentility, a didactic commitment to raising the level of public taste. Walt Disney, battered son of a ne'er-do-well Missouri farmer, preserved nostalgia, clean living, and country kitsch on film and won the accolades of the nation's urban intellectuals and the worship of its middle class. Joyce Hall, son of an itinerant Nebraska preacher and founder of Hallmark Cards, who never graduated from high school, won honorary doctorates from three midwestern universities for printing polite expressions of regard on decorated paper and thereby expressing the social emotions of millions of Americans: today half of all personal mail moved in the United States consists of greeting cards. The common ingredients of Disney's and Hall's products—slickness and corn, politeness and geniality—are ingredients of Unity's products as well. Disney Productions and Hallmark Cards are extraordinary successes, Unity only a modest success, but the name of the game is still the same: packaging. And not Disney, not Hall, and certainly not the Fillmores unto the third generation were ever cynical about the products they manufactured. Prayer as product: it was Charles Fillmore's most brilliant invention. Prayer requires no raw materials. It can be sent in measured quantities by ordinary mail, across a telephone circuit, through a wire. It can be transmitted like radio waves across the invisible ether, without generating equipment. Unity considers it priceless, and does not charge for its production. Those who receive it also consider it priceless, but usually put a price on its effects and remit promptly. Its models need not be changed more than once every fifty years or so, to reflect changes in the language. It does not wear out, needs no special handling, never goes out of style. It is, depending on how it is formulated, a medicine, a service, an investment. And it is tax deductible. As Disney did with character and Hallmark does with sentiment, Unity has done with prayer: categorized all the many varieties so that they may be called up on demand to answer the occasions of human emotion and human need. For years, Unity answered most written prayer requests with form letters supplying standard words of assurance and standard prayers for each correspondent's problem. With the advent of computer technology, Unity is now able to personalize those form letters. An advanced computer system buzzes in its air-conditioned hive on the first floor of the Silent Unity building and helps Unity pray at six hundred lines a minute. "The bread-and-butter operation for our computer," says young Charles Fillmore, "is subscription fulfillment, which seems to be a natural use of our computer. The computer also helps us answer our correspondence. Formerly we answered much of it with form letters, but now we can write personalized letters—actually serve the correspondent better with prayer requests than before. We're not answering prayers with computers. We still have people. The computer doesn't read the letters—'Garbage in, garbage out,' as the saying goes. Formerly it was just 'Dear Friend.' Now we can address 'Dear Bob,' 'Dear Mary.' It's working real well. It's giving better service."

The computer may not read the letter, but an organization which believes that thoughts can fly might soberly consider the power for good stored in the Unity computer's digital interior. If Christianity had ever adopted the prayer wheel, American ingenuity would certainly, before this late date, have harnessed it to the dentist's turbine, and believers everywhere would be flipping messages heavenward at around 300,000 revolutions per minute. Unity, a "here-and-now religion," as Freeman describes it, approaches that accomplishment. No doubt its computer serves.

Unity's formula for Practical Christianity resolves most of traditional Christianity's paradoxes, and makes believing easy. Unity is not a separate denomination but a nonsectarian institution, a "school" of faith. It proclaims no special beliefs, but only what it calls "Truth," which seems to include the irreducible essences of several major religions. "We feel that we don't have a truth that can't be found in any of the great religions if you dig deeply enough," says J. Sig Paulson, director of World

Unity and resident minister at Unity Village, a rangy, athletic man who used to be in the wholesale lumber business in Seattle. "Our idea is to take the message to the individual. We don't care if he goes to church or not as long as he applies it to his daily life. We have no creed or doctrine that anyone has to subscribe to."

Which would seem to leave Unity with no outlines at all, but that is not the case. In its many books and pamphlets, Unity defines itself as an organization which believes in man as God, evolving toward his destiny of immortality and perfection. "We don't believe that man is originally a depraved, sinful creature," continues Paulson. "The only reason he's capable of sin is the fact that he's a god. A dog couldn't sin, just by being a dog, or a cow by being a cow. But a god could sin or fall short, just because of the potential that he has. We feel that man has never discovered his potential just as he's never discovered the potential of the universe in which he lives. Atomic energy is a fairly recent discovery, but it's been here for a long time. Why, there's enough atomic energy in my little finger to light up Kansas City for years, if we only knew how to harness it. Man has to expand his consciousness. The real expansion comes from within."

Freeman is more succinct: "Unity says that evil is unreal—like cold, like dark. The only reality is the good."

The writings of Charles and Myrtle Fillmore do not lend themselves to debate. "I told the life in my liver that it was not torpid or inert, but full of vigor and energy," Myrtle wrote of her first healing experience. "I told the life in my stomach that it was not weak or inefficient, but energetic, strong, and intelligent. I told the life in my abdomen that it was no longer infested with ignorant thoughts of disease, put there by myself and my doctors, but that it was all athrill with the sweet, pure, wholesome energy of God. . . . I went to all the life centers in my body and spoke words of Truth to them—words of strength and power. . . . And neither did I forget to tell them that they were free, unlimited Spirit. I told them that they were no longer in bondage to the carnal mind; that they were not corruptible flesh, but centers of life and energy omnipresent."

Charles was not content merely to heal his body, perhaps because he found himself unable to do so, though he did discard his stacked shoe and minimize his limp as the years went on. "I spent several hours every day in this process [of talking to parts of his body] and I found that I was releasing electronic forces sealed up in the nerves. This I have done for nearly fifty years until now I have what may be termed an electric body that is gradually replacing the physical. It is even more than electric, and when certain spiritual emotions are imparted to it, it fairly glows and blends with an omnipresent etheric atmosphere that is highly charged with life energy. My physical organism is being transformed cell by cell, and the ultimate will be an entirely new body having all the perfections of youth in addition to ethereal life." Charles decided he would attempt not to die, and he lived to be ninety-four. He died in his old body, so far as the records show.

Unity's continuing popularity does not depend on Myrtle's vigorous liver or Charles's etheric transformations, but their writings reveal how much more experimental—is that the right word?—were their ideas than are those of the Unity movement as an institution. Unity's blandness is nearly unique among religious movements. One must look to such purveyors of emollients as Norman Vincent Peale to find a parallel, and Peale acknowledged his debt to Unity several years ago in a celebrated public pilgrimage to Lee's Summit.

The ingredients of Unity's publications combine to create a successful mass product, with affirmative prayers the strings that tie up the package. These from a recent issue of *Daily Word*: I RELAX AND ENTER INTO AND ENJOY EVERY MOMENT OF THIS DAY. I THINK THOUGHTS OF PLENTY, AND I AM PROSPERED. MY VISION IS CLEAR AND UNCLOUDED, MY MIND IS OPEN TO NEW IDEAS. Like horoscopes, Unity's prayers offer a series of abstractions into which most people can read their personal problems. Astrologists learned to construct these bubbles of abstraction long ago, but astrology's reference system is largely outside Christianity, and thus lacks the stamp of Christian authority which is Unity's seal of approval. With Unity, whatever your faith, the interfaces will match, and you also may enter in.

Unity's healing messages offer special compensation to victims of psychosomatic afflictions, for while the ill pray among the parts of their body, they also have the pleasure of thinking about those parts at delicious length—"carnal mind" or not. This from *Divine Remedies*, a Unity book:

> Since constipation and mental tensity in some form are so closely connected, the remedy is: Let go. Imagine yourself in a condition of perfect relaxation. Perfect relaxation can be produced by thinking and speaking relaxing thoughts and words. Say to your bowels: *You now open and let go, as I open and let go that which I hold in my consciousness.*

Cleanliness is next to godliness at Unity Village, ritually and in fact. The printing plant, proudly pointed out to visitors, is the cleanest in Christendom. All mail is subjected to a series of ritual cleansings as it is processed. Workers bless the incoming mail, bless each individual letter as it is opened, bless the love offerings as they are gathered together, and bless the responses Unity mails out. Callers are blessed the moment Unity answers the phone, as if they needed disinfection; workers are blessed by the management several times a day, as if their faith might otherwise flag; and the problems of sinners who contact Unity receive heavy doses of blessings in the perpetual-prayer room, spiritual gamma radiation that should crisp them like cancer cells.

Yet Charles Fillmore's body still proceeded with a limp, and the atomic energy in Sig Paulson's little finger has not yet illuminated the Midwest for even a millisecond. The ritual cleansing goes on, as it must in an organization which denies the corporeal so vehemently, for the corporeal still writhes despite all denials, still smells as ripe and suffers as much—as Unity people have occasion, in the welter of mail, to know. If Unity, on one level, is a helpful and successful tract society and night-care center, on another it must be considered a dismal failure, an experiment in tapping the energy of the universe that failed. But, in all fairness, so must Christianity.

Physically, Unity Village baroquely displays its founders' preoccupations. Most of the buildings on the 1,400 acre tract were designed by Waldo Rickert Fillmore, called Rick, son of the founders and the most sublimated of the Fillmores. Rick wanted to be an artist. He left Unity for a time, studied at the Chicago Art Institute and in Europe, and returned to Kansas City to become an interior decorator before going home to Unity Village and making its physical elaboration his life work.

Rick's was a decorative architecture, an architecture of stage sets hiding practical functions. He experimented, he tinkered, he tried out new materials and disguised old ones. What was once farmland became, at his hands, an ornate park, laid out in the manner of nineteenth-century English estates, with sheds and barns disguised as peasant cottages, with quaint bridges and wandering paths, a hodgepodge of Cotswold outbuildings and Italian Renaissance halls. The balustrades that line Unity's walks look, from a distance, like old stone, but in fact they were molded of stained concrete, with pits and cracks made by mixing clay into the wet concrete and washing it out when the concrete set. Walls of pink sandstone are really concrete dyed to match. Unity's fountains spray all summer, serving as decoration and as cooling units for the air-conditioning system. The School's massive tower, square and pink and 200 feet high, disguises a 55,000-gallon water tank. In the tower, the most masculine of Unity's buildings, Rick had his studio until his death in 1965.

Rick Fillmore was a decorator with a knack for engineering, not an architect. He designed no new structures, but overlaid his favorite European buildings onto pragmatic concrete-and-steel forms. His later work innovates more, structurally, than his earlier. He got interested in concrete prefabrication, learned to mix permalite beads into his cement to make it self-insulating, and devised a single-walled building molded on the ground and simply hoisted, a slab at a time, into place. He learned to locate each apartment's power sources—heating, hot water, meters, fuse box—in a central room off of which four living areas radiated. His monument is probably Unity's main administration building with its pagoda-like central elevation, its ornate, home-grown and home-carved furniture and woodwork, and its 1930s scalloped, edge-illuminated clear plastic valences. Rick himself preferred the detached tower, where he regularly took visitors for a proper overview. He was Unity's one rebel, but he never freed himself from the unrigorous laxities of its intellect. His father still talked about the fourth-dimensional ether in 1933, fifty years after the physicists Michelson and Morley disproved the ether's existence in their seminal experiment, and Rick still built in Cotswold and Renaissance hundreds of years after the sheep and the Borgias were laid to rest. At Unity Village and in Unity, nothing is quite what it seems. Unfortunately, visual and verbal dissimulation muddles more than it clarifies. One of Unity's weaknesses—one of the Midwest's most conspicuous failings, for that matter—is its lack of mind, of trained intelligence. Charles Fillmore would scoff, and say that educated thinking just gets in the way, but it was he, as Freeman notes, who "knew there was no arguing about religion." Certainly not about Unity's. It wouldn't stand up.

Visiting Unity Village today, more than a decade after Rick built his last building, one sees signs of decay. The concrete shales off the sidewalks; the back of the administration building, which Rick never finished, sports a stained dry wall; the toast is stale in Unity's once-popular vegetarian cafeteria. "We serve regular food in the cafeteria now," says young Charles with a hint of impatience. "The vegetarian business gave us a kooky image—though you can still get a completely vegetarian meal there if you want one." The Arches, a picturesque home where Charles and Myrtle Fillmore lived, is occupied by a family of Unity workers. Myrtle refused to allow a kitchen installed in the Arches when Rick built it, despite her husband's pleadings; Papa Charley's mother, come down from her log cabin and living in a house across the road, did the family cooking.

Yet Unity Village is pleasant to walk in, with apple orchards and a golf course, a private lake, a swimming pool disguised as a Roman bath, lodges and cottages and a wealth of trees. A successful Sunday afternoon in Kansas City used to include a drive to the country to buy a jar of Unity honey and a jug of Unity cider, the only cider available near town in those days that wasn't pasteurized. Honey is still for sale at the information center in the base of the tower, and cider in season at a stand across the road.

Charles Fillmore, Rick's son, grandson of the founder, executive vice president and chief executive officer, a man in his forties, occupies an office directly inside Unity's elaborately carved front door. A mounted copy of *Daily Word* glows on his desk; a golf trophy tees off on the bookcase behind him. Like his father Rick, Charles is a stocky, heavily built man with the broad face and twanging speech of a Missouri farmer, and with a farmer's surprising mixture of hesitancy and self-confidence. And toughness, when he talks of Unity's competition.

"The Reverend Oral Roberts came up here with his staff and studied our *Daily Word*, and six months later God told Oral Roberts to publish a devotional magazine and it's just like *Daily Word* except that the Bible verse appears at the bottom of each page instead of at the top. Well, we don't mind." Evidently we do.

"My grandfather was a very practical idealist," young Charles continues. "He always wanted to test things out and see that they worked. He was a human being and he certainly wasn't infallible and didn't claim to be. He wasn't one to go off into the wilderness and spend his life in prayer and meditation. The movement doesn't either, although some of us thought there were signs we were leaning that way. We recently cut the hedge out here, for example, which was pretty symbolic for a lot of us. It was pretty high at one time."

Unity shows signs of a power struggle which young Charles Fillmore won. It must have been fought out between Charles and his uncle Lowell, who is still officially president of the School, and it probably concerned Lowell's dogged loyalty to his parents, Charles and Myrtle. Says the grandson: "Lowell, of the three sons,* was the one—I don't know quite how to put it—he was the one who was very, very dedicated to his parents, to carrying on the work as he saw them doing it. He didn't get out too much. He didn't pursue his formal education past high school, as did the other two brothers. He's never been a civic joiner. The other two were. Lowell has done more writing than any of the rest of us." A self-educated man, a writer, not a Rotarian like his father and brothers and like the grandson: Lowell was different, young Charles implied, from "the rest of us."

"My grandfather Charles Fillmore was ahead of the particular metaphysical thought of his time. However, we've been caught up with, and this is good. He wanted to open up religious thought and let some ventilation in—'blow some minds'! But his followers, despite his wishes, as dedicated followers are wont to do, wanted to deify him—if Charles Fillmore didn't write it or say it, then let's not bother with it. It had a certain crystallizing effect on the movement. As Eric Butterworth† puts it, if we in Unity just settle for Charles Fillmore's legacy, we will have failed him. He believed in truth being progressively revealed. We came to a point where we were pretty self-satisfied. Our membership got older, grew more slowly. It was slow but steady, but not in proportion to the growth made during Charles Fillmore's ministry. Our field

---

*A third Fillmore son, Royal, died while still a young man.
†A Unity sympathizer with an East Coast following.

ministry leveled off in the mid-fifties. We found that more and more of our time was being spent here trying to be a service organization for a growing number of Unity churches and we asked ourselves one day if this was really our purpose. We say we're a non-denominational organization. Charles Fillmore wouldn't even hold his classes on Sunday in the early days so that he wouldn't compete with organized churches. This School was set up not to convert anybody but to try to disseminate a helpful spiritual viewpoint to people in need.

"So we put it to our churches. We said, well, listen, we're trying to be a cutting edge here in the forefront of metaphysical thought, trying to go beyond what our heritage is from our founders. We're trying to reach out to find new and better ways to get in harmony with this universe we live in. So they formed their own organization, the Association of Unity Churches.

"We're glad to have them, of course, and glad to help, but we're trying to get back to our real purposes. I believe that we have stubbed our toe when we have tried to organize groups of students ourselves. You know what can happen with church organization—power struggles, that sort of thing."

Unity's growth slowed during the very years when crowds of Americans moved to the city. Growth has picked up under the practical hand of young Charles, a graduate of the University of Missouri's School of Journalism. Having all but severed Unity's ties with its Centers, he has recentralized the School's power and authority, but he has not acquired a serious professional staff to move the School on. The evidence of Disney Productions and Hallmark Cards is that the founder's faith must be replaced by the professional's skill. Except for a few Unity staff members who are slowly acquiring D.Ed.'s at local universities, and one attending a theological seminary in Chicago, the Unity staff appears stagnant. And perhaps, with its continuing commitment to the personal belief of each worker in Truth, Unity cannot adapt itself to a world where packaging is at least as important as revelation. Young Charles Fillmore, it seems, despite his aging uncle's reluctance, will nevertheless make the attempt.

We all learned to be nice, years ago, as nice and clean and white as Charles and Myrtle Fillmore hoped we would be; out of that niceness the United States is now emerging to confront the ugly problems which gentility disguised. Unity has never confronted its own contradictions; symbolically enough, its beacon light shines not from its tower, where the light belongs, but from a low and feminine building sheltered behind the tower, a building that appropriately houses *Silent Unity*. Today the tower peels with disuse and Rick Fillmore's studio is shut up. The information center in the base of the tower sells honey and tracts.

The tower elevator struggles between the seventh and eighth floors. They are spaced far apart to accommodate the massive 55,000-gallon water tank. Riding along outside the tank in the elevator, you hear undersea echoes, ripples, ominous clankings, a hint of death by drowning, a reminder of the soulless waters from which we all emerged, a dark and liquid world that has little to do with affirmative prayers and honeybees. Rick Fillmore, Unity's Faust, designed his massive but amateurish monument here, and perhaps the presence of that vast tank of water next to his studio served him better than Unity knows.

When you emerge at the tower's open observation floor on a foggy day the structure seems to occupy a rarefied and spirited space of its own. You can barely see the Unity School of Practical Christianity far below, pastel through the mist. The scene recalls DeMille versions of heaven, fog pumping out of dry-ice machines, dialogue lofty, he-man actors wearing gossamer wings. Yet this foggy tower is far more real than the activities below, because you do not approach the railings around the tower's edge, amid the leftover wiring of Christmas lights, without understanding the distance that you could fall. The fog itself is more substantial than the gentle words that drift these days from Unity; it is water vapor, and they are metaphysics, less than motes of sunlight, which at least imply black night.

Unity's affirmative faith, its belief in God's interiority, requires of its students a terrible denial of self, for if it is not oneself inside there suffering and sinning, if to give up sin one must give up oneself and find merely God lurking in the corners of one's liver and the passageways of one's bowels, then one sacrifices the very thing Christianity has promised, almost alone among the world's religions: the persistence of individual identity: the privilege of personal existence now and through all time. Unity students pay a price for their faith in loss of identity. Perhaps they do not consider that price too high.

Charles Fillmore, successfully coaxing orchards to bloom and affirmations to ring; Myrtle Fillmore, gentle with people and generous with love; both made heavens on earth. They were rewarded in due portion: their followers recognized their happiness and, happiness being the rare commodity it is, paid generously to be near it in spirit and in flesh. It was a sideshow of sorts, the progress through life of Charles and Myrtle Fillmore, the snowy-haired, handsome man, the snowy-haired, lovely woman, a sideshow where the maimed crowded in to see the perfect: despite their physical afflictions, the Fillmores deserved their places above the crowd. Myrtle was a saint, Charles a crazy genius, and they got on in life by doing exactly what it pleased them, within their intellectual and spiritual limitations, to do. That era of Unity's development is over; the lights have been taken down; and now Unity is left with itself. So far it has found no new purpose that can match, in glamour or in seriousness, the old. Better to have an electronic body than a pedestrian soul, and today, amid computer tapes and its cult of normalcy, Unity has gone pedestrian. One can only hope that the founders' schizophrenia may be inherited somewhere down the line. The world has need of such wackiness.

# 8 / Death All Day

*I suppose, from a modern moral point of view, that is, a Christian point of view, the whole bullfight is indefensible; there is certainly much cruelty, there is always danger, either sought or unlooked for, and there is always death, and I should not try to defend it now, only to tell honestly the things I have found true about it. To do this I must be altogether frank, or try to be, and if those who read this decide with disgust that it is written by some one who lacks their, the readers', fineness of feeling I can only plead that this may be true. But whoever reads this can only truly make such a judgment when he, or she, has seen the things that are spoken of and knows truly what their reactions to them would be.*

—Ernest Hemingway, *Death in the Afternoon*

WHO WOULD HAVE THOUGHT THE OLD MAN TO HAVE had so much diffidence in him? He was a young man then, in 1932, and of course his apology to the high-toned Christians he despised is ironic. But the earnest apology is there too, the apology for enjoying a spectacle that expressed no sweat from the Anglo-Saxon brow nor added any treasure to the Anglo-Saxon glory vaults, as did the war he had survived a decade before. Other wars since have darkened that brow and emptied those vaults, wars so bloody and so relentlessly brutal that the gutting of horses in the Plaza de Toros—or the tearing of coyotes and cocks on the Kansas prairie—must seem antique entertainments. Today there is little need to apologize for killing merely animals. We have learned subtleties of husbandry unknown to Hemingway in 1932.

My own husbandry was developed during the six years I spent on a Missouri farm. For three of those years I butchered a steer every month and helped butcher a dozen hogs and several hundred chickens every quarter. Those with fineness of feeling may make of these facts what they will, but should consider that they eat the flesh of animals every day, only cutting meat from bone with smaller knives. I left the farm for the city at eighteen, and would be as squeamish about butchering today as any other citizen, though I might sooner get on with it.

Portis, Kansas, I discover on my Standard Oil map, is located within forty miles of the geographical center of the forty-eight continental states. That makes it precisely the heart of America, or at least of America before Alaska and Hawaii joined the fun. Portis is a knot of pitch and wood in north central Kansas surrounded by wheat fields, a village of 200 souls that is not even listed on my map's index of Kansas communities. As in every small town in Kansas, its landmark is a grain elevator and adjacent grove of storage bins rising high above the one-story houses around it, the town's name printed in block capitals—PORTIS—on the side of the elevator.

Dodge City remembers its gunsmoked past, Holcomb its murders, and Abilene its Eisenhowers (the latest grave is fresh there as I write). Portis notches its years on the performance of its high-school basketball team. The children depart for the city as regularly as cattle go to market, leaving behind cooling scores and tarnishing trophies that recall years when their parents were young and their families united. Such memories the parents value. Portis used to support a population of 240, and as the children move out no new families move in, and those who live there know the town will go to ghosts soon enough.

Portis remembers basketball; its young people remember coyote hunting, a sport or art form less venerable than bullfighting, and less elegant, but hotter. Everyone who goes on a hunt, young or old, takes part; cruelty, if coyote hunting is cruel, is shared, and so is such excitement as a wild-assed chase at fifty miles an hour over broken ground can supply.

We are three in Kansas City preparing to leave for Portis on a Friday afternoon in April, late season for coyotes but the weather has been impossible all winter. Dan Cram, D.V.M., a Portis boy now settled in Kansas City as associate veterinarian at a dog-and-cat clinic, will be our guide. Leaving the clinic, he carries a lithe breakdown .22 rifle he will take along to side-hunt prairie dogs and not have occasion to use. Portis hunts coyotes with hounds, not with guns. One of Dan's patients, an enthusiastic cocker, passes him in the parking lot with a little girl holding its leash. "Mommy, what is that gun for?" the girl querulously asks her mother, meaning, "Is that how they put animals to sleep?" The clinic is longer on service than on public relations. Dan's boss, the owner, hangs animal pelts, including the pelt of a bear cub, in his office and hunts big game in Canada and the Pacific Northwest. A lady, says Dan as we begin the drive to Portis, brought her child's stool sample into the clinic last week to be checked for worms, and when a pet bites a child the clinic is as likely to be called as the family physician. Hunting, for Dan's boss and for Dan, may be a healthy response to the overpressures of Kansas City pet lovers.

The other third of our party is Ron Nolan, an Ohio boy who overcame New York a few years back to homestead a two-room cabin in the woods outside Kansas City. His cabin contains an Italian racing motorcycle, a KLH20+ stereo, a wall of books, tennis rackets, board games, a hookah, rifles, pistols, a Beretta Golden Snipe .12-gauge over-and-under shotgun, a Pacific shotshell reloader, and, outside, a golden sand Jaguar XKE convertible and for short hauls an aging Morris Oxford station wagon, likely the only one in the Midwest. Ron is a bachelor.* He has lately acquired a faithful dog, Nolan's Irish Clancy, and currently pursues goose and duck and quail in season, trapshooting on Wednesday nights. He is thinking of raising bees in the woods behind the cabin as a crop. For the trip to Portis he has left red Clancy at home to gnaw on the cabin siding, but brings along a guitar.

Eastern Kansas, through which we now drive, is an area of enclaves like those General Gavin proposed for sanity in Vietnam. Lawrence, the first big town beyond Kansas City on the turnpike, encloses the University of Kansas, a respectable school with Oxonian pretensions. K.U. annually holds a festival of the arts which trucks in New York critics for what may be their once-in-a-lifetime glimpse of the Midwest. The school also boasts a Shakespearean scholar who capped his distinguished career by subjecting the First Folios to an exhaustive textual analysis using methods adapted from aerial photography. He discovered that the printer's devil couldn't spell and that one of the typesetters was a drunk. And established texts that approach Shakespeare's originals—not bad for prairie man.

Topeka, on down the Kansas Turnpike, the state capital, embraces the Menninger Clinic, with more shrinks per capita than any other city in the world, a great place for cocktail hours and late dinners, plump with Viennese *Gemütlichkeit*. When Anna Freud came to visit, the entire establishment

---

*Was. He has since married an intelligent, attractive, long-legged mathematician of a girl, and settled into prosperity with only an occasional huckleberry.

turned out, as if Mary Magdalene had returned to tell her tale of miracles and resurrections. I have heard of people who moved to Topeka just to be near the Menningers, and not as patients, either. Hemingway never visited Menningers', though an ill-advised staff member allowed, soon after the old man's death, that the Clinic could have saved his life and even set him writing again, and perhaps it could have. It has done as well with others. Across the street from the Clinic's front gate a solitary buffalo stalks the fence of the city zoo. Down the road a battalion of grain elevators marches west, aromatic of bran. Most of the Clinic's patients grow flowers. I wonder what variety Hemingway would have planted.

Beyond Topeka, big enclaves give way to small towns. Trees disappear except for scattered huddles of cottonwood, and the population thins in inverse proportion to the thickening of the wheat fields. It is a region most people fly over. Driving through it on an April evening, we count five jet contrails above us at the same time, the jets playing high, silent games of tag, racing each other for Kansas City, of all places, or seeming to collide head-on as they pass east and west at different altitudes. Farmers are burning off their pastures; in the dusk the fires glow like minor sunsets. The wheat is green in April, spraying in explosive tufts from holes drilled at precise intervals in the hard ground. The rest of the land is brown, the grass short and sere, the milo and corn fields knee-high brown stubble. In one farmyard we pass we notice an old Chevy panel truck painted in psychedelic swirls, an April Easter egg nested against a weathered gray barn.

Junction City, where we leave the turnpike for a two-lane highway, feeds on Fort Riley, a military camp twice as large on the map as the shrunken Pottawatomie and Kickapoo Indian Reservations north of Topeka. Crowds cheered when Riley sent its Big Red One off to Vietnam in 1968, despite the loss of local revenue. The only movie house I find on Junction City's main street features *Animal Lusts of the Night*, but there are no posters in the display cabinets to define which animal or whose lusts. That is Junction City's sort of compromise. In the black end of town, whores are no longer allowed to hook from street corners, but everyone knows they are still available. White whores, better camouflaged, man roadhouses staked out around the Fort. Junction City is hog heaven for the troops, its main drag a progress of beer bars. It preserves its country character with balloon-frame gothic houses jammed in among the storefronts and pungent assertions of skunk blowing through the streets.

In a Junction City diner where we stop to eat, a sunburned young farmer comforts his squirming son while his wife sips coffee and recalls the high-school prom. Ron orders pineapple pie, hoping its rich homemade goodness will set the tone for the trip, but the pie is store-bought. Through the window at my elbow the wooden scrollwork on the diner's marquee glows red and yellow, garish lights from a neon sign across the parking lot, and around and above the sign swells the vast Kansas sky, black as space. Dick Hickock and Perry Smith, diabolic engines with oddly ordered gearings and photocell eyes, also made this trip on a windy night. It's no wonder, under such a sky, that Perry killed, rived his gentleman's throat, narrowing the vastness into violence. The mantle of that violence must have covered him just long enough to get him safely back to Olathe. *The plains of Kansas are even lonelier than the sea*, a friend of mine once wrote, reviewing *In Cold Blood*. They are, and they would madden the battered children of our cities. What balances the people who live out here, most of them, is humility. They gird themselves in shyness and sleep well. And, when the loneliness echoes, fish and hunt.

Beyond Junction City, heading northeast now, we travel state highways, two-lane asphalt roads lit only by our headlights and the yardlights farmers leave on all night to keep the local kids away from the farm gas pump. And to say hello. Everyone hellos everyone in Kansas country, even with yardlights late at night. Ron breaks out his guitar and gives us ten verses of his favorite song:

Every time I go to town,
The boys keep kickin' my dog around,
Makes no difference if he is a hound,
They oughta quit kickin' my dog around

and falls asleep among the boots and the guns. Dan, wild farm boy turned dog doctor, drives on, pushing ninety, scanning his rearview mirror for the state patrol, confident that beyond the next hill or around the next curve no car will appear to destroy us at the desperate country hour of eleven o'clock.

We core the blackness with the tunnel vision of jet pilots, but start jackrabbits and possums on the ground. I am convinced Dan would hit one if it got in his way and drive right on. It would be an act without malice. He throws his beer bottles out the window too, as later, at the hunt lunch, we will leave our orange peels and bread wrappers on the roadside. Petty desecrations irritate me because I know how little of the country is left for us to litter, but for Dan, as for Portis's hunters, open land is the commonage of the people. It is also Kansas' most apparent natural asset, and perhaps there is irony in the littering of it: most of America spurns Kansas anyway as the Great American Desert, where the sedge is withered on the creek and no birds sing.

Dan's parents have waited up for us with Johnny Carson and Ed McMahon. Mrs. Cram appears to let us in—a slim, pleasant, dark-haired woman in a quilted robe, feminine without fluffiness, with delicate and graceful hands. She does not, as a farm woman might, leave the conversation to the men; as she asks her questions her eyes examine her son, assaying his health, his appetite, his state of mind. Married only ten months, Dan has not yet finally left home, and between his mother and his grandmother, in the next twenty-four hours, he will receive more attention than makes him comfortable, as befits a former Portis high-school basketball player. His father, Wendal, is an older and easier version of Dan, trim, built for endurance, a little shy, a World War II navy man and small-town banker who will soon marry off his last child and only daughter. The house is what we used to call "spick-and-span": landscapes painted by Mr. Cram on the walls, a bonsai sketched in wallpaper across the living room's west end, a nubby carpet on the floor. We sip instant iced tea and itemize the town's eccentrics. A lady down the street raises magpies for company and gives them the run of her speckled house. Old Les Wolters lost all his teeth twenty years ago and refuses to wear his plate—we will meet Les again on the hunt. A chauvinistic spectator made a Portis basketball referee so mad once that he kicked the spectator out of the gymnasium on a technical foul. And so to bed. Ron and I are offered, in frontier style, a double bed, which we find awkward: I haven't slept with a male since my brother left home; Ron hasn't slept near a male since Korea. We bed down uneasily. His snoring wakes me at six-thirty in the morning, and Mr. Cram is already making coffee.

Harold and John Wolters, toothless Les's brother and nephew respectively, call for us at eight o'clock. The Wolters are a Portis legend. Harold is seventy-four, all sockets and wires, gold front teeth, a weathered hatchet of a face half hidden beneath a plaid cotton baseball cap that is several sizes too large and settled on his ears, bib overalls harnessed over a thick plaid shirt with its collar buttoned and turned up against the morning chill. He is a man completely at ease, patriarch of his clan and unofficial master of the hunt; a man who will drive all day and not appear to be tired, certainly not as tired as I will be; a man who hands down his cars and his farms to his sons and sons-in-law as easily as younger parents hand down children's clothes. John, in his early thirties, is solid, honest, reliable, but otherwise his father's opposite: big-bellied, heavy-fleshed, stubby-handed, strong as an ox. John has laryngitis, and his voice is cloudy and uncertain. Harold's voice is clear, and after an hour on the road of uncanny *déjà vu* I place it: in pitch and cadence and dialect, and in a certain tendency to loquaciousness, Harold sounds exactly like Hubert Humphrey.

The Wolters pickup truck, a broad-beamed Ford, startles me with its sweet reek of cow manure rising up from a robe of beige carpeting laid over the seat cushion. Former butcher boy and cattle feeder, I had forgotten the smell. By the end of the day I feel at home.

We rendezvous at the Co-op filling station in Portis with three other trucks of hunters. We will acquire three more at Long Island, Kansas, another town that isn't on the map despite its portentous name. It is the largest hunt, Harold tells me, he has ever gathered together in fifty years of coyote chasing. The presence of two women among the trucks reduces the badinage on the two-way radios to awkward gossip and hurried speculations about the weather. From down around Lincoln, Kansas, someone named Harry overtakes us, and at our grocery-store rendezvous schemes with Harold to call the girls "fuzzy-tail." The scheme works for a while. "Guess he just doesn't want to catch that *fuzzy-tail*," quips Harold over the radio when one of the party lags behind, and jabs a bawdy elbow in my ribs as old Harry cuts in over the radio with a guffaw. "Fuzzy-tail" gets forgotten in the excitement of the chase, except when we stop to relieve ourselves; then John scouts fuzzy-tail while Harold and I wet down the dust on the womanless side of the truck.

I ride between Harold and John in the middle of the wide seat, my legs hanging over John's side of the transmission hump. A riding crop coils on the dashboard; a hammer hangs in a loop of binder twine from the floor-mounted gearshift. The crop will discipline the dogs; the hammer will quiet the coyote.

The pickup has been stripped to its floorbed in back, and mounted on the floorbed is a box the size of a shipping crate. In two compartments, their heads stuck out through a narrow slot cut the length of the box, stand the dogs. They are greyhound, mostly, with some staghound mixed in for endurance. Names you would expect: Blue is blue-black, the color of gunmetal; Nig is night black; Ring sports a white ring of fur around his neck, the rest of him black; Red is red; collectively Harold calls them "you bastards," but treats their hunt wounds with care, dousing them from a plastic squeeze bottle of methylene blue. They are big dogs, nearly as big as a man on all fours would be, but light; Dan estimates their average weight at forty-five or fifty pounds, though they look seventy-five. Their mass is all long legs with sinewy muscles to move them and a deep barrel for wind, and even then the coyote, at thirty pounds, can outrun them if the chase goes anything over a mile. "I always say you can run a little faster if your life depends on it than if you're just doing it for fun," one of the hunters will answer my question as we drive back from the hunt.

Poking their long greyhound muzzles out of the head slot of their box, they are docile animals with soft eyes, expressions made downcast by their tough training and uncomfortable quarters. They must twist their heads to force them through the slot, and their necks rub uncomfortably against the bare plywood edges. Harold has carpeted the compartments in his dog box with pieces of an old Oriental, and the traps also are carpeted—so that the dogs can spring onto them and into the box from the ground, a leap of five feet which they make with complete ease even when winded from the chase and the kill.

We arrive at the area where the hunt will begin, an hour northwest of Portis, and the trucks fan out around four sides of a mile-square section of land. The sport of coyote hunting, Portis style, is founded on the section, the basic division of land on the plains, 640 acres bounded on four sides by barbed-wire fences and usually divided inside with other fences into quarter-sections.

Dirt ruts along the half-mile lines inside—Harold calls them "by-roads," the old term—give access to each quarter-section, but the placing of gates is capricious, and more than once a hunter lost a coyote to a fence he couldn't find a way through. The land is broken up by copses of trees, by deep gullies and draws, by high contoured terraces and by young wheat fields which the code of Kansas hunting requires the farmer-hunters

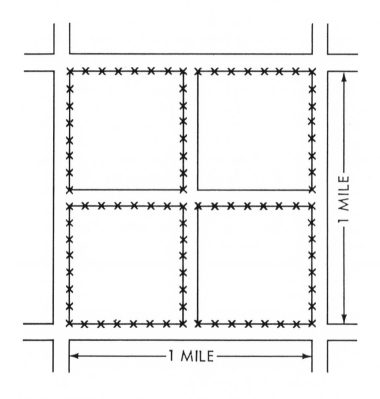

to avoid. The land's roughness further complicates the chase—Harold buys a new pickup every year, and ravages it in one winter's season of hunting. If there had been no fences in the area we would have caught more coyotes, but not in sport. For sport, the animal must have a reasonable chance to escape; with fences and wheat fields it has that chance. Some Kansans hunt coyotes with light planes or helicopters, driving the animals to the road, where they are shot by men in trucks: that is no more sport than a Saturday-night rat shoot at the city dump would be, and perhaps less. At least the rats have holes to hide in; with a plane overhead, the coyotes do not.

Coyote hunting, Portis style, is coursing, the sport of czars and kings, for which the greyhounds and borzois and staghounds of the dog kingdom were bred long ago. It is a sport almost completely unknown in the United States except in the western ranges of the Middle West. The Duke of Norfolk first established its rules in the days of Shakespeare's Elizabeth; England unfortunately lacking coyotes, the sport was practiced there on hares, which are not animals renowned for their ferocity. Coursing differs from other types of hunting with dogs in one important respect: coursing dogs hunt by sight, not by smell, and the dead trophies—coyotes the size of young children, looking like foxes on the bum, with narrow yellow teeth bared in death as in life—may be slung from the top of the dog boxes, out of sight but very much in smell. Coursing dogs do not attend their noses. They are, like man, all eyes.

With the trucks deployed on four sides of a section, the first we surrounded during the long day, Harold turns in at the south gate, drives up a by-road, and heads through a field of milo stubble. He extracts a nine-shot .22 revolver from the glove compartment and fires into a long draw at the edge of the field. Nothing emerges. John swings out of the cab onto the side of the dog box, which has a length of water pipe bolted on at the top for a handhold. Through territory that will throw me all over the cab, John holds on easily to the outside of the truck.

"You just kinda relax and bend your knees," he explained later. Even inside the cab, I found that hard to do.

A second gate at the "old mile road"—the half-mile by-road in the middle of the section—lets us into the northeast quarter, and in the first draw we start a pair of coyotes that divide, one heading northeast in the same direction we are traveling, the other, the bitch as it turns out, heading southwest along the center fence. Ron and Les, alerted by Harold on the radio, head south along the west road outside the section to intercept the bitch; we accelerate to chase the dog coyote, Harold in second gear racing the engine up to a turbine-like whine, taking terraces at a sixty-degree angle that he jerks the truck out of as soon as the front wheels clear the top, throwing us back and forth in the cab, John still spotting the coyote as it runs through the stubble down to a brush-surrounded creek. We hit fifty miles an hour, dry weeds slapping the hood and filling the air with chaff; we brake abruptly and smash down a dropoff that jams me to the bottom of the seat, the coyote veering back southward to cut by us and escape, Harold slamming on the brakes full force and yelling to John to release the dogs, John pulling the release rod, the dogs out of the truck now, yelping and barking and closing on the coyote at the bottom of the contoured hill. I jump from the truck and run down the hill to find the dogs, five of them, all over the fighting coyote, biting at its neck and legs and groin. It is still alive; it locks one dog's ear in its jaws, its narrow yellow teeth bared. The dogs have it on its back, one is trying to clamp its neck and cut off its wind, another pulls on a hind leg, another clamps the neck from the opposite side, with yelps when the coyote manages a hit. It stares at John and me as we move to it with an expression in its eyes strangely detached for an animal being torn—"What the hell am I doing here?" John motions me back and works in toward the head. The coyote catches his leather glove and he pulls away just in time to avoid a bite, tearing the glove. He moves in again and pries the coyote's mouth off a dog's lower jaw, then maneuvers his boot onto the coyote's head and hits the skull with the hammer, the sound like driving a nail into hard oak, resonant but damped at the same time, tunk, tunk, tunk, tunk. Sensing the coyote slumping beneath them, the dogs relax, and John begins pulling them off. Their mouths drip with blood, their own and the coyote's; one has a hole the size of a quarter in its upper lip that I can see the sky through, another a deep gash on its neck, another a torn foreleg. Blood-thirsty as they have been—they showed the coyote no mercy once the braver dogs began the kill—they display no anger when John takes them off their catch, as even a house pet would if you pulled him off a bone. I hold two of them by the collar while John works at the others, and except for a slight straining away from me they are entirely docile.

By the time we get the dogs off, Harold has clambered down the hill. He flips the coyote over and reaches between its legs, encountering a small black bag. "Why, it's an old dog coyote," he says, and pulls back the lips to check the teeth. "Big one, too. Looks to be about four years old. We got us an old dog coyote. Them's the hardest kind to catch." He is obviously pleased with the first catch of the day.

Back in the truck, over the radio: "WE GOT US A OLD DOG COYOTE, 'BOUT FOUR YEARS OLD. YEP, IT'S A GOOD 'UN. ANYBODY SEE THAT OTHER ONE? WE STARTED TWO OF 'EM DOWN IN A DRAW." Les reports in: "WE'RE AFTER THAT ONE DOWN HERE IN THE NEXT SECTION SOUTH. HE'S RUNNIN' TOWARD A PATCH OF TREES. WE DROPPED OUR DOGS."

In the background I could hear the dogs yelping. Ron told me later they dropped the first box of dogs at the east fence to keep the coyote in sight while they raced to the south fence to find a gate. Halfway across the section, going west on its south road, they saw the coyote crossing the road in front of them with the dogs a hundred yards behind. They found an opening in the north fence of the next section south, which the coyote by then had entered, and turned through it into a stubble field, driving fast right through the dogs. Then they dropped their second box of dogs, which closed on the coyote just before it reached the copse. "If it gets to the trees, it'll get away," Les told Ron. The dogs stopped the coyote in the last seconds before it entered the trees. It was the bitch from the pair we had started almost two miles back.

The chase, Harold tells me later, requires two types of dogs—catchers and fighters. The best dogs will catch and fight both. "I'll pay $200 for a good coyote dog any time," he says. Coyote hunting is not an inexpensive sport.

Our first coyote turned out to be the only one we would catch that day, though we scouted as hard as anyone on the hunt. Les, canny operator that he was, usually waited out on the road for someone else to flush the coyotes his way, but even with that tactic he caught only two. Someone else got three. Old Harry, the wrong man in the wrong place at the wrong time, got none. The star of the day was a twenty-five-year-old county employee and novice coyote hunter named Johnny Wagonblast, who took Dan on as a rider—which means spotter and aimer and dog-dropper—and caught no fewer than five coyotes, his shy, sunburned grin stretching wider and wider as the day progressed.

We draw the trucks together on a north-south stretch of road and drop the dogs a box at a time to relieve themselves, which they do by finding a fencepost, strange habit for dogs of the treeless prairie. One even settles for a dry weed. Ron is grinning when we meet; so am I. The men look over Harold's catch, which we have thrown onto the top of the dog box with one of its hind legs hooked into a piece of bailing wire attached to the pipe rail. They seem to make a ritual of squeezing the dog's bag, but that may be a city fancy.

After the rest we search resolutely westward, as Thoreau advised. The remainder of the day's hunting will exercise Harold and John's patience. We hunt hard but catch no more coyotes, though once we come close enough to release the dogs only to see them miss the coyote's sudden northward turn—they are coursing west behind it—and head for a pickup truck stationed opposite us. Good soldiers all, the dogs have only responded to their training, but with the perversity of field marshals we want them momentarily to forget training and think for themselves. The dogs' confusion makes John mad. "Goddamn it, Dad, if you'd released the dogs back in that wheat field they could of headed that coyote off before he got to the brush. We'd of caught the son of a bitch"—which angers Harold enough that he tells his son, who outweighs him by at least a hundred pounds, to shut the hell up, which John, being a good son, does. Even lucky Johnny Wagonblast's dogs will miss an easy catch when the coyote they are chasing veers across a road and they, yelping like a neighborhood pack harassing its favorite garbage truck, home in on a passing car.

Before that time, most of us still fresh from other chases of the morning, we stop for lunch, and one of the hunters, a drugstore cowboy in Stetson, Western shirt, Levi's, and tooled black boots, announces that we are in Nebraska. We have hunted our way northwest over an area of fifty miles, and searched most of the one-mile sections along the way. We have seen no towns and only a few occupied farmhouses. That kind of range is possible with seven trucks. Harold's prediction that with so many hunters we would be "falling all over each other" has not come true. The large number of trucks simply makes it unlikely that the hunters who flush the game will get the kill.

We park on a gravel road, completely blocking it. Harold hauls out a brown cardboard box and sets it down by John on a ridge next to the road. In it are hamburger buns, lunch meats, American cheese, potato chips, bananas, oranges, and chocolate-covered fudge sandwich cookies. "Help yourself—just pile it on like you was at home," Harold tells me. Les sits down next to Harold, unpacks his own supplies with Ron, and is soon happily gumming a cold hotdog which he douses from time to time with ketchup. The ladies eat discreetly in the trucks. I make a sandwich with a little of everything at hand and peel an orange for fluid. Les brings out a thermos jug, swigs from the spout, and announces to Ron that it contains "Portis brew." The conversation swerves from reconstructions of the morning's chase to the problem of Nebraska coyote-hunting licenses. "The game warden stopped me up here one time," someone says. "I had two coyotes on the truck and he asked me if I'd caught them in Nebraska. I said I had, and he wanted to know if I had an out-of-state hunting license, since the truck has Kansas plates. I said I didn't, but I owned some acreage in Nebraska and caught the coyotes on it. He let me go that time."

"The warden down by Russell is a real hardnosed old bastard," someone else says. "He caught those Nebraska boys down there one time and fined them heavy."

The cowboy, who is in fact the owner of a sales barn in Mankato, northeast of Portis, suggests we turn the hunt southwestward after lunch to avoid the river to the north and to get back into Kansas. Soon we pack up our gear and start off.

While Johnny Wagonblast, with Dan beside him, sweeps up the afternoon honors, Harold and John and I dig into every gully and ditch and copse we can find. We buck down by-roads washed out by spring rains, thread around creek beds still soft enough to mire the truck, fire into milo fields and draws, and never see a coyote. We flush pheasant and quail and jackrabbits, which we leave alone. At one point we race up a forty-degree bluff, slip back down, gun up twice more, and finally make the top only to find our way barred by a fence. And all the while we listen to the cowboy come on over the radio like Red Barber announcing the Yankees as the other hunters rack up their coyotes for the afternoon: "THERE HE COMES, LES, OUT THAT SOUTH FENCE—GO SOUTH, LES! GO SOUTH, GO SOUTH, HE'S CROSSED THE ROAD, HE'S IN THAT SOIL BANK IN THE NEXT SECTION, BETTER GO WEST AND HEAD HIM OFF, LES, JOHNNY WAGONBLAST, WHERE ARE YOU? YOU OUT ON THE WEST ROAD? COME NORTH, JOHNNY, HE'S IN THE NORTHWEST QUARTER, COME NORTH," and Harold nudging me, Harold in love with his radio, "See, I told you he was a real good boy, regular sportcaster," and then the sound, sweet jealous sound now, of the dogs dropped from Johnny's truck, and cowboy back on the horn, "HE'S GOT HIM, JOHNNY WAGONBLAST'S GOT HIM, THEY GOT THE COYOTE!" John riding up on top without a word, Harold crashing his truck through the thumping stubble, coyotes anywhere but here. "There's days like that," Harold tells me. "That's what makes it such a sport. Some days a man can't do nothing wrong, other days he can hunt as hard as hell and still get no coyotes. I thought we'd see more out here, though. Don't know where they've all got to."

Then the near-miss when we dropped the dogs, and the flare of anger between father and son. John thought Harold spent too much time on the radio—"If you come out here to catch coyotes you got to *drive*, not talk on that damned radio all the time"—and more futile hunting. The afternoon sky has clouded over and the air cooled, but after our second and final dog-drop I can hear the animals raggedly panting, a torn, screeching pant that rips great chunks of air from the road to feed tissue completely used up in the chase. I have heard such a sound only once before, at the finish line of a two-mile cross-country race, the runners vomiting green bile and packing their lungs with air as if they might never breathe again.

We stop at a pond and John carries a number-ten can to the water and brings it back for the dogs. Harold holds it up to them, and they jam their muzzles two at a time into the muddy froth and drink. He moves quickly from dog to dog, allowing them only enough to wet their throats, avoiding the tanking that would cramp them. Their condition leaves me wondering how Johnny Wagonblast's dogs have lasted the afternoon, especially since he announced coyly at one of our rest stops that he almost missed the last coyote because he dropped his "cripples" instead of his good dogs. Almost.

A coyote hunt has no official end. Portis men, like country men everywhere, practice indirection in all matters of public behavior. Harold continues to search for coyotes until the light begins to fail, and so do the others, but the hunt turns from west to southeast, and without perceptible effort we find ourselves searching a section only a mile outside Long Island. We drive into that village to get gas for the pickup. Everyone else has had the same idea and we are soon swigging Coca-Cola at the filling station. Even then no one admits he has to get home to chores. The closest anyone comes to announcing his destination is a laconic "Guess I'll head on in." By this time old Harry has started to drink, someone says. He still wants his coyote—do the wives judge their husbands' *cojones* by the quantity of their kill?—and Harold senses his discomfort and offers to work over the hills outside Long Island on the way back to Portis. Harry agrees and we set off once more, all of us tired now and half-hearted. We fire into several promising draws, but no coyotes emerge even though Harold and John, who have phenomenal memories for past kills, recall having caught several coyotes there two years before. Finally we leave Harry to his own diversions and drive back to Portis. Together, all seven truckloads of us, we have caught thirteen coyotes.*

At dinner at the Crams', Ron entertains us with Wolters stories passed on to him by Les, a non-stop talker. The Wolters are a fighting family, he says, squabbling among themselves, but they turn a solid front to the world. They are regionally famous for their coyote hunts. They usually pile their entire

---

*It was Harold's last hunt. His father rode out for buffalo; by the time Harold was old enough to hunt, the buffalo were gone, so he switched to coyotes. He caught more than 6,000 of the animals in his fifty years of hunting, raised a large and able family, and made himself and his sons into prosperous farmers. "The abler spirits of the pioneers," writes William Carlos Williams in "The American Background," "cut themselves off from the old at once and set to work with a will directly to know what was about them. It set out helter-skelter. And, by God, it was. Besides, it couldn't wait. Crudely authentic, the bulk of a real culture was being built up from that point. The direct attack they instituted [was] shown in many cases by no other results than the characters of the men and women themselves. . . ." Born on the 29th of April, 1894, Harold Wolters died of a heart attack on Friday, the 13th of June, 1969. *Sic transit gloria mundi.*

winter's catch of coyotes in their front yards, or line them up along the road. Harold averages more than 150 coyotes every season. Someone once came by at night and snipped off all the ears of Les's collection, which made him furious. The ears are required to collect the two-dollar bounty the county still offers for coyotes, though the bounty is not enough money even to pay for the gas used on the hunt, much less to support each hunter's ten or fifteen dogs year-round. Les's dogs, Dan remembers, can be identified by a brown streak of tobacco juice across their muzzles. Les chews Red Man tobacco and spits the juice out the window; the wind carries it back across the dogs' heads as they stick out of their boxes behind the cab.

We are tired from the hunt, but Dan has described to us the Saturday-night chicken fights in the nearby town of Minneapolis, Kansas, and after supper we pack up and head east on Highway 24.

Dan says the town has held chicken fights on Saturday night for years. They are open to the public for a fee, and legal, according to a local handler, as the result of a test case brought by the A.S.P.C.A. and carried to the Kansas Supreme Court which held that the Kansas statute concerning cruelty to animals did not apply to chickens since they are technically not animals but fowl. No record of such a judgment exists. According to the statutes, chicken fighting is illegal in Kansas only on Sunday, a day of rest for fowl.

We pull into the parking lot of the Minneapolis Pit, a converted auction barn, at nine-thirty in the evening and enter through a screen door into its small anteroom. Our tickets, $1.50 each, are white tags with the words "received," "ready," and "bundle" on them—laundry tags, probably—which we are supposed to hang onto a shirt button in plain view.

Inside the barn, an amphitheater full of smoke. I had expected to find men; instead I find men and women and boys and girls and little children, and not much animation among them. A few of the women look well-to-do, and none looks poor. The best seats, on the south wall above one long side of the pit, are filled; on the north side of the pit stands a line of men, some of them handlers, some there to take the crowd's bets. The main pit, painted white, is sunk into the center of the floor, an oval twelve feet wide and eighteen feet long with twenty-inch walls dropping to a sand base littered with short feathers and spattered with blood. Wooden steps lead up steep benches to a top loft near the ceiling.

Below, the lurid pit, a pygmy Colosseum floored in dirty sand; above, the sober crowd, pewed on gray, siding-faced benches that might have come from a Puritan meetinghouse or a medical-school lecture hall. The abrupt change in scale and lighting shocks, as if the pit were shrunken to obscure the brutality of the spectacle enacted there. Even the lights over the pit—a rectangular bank of fluorescent tubes—enforce the dislocation, the fluorescent light cold and narrow as the light in an autopsy room while the crowd above is warmed and enlivened with incandescent bulbs.

The birds themselves seldom weigh more than five pounds; dressed, they would hardly match a good boiling hen. They fan their neck feathers vainly to frighten their opponents, and admit their size by leaping easily over each other, a feat for lice and lizards and birds, not for men. Even their red and brown feathers conspire to diminish the bloodletting by masking, in their colorful profusion, the wounds. The birds predominantly white still sport a mingling of red feathers. But red and black were the colors of the evening: red of feathers, of fresh blood, of lung tissue coughed from a stricken bird's yellow beak; black of feathers also, of dried blood, and of the darkness at the height of the room.

The spurs—they are gaffs, not slashers, pointed miniature foils two and a half inches long—jut out of scale, cold man-made weapons that connect the two perspectives. No bird could grow such spurs, the length of a man's index finger slightly crooked, the tempered steel of scalpels and clamps and interrogation chambers. They penetrate so deep into the victimized bird that the cock cannot pull them out. The referee must stop the match and carefully, in a parody of concern, extract them as a claw or a fang is extracted. A man with a sword in his hand would not match the scale of those spurs.

The handlers carry their cocks to the edge of the pit. They cradle them in the nest of their arms like infants, talk to them, croon to them, baby them as soldiers baby their weapons in the seconds before battle begins. The referee jumps into the pit, absolute authority in cockfighting from whom there is no appeal. The handlers bring their cocks to the center line, jam the birds together to anger them and give them a taste of blood. No horses here. They warm up on each other. The birds click at red combs, sample an eye and a wattle, alert red instincts honed on a diet of cracked corn and pep pills.

Set down on their starting lines, they strain toward each other, held by their handlers by the tail. The referee signals and they go forward, flare their feathers, dance, circle, leap over each other, peck, jab, jibe, close, seeking the head, the eyes, the spurs an afterthought, and above them the crowd stares almost without sound until a plump woman in black pants with cash wadded in her fist yells, "Shoot 'em! Shoot 'em!"—shoot the spurs in. A spur stabs underneath the white cock: "Handle them!" says the referee, and he comes to the end of the pit to calculate the hit and extract the spur. Drawn back to its end of the main, the white cock appears dazed, flicking its reptilian inner eyelids. Its handler is a young man, thin, dark, breathing hard, new to cockfighting and intent on winning. He pinches the back of his bird's neck, draws out its beak, raises its tail feathers and blows on its vent.

Matched again, the recovered white cock scores on the red, and after the spur is drawn the red reels. A florid man in an orange polo shirt, receding hairline, bulging eyes, bulging belly, handles the bird, sticks his finger down its throat and stretches out its neck to bring it back. He sends the red cock out again to fight the white, and again the red is hit and loses ground. The referee calls time and the two men pick up their cocks and leave the main. Two smaller pits—"drag pits"—have been laid out at right angles to the main in a side room that opens into the arena. The drag pits are smaller than the main because by the time the cocks reach them one of the birds is usually wounded and no longer has the strength to maneuver. In the drag pit the slaughter continues, the red bird set on its feet at the starting line immediately falling over, the white cock with its furiously intense handler behind it advancing to tear at the red's head and eyes. Before the red cock dies, the white will peck out both its eyes.

> *Before the red cock dies*
> *The white will peck out both its eyes.*

The white cock has already lost an eye.

The red flops onto its back, breathing in gasps, but the fight still continues, timed and counted out by the referee, who consults a stainless-steel watch and scolds its luminous sweep second hand. The boy blows on his bird's vent; the florid handler sweats with anger, working over his bird as if it were a mis-sighted rifle or a dull knife which exasperates him because it needs unavailable repair. At the edge of the drag pit stand two blonde college girls, sisters perhaps, attracted by the boy's passion but uninterested in the match. When a bystander remarks the white cock's missing eye, one of the girls says casually, "Oh, he'll never fight again, that's too bad." Then the white spurs the red fatally and the red convulses, dead. The florid man picks it up by its claws, snips the waxed threads that hold on the spurs, and tosses it onto a pile of dead birds in the corner. He wipes the spurs and returns them to their case, worn like a slide rule in a holster on his hip. The boy, tightly smiling, cradles his winning cock out a side door.

I glimpse the evening. Two boys, eight or nine years old, lying on a bench head to head before a window at the top of the stands, talking to each other and the moon. Fresh cocks in their narrow varnished pine boxes, with small screened windows in front, crowing as if at sunrise. A keeper raking a billow of pinfeathers out of the main. A mustached, bib-overalled, be-reted handler coaching his cock in the moments before its match. A pretty, dark-eyed country girl with black hair falling down her back, in sandals and a poor-boy and pants, country hip, posing for such eyes as might find her. A sign on the wall advertising chicken feed. The florid handler's cleft butt squeez-ing out of his pants as he squats to eke another stand from his dying bird. A slumming college girl in a linen pantsuit leaving abruptly when a cock shoots its spurs. Wives gossiping easily at tables in the anteroom, waiting for their husbands as they might wait at a bowling alley. A white cock with both eyes torn out running in blind fear from the drag pit to be caught and brought back for another round, the fight finally conceded and the cock taken outside and its neck wrung. Dan's protective boredom, Ron's protective silence, my protective curiosity. The smell like a chicken house of dust and ammonia, the smoke like a hustled poker game stinging and blue. From the look of the spectators they might be conspiring a town orgy, sex in the pit, casual lays arranged in the stands, silent onlookers breath-ing hotly from their seats. But the children wouldn't be present at an orgy, whispering to each other of alliances and tomorrow. Sex is more private than death.

Enthusiasts, the books say, justify cockfighting for the gam-bling it generates, continuing through the main as the fortunes of the two birds change, and Ron brings me tales of Kansas City gamblers motoring out to Minneapolis for big stakes, but the bets I see at the fights are low, a dollar or two, seldom five, rarely ten, and they do not continue through the main. The Minneapolis fights are held not for gamblers but for kids and married couples, who watch with little apparent passion, as they might watch a favorite TV show on an easy Sunday night. "Chicken fights," they call them in Minneapolis, banally, and all of us who know the farm know the banality of chickens.

The schoolmasters of Victorian England judged their pupils' cockfights to earn the dead birds for food; in prosperous Kansas the birds lie rotting in a corner, to be burned tomorrow with the trash. Conspicuous waste, the beer cans at roadside, the cocks in the corner: it is the American compulsion going back as far as the slaughter of the Indians, the slaughter of the buffalo, the littering of the Oregon Trail when the emigrants' wagons proved too heavy for the march with heirloom chests and Eastern frocks and family quilts and hopeful pianos. We have always littered the land, and pious folk have always deplored our littering, but it has measured our desperation, our determination to move on before we are found out. We have not needed to hoard, we say, the promise being rich before us. It is truer that we have understood the death the hoarder dies. We have moved west as a hounded people moves, fleeing the destruction of Sodoms. The Jews of Europe who could not litter— who could not leave house and home and position, walk out their doors for the west and not look back—lost everything. We have ever been a people who could litter.

And now, the oceans having bound us, we devour the land and each other. We thought we were peaceful, but a pair of coyotes sniffing rabbits in the brush are peaceful, cocks crowing pride at each other across a barnyard are peaceful, dogs rolling in the grass are peaceful. Guns are not; trucks across broken fields are not; lean sutured spurs are not, nor are we who devise them. "Ah! what a plastic little creature he is! so shifty, so adaptive! his body a chest of tools, and he making himself comfortable in every climate, in every condition."* We need not fear our machines. We become them on this late continent. We are the avant garde of our race, locked in continental sanctity, feeding on roots and carrion, stripping ores and oils down to the hot core of the earth, sparing not even the small fossil shells.

There is no darkness of nature so dark as the darkness of men. We observe with a cold agreement of brain cells that do not reproduce and feel no pain. We stare, unblinking eyes, at dying beasts and see only casual transformations. Corn grows,

---

*Emerson, in rare humor, mocking Hamlet.

and we pluck it; wheat grows, and we cut it; coyotes run, and we tear them; cocks crow, and we murder them; men die, and we send others after them. We are nature's full circle, the end product of her millennial butchery of forms, form feeding on form unto the ends of the earth. We nest as animals: we hunt as men. We huddle as animals: we murder as men. We are most extraordinary where we appear most common, as in a cockfight in central Kansas. We are backward and spare in our kindnesses, and even these will not abide.

Beyond Portis, now far behind, the land stretches west to the Rockies. Shallow hills blow barren of houses and men, fertile in wind and wheat and coyotes. Ghosts of Indians and buffalo wander the steppes, but the short grass preserves no mark of their passing or of ours. The plains of Kansas are even lonelier than the sea. They are lonely as men are lonely who seek, as we seek beyond all civility, blood to freshen us, wounds to warm our hands. Perry Smith's glowing mantle of violence is ours also, and only our flesh shrinks below that shelter. We would eat the moon and rape the sun if we could. Hemingway did well to apologize, but not to the Christians.

Out here in Kansas, I say now in impulsive justification, "having suffered myself and learned mercy,"* we murder animals more often than we murder men. We are the old primitives of the country set against the city's new.

And what is local of this? The surprising appropriateness of cockfighting in Union Kansas, spiritual home of John Brown. The earnest indifference of the handlers, who pit their birds for gain, not for love—some were exceptions, but most were not. The stolid audience of spectators, plainly watching murder with no English lust or Latin ardor. The penny-ante bets in a

---

*The English naturalist Charles Waterton, defending from slaughter the ghostly and superstitiously feared barn owls on his estate: "Having suffered myself and learned mercy, I broke in pieces the code of penal laws which the knavery of the gamekeeper and the lamentable ignorance of the other servants had hitherto put in force...." Our mercy is not of that quality. Not yet.

society which creates capital faster than it can destroy it. The human warmth of the Portis people, who seemed, plain truth or proud face, at home with themselves and with strangers, pleased to show their ways, comfortable in judgment and unwilling to judge. Their care with each other, pride meeting pride across politeness and indirection. The coyotes. The cocks. The yardlights. The wheat. The sky. The sky.

And Dan, and Ron? Ron went to Portis and to Minneapolis for a manhood ceremony, as he goes to all festivals, and passed the test of the coyote hunt by doing it better than a novice should, and passed the test of cockfighting by despising its brutality. Dan went and came home and kept his counsel; I saw him the following Saturday cheerfully treating a clinic full of cats and dogs, and at the hunt and the fights and the clinic he wore the same honest face.

And I, since I am of this place and this time also? Old veteran of the knife and the noose and the capsule, I found nothing amiss. Did you?

# 9 / Cupcake Land

ON ONE CORNER OF A DECORATIVE BRIDGE ON THE
Country Club Plaza, a shopping district in Kansas City, Missouri, a massive bronze sculpture attracts the attention of tourists. They are drawn to the work first of all by the colorful
flags—of the United States and Great Britain—that fly overhead and seem to proclaim for it some undefined official status.
Approaching the display they discover that it depicts a man and
a woman seated on or emerging from an undefined bronze
mound. The man and the woman turn out to be Winston and
Clementine Churchill, Winnie staring moodily ahead, Clem-
mie at one side with folded hands observing her husband be-
nevolently. "Married Love," the sculpture is titled. By pushing
a button on a sort of wooden juke box behind it, one may listen

to a scratchy recording of Churchill speaking to the British people in the dark days of the Second World War; "blood, toil, tears, and sweat" is sometimes discernible over the noise of traffic, Kansas Citians approaching the Plaza to shop.

"Married Love" originated as a coffee-table piece by the late Oscar Neman. Neman was an acquaintance of a Kansas City dentist, Joseph Jacobs, who saw a model of the Churchill piece in Neman's Oxford home several years ago. Impressed, Jacobs brought home a photograph. One of his dental patients was Kansas City business leader Miller Nichols, whose father, J. C. Nichols, built the Plaza and whose realty company operates it today. With Miller Nichols captive in his dental chair one day, Jacobs confronted him with the photograph. "It's no wonder that our young people have gotten away from traditional values," the dentist says he told the realtor, "when they don't have symbolism to inspire them." Nichols liked the idea of a Churchill statue on the Plaza; it has been fashionable in Kansas City to celebrate the wartime British leader ever since Joyce Hall, the founder of Hallmark Cards, courted his friendship back in the 1950s by sponsoring a national tour of Churchill's leisure-time paintings. "Get that sculptor over here and let's talk about it," Nichols told Jacobs a few weeks later. Neman was only too willing to scale the little sculpture up to heroic size. A man who pinches his inherited dollars until the eagles squawk, Nichols wasn't about to pay for the work himself. He turned fund-raising over to his wife, Jeannette, who assembled privately the nearly $500,000 that the statue and its endowment required. Jacobs says he suggested the title "Married Love." What was kitsch at coffee-table scale thus found epic realization in bronze; the Country Club Plaza, with statuary already at hand of penguins, Indian braves and sleeping babes, acquired the world's first Chatty Churchill.

Welcome to Cupcake Land.

Though Cupcake values have spread like sugary icing to cover much of the United States in the years since the Second World War, Kansas City is the capital of Cupcake Land, and the

Country Club Plaza, injected into it like a fulsome puff of cream filling, is its essential center. I lived in Kansas City most of my life and watched Cupcake Land rise. We were more Elmer Gantry here once than George F. Babbitt: what the hell happened to my town?

Curiously, although the East and West Coasts regularly forge ahead of the Midwest in many other aspects of popular culture, in Cupcaking the Midwest has permanently held the lead. The Holy Grail of Cupcake Land is pleasantness, well-scrubbed and bland, and the Northeast Corridor is too crowded and dirty and ethnic, California too highly coveted, too expensive and therefore too much on the make, quite to measure up. Not by accident is Kansas City the best test market for new products in the United States; what Kansas Citians consume (to paraphrase Walt Whitman) you shall consume, for every longing belonging to them as good belongs to you.

Cupcake Land is petit point and paisley and white wicker. It's professionally catered deb parties featuring miniature hamburgers from Winstead's (the mediocre Country Club Plaza drive-in that Calvin Trillin sometimes celebrates in the *New Yorker*). It's the Kansas City standing ovation, a tribute audiences accord to almost every performance of classical music or ballet or theater that comes to town, preferring effusion to critical appreciation and too timid to remain seated when fellow Cupcakes stand.

Cupcake Land is Laura Ashley and Buick and Pierre Deux, yellow ribbons on every tree to declare Cupcake solidarity with distant hostages, memorials to Christa MacAuliffe—the *Challenger* teacher—a thousand miles from Concord. When the goods at a bake sale staged to raise money for charity cost more to bake than they return in sales, I know I'm in Cupcake Land. I know I'm in Cupcake Land when a thorough search of an expensive, well-furnished house turns up not one serious book. When a movie audience giggles appreciatively at jokes that allude to scatology but greets sexual humor with nervous silence, denizens of Cupcake Land surround me.

Cupcakes wear Ivy League styles of clothing, sort of: button-down shirts for the men in easy-care Perma-Press, demure skirts, shorts, and one-piece bathing suits for the women. Cupcakes usually do not attend Ivy League schools, however; they attend state universities, because they believe that going to school out of state looks pretentious, isolates them from the gang and excludes them from the network of potential business contacts they will need after graduation. Cupcakes do pledge fraternities and sororities; Cupcake Land itself is a working out in maturity of the values, such as they are, learned so painfully in the crucible of the fraternity and sorority house.

Cupcake men drink beer in moderation at backyard barbecues; Cupcake women don't drink at all, fearing to misbehave ("I get so silly"); or drink hard liquor in milliliter quantities mixed with diet Seven-Up; or drink "A glass of white wine, please." If the waiter specifies "Chablis?" they answer "That will be fine." "Chardonnay?" would elicit an identical response. Since to Cupcakes the point of ordering a glass of wine is not to seem standoffish about drinking, variety isn't an issue, and since Cupcakes in general know little about wine beyond what they've learned from television advertisements, making it an issue would appear snobbish to their friends. So of course they don't.

The suburban home and yard are the sturdy trunk and root of Cupcake Land. When Houston, Texas, decided to resettle some of its urban poor in suburban houses abandoned by Cupcakes who lost their jobs to the Oil Glut, it fended off Cupcake outrage by requiring the impoverished to attend a course in suburban living; a key topic for review was yard care. The ideal yard in Cupcake Land is a monoculture of bluegrass or Zoysia (a hardier Southern hybrid), a carpet of brilliant green maintained unvarying through the vicissitudes of summer with herbicides, pesticides, fertilizer, mowing, trimming and irrigation. Paleoanthropologists examining the Cupcake past have theorized that the home and yard are symbolic attenuations of the family farms whence Cupcake antecedents emerged, but the true original of the home and yard is the rich man's country estate. Farmers don't have yards, as such, or didn't before the practice spread from the suburbs to the country.

The front yards of Cupcake Land, whatever their extent and however inviting their shaded green swards, aren't used. They're purely decorative, like the pristine curb spaces in front of Cupcake houses, where cars in urban neighborhoods would be parked. Cars in Cupcake Land belong in built-on garages with the garage doors closed and front yards are not for idling, although driveways may be given over at appropriate times of day to pick-up basketball games. Garages for cars exemplify the Golden Rule of Cupcake Land, which is, *A place for everything and everything in its place.* In the spotless kitchens of Cupcake Land, hoods like the hoods condemned criminals wear to the gallows hide the blender and the food processor and white-enameled tin lids painted with meadow flowers disguise the plain, functional heating coils on the electric range; in Cupcake bathrooms, an opalescent plastic box, blue or pink, slotted on top and bottomless, slips over the Kleenex box; and cars belong in garages, behind closed doors, not on the street.

Cupcakes go to church. They're comforted to find so many similarly dressed and like-minded people gathered together in one place. If the sermons are dull, the setting is peaceful. God's in his heaven; all's right with the world, except in unimaginable places like Russia and Nicaragua and Iraq. (During the Reagan Era Cupcakes honestly believed that Central American Communist guerrillas were poised to invade Texas, as if all the hundreds of billions of dollars devoted in that era to the defense budget had gone for naught; as if Texans with their vast personal arsenals couldn't take care of themselves.)

The Empress of Cupcake Land was Nancy Reagan, whom Kansas City Cupcakes adored—always impeccable, all her deals under the table, devoted to a cause for which she found a genteel, simple-minded solution ("Just say no") that was the equivalent for drug abuse of Cupcake Land's standard solution to poverty ("Just get a job"), to AIDS and teenage sex ("Just keep your legs crossed") or to the national debt ("Just quit spending"). Ronald Reagan was the Emperor of Cupcake Land, of course, pleasantness personified, resplendent in his new clothes.

THERE WASN'T ALWAYS A CUPCAKE LAND. I'VE HAD some luck identifying when the territory was ceded. The late Edward Dahlberg remembered a brawnier and more vigorous Kansas City, for example, in his 1963 autobiography *Because I Was Flesh.* "A vast inland city," he described it, "a wild, con-cupiscent city." He recalled "a young, seminal town" where "the seed of its men was strong." Clearly this is not yet Cup-cake Land; the period Dahlberg is evoking is the decade before the First World War, when he was a small boy. "There were more sporting houses and saloons than churches" then in Kan-sas City, he says. Remembering those forthcoming days he asks heatedly, "Could the strumpets from the stews of Corinth, Ephesus or Tarsus fetch a groan or sigh more quickly than the dimpled thighs of lasses from St. Joseph or Topeka?"

But by the 1930s, on the evidence of Evan S. Connell's auto-biographical 1959 novel *Mrs. Bridge,* Cupcake Land was up and running, as if it came along one sinister Christmas complete and fully assembled, in a Pandoran box. Mrs. Bridge, a young Kansas City society matron, already shops on the Country Club Plaza, where presumably she bought her guest towels:

> She had a supply of Margab, which were the best, at least in the opinion of everyone she knew, and whenever guests were coming to the house she would put the ordinary tow-els in the laundry and place several of these little pastel towels in each of the bathrooms. They were quite small, not much larger than a handkerchief, and no one ever touched them. After the visitors had gone home she would carefully lift them from the rack and replace them in the box till next time. Nobody touched them because they

looked too nice; guests always did as she herself did in their homes—she would dry her hands on a piece of Kleenex.

Mrs. Bridge is conversant primarily with just such matters as towels, Connell observes, as well as "the by-laws of certain committees, antique silver, Royal Doulton, Wedgwood, the price of margarine as compared to butter, or what the hemline was expected to do." She knows the bedrock rules of Cupcake Land, which would seem not to have changed much these past sixty years. "Now see here, young lady," she scolds one of her daughters typically. ". . . In the morning one doesn't wear earrings that dangle."

Christmas decorations interest Mrs. Bridge and her circle as they continue to interest Cupcakes today, though "they presented her with a problem," Connell writes: "if you did not put up any decorations you were being conspicuous, and if you put up too many you were being conspicuous." That much at least has changed; decoration in quantity is now acceptable provided the lights are fashionably white.

The use of small white lights to decorate winter trees, I'm informed, originated at the Ritz Hotel in Paris. Eventually, as all things decorative do, the custom found its way like a new strain of influenza to Kansas City. First the twinkling little lights appeared on the skeletal trees that landscaped the entrance drive of a local hotel. They spread quickly, virus-like, from one hotel to another. Next they blanched the formerly multicolored Christmas lights outlining a tower or two of the Country Club Plaza, where tens of thousands of Kansas Citians crowd together each Thanksgiving Eve to watch hundreds of thousands of light bulbs turned on. By last Christmas, the plague of fairy lights had spread to private homes all over the city, luridly netting junipers framing porches and dormant front-yard crabs. The spread appears to be exponential; in a few years Kansas City may very well be visible, a twinkle of white, from the moon.

Edward Dahlberg revisited Kansas City late in life; his cantankerous but perspicacious reaction confirms the areas's annexation to Cupcake Land:

These cities, which are full of every kind of man and woman dirt, and have the most repulsive sex and movie dives, and prurient penny arcade nudes, and pornographic post card streets like Twelfth, have citizens, who are crazy about the word CLEAN. Clean health, clean living, clean politics! Only the corrupt can use this tabu word so easily.

Not many blacks live in Cupcake Land; white flight, after all, was a major force behind its founding. A few years ago I rented an apartment in an old restored building in midtown Kansas City. "Funny thing," the rental agent told me, "the people who rent here are almost always from somewhere else. Kansas Citians all want new." To find the new, however diminished—and to escape the desegregation of the public school system that began in 1955 and was still not complete thirty-five years later—Cupcake recruits moved en masse across the state line into Johnson County, Kansas, last year's cow pasture become this year's ersatz Colonial or French Provincial suburb. If all the millions invested in building the suburbs had been invested in restoring its downtown and its older neighborhoods, Kansas City would be a paradise. Freight wagons used to follow the Santa Fe Trail from Kansas City out through Johnson County; developers today, putting up houses and shopping malls along that trail, seem bent on moving the city itself to Santa Fe.

Housing developments and apartment complexes in Cupcake Land evoke a nobler past, in name if not in quality of construction. The real-estate section of the Sunday *Kansas City Star* offers Colonial Gardens, Cherbourg Apartments, Fox Run, Kings Cove, Hampton Woods, London Towers, Candlewyck, Fountainhead and—for a walled compound on the Missouri side of the state line—Churchill's own beloved

Chartwell. Hyping the virgin prairie with historic place names is an old practice, to be sure; the United States would be a different and bigger-hearted land if it had ever sponsored even one Shit Creek Estates.

Not that Cupcakes dislike blacks, exactly. They avoid them not because they think them inferior but because they know them to be different, Cornbread rather than Cupcake, just as the blue-collar whites who live south and east of Kansas City in Pancake Land are different. In that difference Cupcakes measure a strong potential for unpleasant encounter. "What would I *say* to one?"

Connell, in *Mrs. Bridge*, reinforces this analysis, depicting discomfort rather than active hostility in black-white relations at the borders of Cupcake Land. "The niggers are moving in," Mrs. Bridge's daughter announces provocatively one day:

> Mrs. Bridge slowly put down the tray of cookies. She did not know just what to say. Such situations were awkward. On the one hand, she herself would not care to live next door to a houseful of Negroes; on the other hand, there was no reason not to. She had always liked the colored people she had known. She still thought affectionately of Beulah Mae [a laundress long departed for California] and worried about her, wondering if she was still alive. She had never known any Negroes socially; not that she avoided it, just that there weren't any in the neighborhood, or at the country club, or in the Auxiliary. There just weren't any for her to meet, that was all.

As a minor poet once complained of Chicago, in Cupcake Land deep arguments end in dull commercial liturgies. The Country Club Plaza is a showcase of commercial liturgies. There Gucci sells his wares and Saks, Brooks Brothers and Polo; Tiffany tried, but gave up for lack of customers: so awesome to Cupcakes is Tiffany's reputation that hardly anyone dared to enter the premises.

The Plaza is supposed to be a place for strolling, window-shopping, watering at one of its several outdoor cafes. (Alternatively, one may ride in a horse-drawn carriage, à la Central Park, another epidemic proliferation: at the height of the season more than a dozen carriages work the Plaza, an area only about ten city blocks in extent. They do not want for customers.)

A little posse of black children biked into this pleasant setting one afternoon in the heyday of break dancing. They unrolled their pads of cardboard and linoleum, cranked up their ghetto blasters on a centrally-located corner outside a men's clothing store and got down. They were good; spinning and double-jointing through their repertoire they drew an appreciative crowd. But the Nichols company doesn't want vulgar street entertainment within the confines of the Plaza, particularly when the entertainers are unlicensed and black. Security guards elbowed through the crowd, spread-eagled the children against a wall, handcuffed them (or tried to—the cuffs kept slipping off one small boy's wrists) and dragged them away.

Kansas City renounced its heritage when it pledged allegiance to Cupcake Land. The brown, torrential river that justified the city's founding in the first place, that Lewis and Clark explored, that river boats filigreed in Mark Twain's day, flows disregarded past the old city landings at First Street, its potential for recreation and for civic renewal ignored because its history is local and vernacular rather than European and genteel.

To obscure its bawdy history Kansas City lays claim to an ersatz nobility. Its livestock show is the American Royal, its debutantes debut at a Jewel Ball, and the trademark of its best-known local industry, Hallmark Cards, is a crown. Its professional football team ran the royal theme through a Native American filter and came out the Kansas City Chiefs. An exhaustive Name-the-Team contest that received some 25,000 entries preceded the establishment in Kansas City of its 1985 world-champion baseball team; we were asked to believe that team owner Ewing Kauffman, a self-made pharmaceutical tycoon, considered those thousands of alternatives seriously before he came up with his all-too-predictable choice, the Kansas City Royals, and with the team logo, a distinctly Hallmark-like crown.

The apotheosis of such pretensions was a wedding party in London one recent June for the twenty-year-old stepdaughter of Ronald Reagan's Ambassador to the Court of St. James Charles Price II, a good-old-boy Kansas City banker whose wife, Carol, is heiress to Omaha's Swanson TV-dinner fortune. Melissa Price's wedding dominated the pages of the *Kansas City Star*—a headline I particularly cherish read SIX-TIER, 500-EGG CAKE WILL BE SHOWPIECE OF RECEPTION—and nearly one hundred of Kansas City's elect flew to London for the event. "Sensible young people," the *Star*'s society editor wrote of the couple thus honored, "who believe in some of life's solid dividends, such as friendships and careers." The name of the Berkeley Hotel, the editor noted in a helpful aside, is "(pronounced Barkley)." There was breathless speculation that Nancy Reagan might attend the wedding, her presence transmuting Cupcake into Pound Cake—the Prices are inevitably canonized in social notes as Reagan intimates—but no such imperial benevolence was bestowed.

I've concluded that Kansas Citian Calvin Trillin declared Arthur Bryant's Kansas City barbecue to be the best in the world to gull such pretensions. Bryant's isn't even the best barbecue in Kansas City (their sauce, for one thing, which Trillin seems to have confused with Lourdes water, tastes unsubtly and overwhelmingly of cayenne). Bryant's is situated in the heart of Kansas City's black ghetto, a place very few Cupcakes normally, by choice, even remotely approach. Arthur Bryant is gone now, but in his day the tables were rickety, the windows dirty, the neighborhood risky and the barbecue bad. Back in the 50's, Bud Trillin's high-school crowd went to Bryant's for barbecue to be daring. Cupcakes traipse down to 17th and Brooklyn now because they think it's sophisticated. Eating greasy cayenne-embittered pork in a ghetto barbecue joint identifies them, *mirabile dictu*, as *New Yorker* readers.

On the dark side, Cupcakes, most of whom work for large, impersonal corporations, commute home to the suburbs of Cupcake Land every afternoon fearing for their jobs, and the angst such fear engenders colors all the other hours of their lives. I have heard bright and talented adults, who do not hesitate to speak up on issues of national politics, lower their voices in public places when discussing the doings of their corporations, afraid they might be overheard by someone who might pass on their usually innocuous testimony to the *eminences noires* of directordom. The Soviet Union can't have been any worse in this regard in its Stalinist heyday. If you can't say something good about something, as I was told many times in Kansas City, don't say anything at all. Cupcakes don't. They don't dare.

The corporation is the Darth Vader of Cupcake Land. Corporations brood in our midst like brown dwarfs, those stillborn stars too small to achieve full-scale thermonuclear burning that never quite light up. As political institutions, corporations aspire to nationhood but lack a sufficiently numerous and distinctive polity, though they often command budgets larger than most of the nations of the world and expect their employees to die for them. In dispensing raises and advancement they make it clear that they value loyalty more than achievement. Within such total institutions even the most talented employees frequently come to believe that they are qualified for no other work (the Man without a Country syndrome), that only the corporation's benevolence sustains them.

At the bottom of the cup in Cupcake Land is a deep insecurity about the consequences of individual expression. Cupcakes are usually only one generation removed from the urban working class or the farm. They wear their new-found bourgeois respectability awkwardly. Like the maids and nannies of Victorian England, but with no such compelling evidence walking the streets around them, they believe that only their conformity to the narrowest standards of convention protects them from the abyss.

Their fear stales friendship and love; in personal relations Cupcake men and women give off a continual sense of disapproval and unease. They don't mean to be difficult; they're only continually fearful that your actions or theirs might reveal them to be parvenus. "Between you and I" is standard English in Cupcake Land, Cupcakes working too hard to get their grammar right. When such hypervigilance extends to sex it's deadly; in bed with a Cupcake (to speak in the simplified but useful jargon of transactional analysis), child encounters parent instead of child encountering child. "I don't mind. I enjoy cuddling. Let's try again next time." Cupcakes, I'm afraid, lack spice.

ONE YEAR I MOVED TO THE MISSOURI COUNTRYSIDE TO find out what rural life had become in the thirty years since I left the farm. The morning of the first day of my visit I met the farmer I would be following, whom I call Tom Bauer, at the outdoor feeding floor where he finishes hogs for market. One of the hogs had a prolapsed rectum, Tom explained, which he was going to try to fix.

I had no trouble identifying the afflicted animal. Knee-high, weighing about one hundred pounds—half-grown—it was pink, with coarse white hair, and a swollen, bluish tube of tissue protruded from its body behind. Because of attacks by the other hogs the prolapse was bloody. "You cain't always fix 'em," Tom told me. "Sometimes you work them back in and they come back out. Then you've lost the animal for sure. But we're gonna try."

Tom's big sixteen-year-old son, Brett, was at hand. He slipped into the pen and skillfully caught the hog by a back leg and dragged it out into the aisle. His father pulled on a sterile plastic glove. "We got to haul it up by its hind legs and hang it over the gate," Tom directed. Brett caught the other leg and worked the animal around as if it was a wheelbarrow until its belly approached the gate, which was framed with smooth iron pipe. But the hog's legs were slippery with brown, pungent hog manure. Strapping kid though he is, a reserve guard in high-school football, Brett struggled to lift the animal into position.

I didn't think I was being tested, that first day on the farm after a long absence, but on the other hand, the boy needed help. I took a deep breath—not, in those redolent surroundings, the wisest decision I ever made—stepped to Brett's side, grabbed one shit-covered leg, timed my effort with the boy's and heaved the hog over the gate so that it hung down bent at the hip, its butt in the air. Brett and I held on then while Tom carefully worked the poor animal's rectum back into its body, the hog screaming in unavoidable pain. "Gross," Brett said. Then his dad was finished and we let the animal gently down. It didn't prolapse again—it lived, to be trucked at 250 pounds to the slaughterhouse for pork chops to grace the tables of Cupcake Land.

I adjusted to the realities of farm work quickly enough, having grown up in the trade. But I realized that first morning as I pushed through my initial cultural shock how far removed the city has become from the countryside that sustains it. Cupcake Land is farther removed yet—too far, I fear, for any straightforward recovery. To make life pleasant seems a worthy enough goal in the abstract, but increasing control and decreasing surprise is finally stifling. Full-blown and pathological it results in life-threatening sensory deprivation like the cocoon states that Howard Hughes and Elvis Presley suffered. Cupcake children in their pervasive and much-remarked ennui show symptoms of such deprivation, children like the crowd of well-provisioned Johnson County Cupcake teens who raged through their suburban neighborhoods one recent spring smashing cars; Cupcake opinion of the rampage blamed permissive education.

Some foresee a brutal recession in the last decade of the century, the ugly sequela of the Reagan years. That would be a terrible betrayal of Cupcake trust. Chatty Churchills won't guard the gates to Cupcake Land then, or tea-cozies hood the disaster, or cuddling comfort the bewildered, or credit cards pay the bills. If any good might come from such a consequence it would be the lifting of the burden of pretension from Cupcake backs.

It's possible, barely possible, to imagine a future where Kansas City's front yards have all been converted to vegetable gardens, back yards to lots where a hog or two fatten and a milk cow grazes, and where Cupcake children, grown lean and vigorous, play at hoops or mumblety-peg as they walk themselves to school. It's possible, but the odds aren't encouraging. Like other Cupcake outposts across the land, this plain-spoken river-bluff city I know and still grudgingly love has glazed over its insecurities with pretension. Sooner or later, such artificial barriers always collapse. The Missouri River will still be around then, ready in its brown flood to sweep the stale crumbs away. People I respect who care about this place counsel patience, but it's been a damned long wait.

# 10 / Wheat

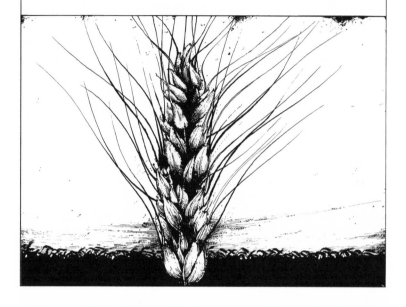

WHEAT. FOR MORE THAN FIVE THOUSAND YEARS THE mainstay of Western civilization, shaping our culture and our ways as rice shaped the East. More than racial traits, the primary division between East and West is the division between wheat and rice. Did not Christ break bread, elucidating the ancient mysteries, packaging them into conveniently portable form? "Jesus took bread, and blessed it, and brake it, and gave it to the disciples, and said, Take, eat, this is my body." And thereby invented the individual.

Wheat, but Americans adore it more than they live by it. We are meat-eaters, not bread-eaters. Ours is a culture of animals more than grain, or rather, grain for animals more than grain for people. We eat bread, or something that goes by that name, but our primary source of protein is meat. The Roman armies lived on their standard issue of three loaves a day; we must have our steaks and chops or believe ourselves deprived. We eat more meat than any other major people of the world, and that fact is food for a metaphor of social Darwinism which would delight the Victorians. Tall, brawny, meat-eating Americans, we are the Huns of the twentieth century: meat-and-potatoes people despite the amber waves of grain in our favorite national hymn.

We grow wheat where we cannot grow other crops, and such is our landscape that we produce millions of bushels more than we can consume. California was once our national wheat field, so broad and sunlit that the first combine, a fifteen-ton machine that cut a thirty-five-foot swath and was pulled by forty mules, could do duty there in the 1840s. But irrigation made other, more lucrative crops possible: dairy cattle, hops, grapes, oranges. In parts of Kansas, Colorado, and Nebraska where once wheat was grown, irrigation has planted sugar beets, a crop that produces twice as much income per acre as wheat.

Yet wheat is our flag, our glory, as American as the Fourth of July. It looks like gold; we pan for it in the interiors of combines as once we panned for gold; and the smell of bread freshens racial memories older than the green continent where we have lived these few hundred years. Everyone knows where wheat is grown: in Kansas. That Russia's immense wheat fields stretch north to the Arctic Circle, that wheat is a thick blanket laid across Italy and Turkey and Afghanistan, we are hardly aware: America is wheat, breadbasket of the world. We ship it to India; we win wars with it and feed the starving losers with it; we grow so much of it we must watch it rot in the holds of pastured ships: to the victor belongs the spoiled.

Ours is the best wheat in the world, hard winter wheat, long-grained, for bread, not for spaghetti, high in protein, glowing with American sunlight, clean as a blond American child playing in the sun. But wheat breaks men's backs, too, the hottest and dirtiest and most intense harvest of the year. Corn? Corn is four months from planting to harvest, something to crop out in the cool of fall; wheat is nine months, a work of long summer tillage, the wait of winter, the panic of weather and haste and fickle prices in June or July, and then the long round of preparation again.

This is wheat and the wheat harvest, not at all what it has seemed to sentimental eyes.

THE WHEAT IN CENTRAL KANSAS IN LATE JUNE STANDS waist high. Each stalk is buff yellow, a hollow tube that no longer carries nutrients to the grain head, tapering to the diameter of a pencil lead at the top. Two, three, four joints along the length of the straw indicate the spurts of its growth through the long winter and short spring. At the top of the straw, bent over in the curve of a cobra's head, hangs the head of wheat, scaled and overlapped like a rattler's tail and loaded with about twenty-five grains of wheat, hardly enough to fill the palm of a cupped hand. But not like a rattler's tail either, for the grains in their husks advance up the head in a hardly noticeable spiral. From the cunning point of each husk of grain protrudes a fine tapering wire of straw; together these wires make up the wheat's beard—that is its name—and it's these wires of beard scraping together in the wind which give the wheat field its characteristic sound, a dry whisper, a rustle, a high rattle as of some convention of small snakes; a miniaturization of cicadas, something insect-like, dry scraping of scaled legs. Our thirst for the oceanic must have led us to hear the ocean in a field of wheat, for that is not its true sound, but an insect concert; and part of the horror of the great locust plagues of the last century must have been the realization that the green horde outside the screens and windows and quickly stuffed chinks of the cabin sounded like nothing so much as a field of wheat come to terrible life. For if we eat the wheat, can it not also eat us? It is a fantasy any child might have, or any saint.

Break off one bearded husk and the image changes abruptly. The individual husk appears suddenly delicate and marine, an opalescent shell through the cracks of which appears the golden-brown nugget. But before you notice the nugget you notice something else: that the pearly husk with its beard curving out behind is the model, magnified ten thousand times, of the human sperm cell, another repetition in nature's economy of forms, and perhaps our sperm grow in spiral clusters in some gonadal wheat field of the body. But we do not waste wheat as we waste our own seed; in the fields and in the elevators every grain is swept up and preserved, since it is worth money as our body's seed is not. A billion grains of wheat in every truckload, but the floor of the truck and of the elevator are carefully swept.

Crack the spermy husk and the golden grain slides out, hard, brown, its illusion of goldenness the result of its translucence, like the goldfish, which, though tailless, the tiny grains with their eyes of wheat germ resemble. Each grain has a white center, the flour we all cherish, but before and around and above that center circle the translucent layers of bran which give wheat its characteristic appearance, and which may be selectively flaked off, so: epicarp, mesocarp, endocarp, episperm, tegmen, perisperm, and chit. And below those, the endosperm, the flour. At the top of the grain, a small brush. At the bottom, the germ. A fruit, if truth be told. A living thing, still alive when it hits the first punishing rollers at the mill, with its own vascular system and the capacity to reproduce itself. A grass seed made huge by cultivation and breeding. Oats would do as well, or rye, or barley, but wheat is the king of grasses and the emperor of grains. It fought with rye in Russia and won; it fought with our American corn in Europe and won; it has lost only to meat in our own land, though Lord knows we like corn well enough.

Each small grain curves round to a cleft, a butt, a vertical indentation, a way for the layers to grow out from a common center of nourishment, to begin or to end not as an egg, with an outer shell enclosing inner liquidity, but as a living fruit locking in upon itself, asking to be divided down to the white clean marrow. It is a miniature storehouse, an energy system devised by nature merely to feed the germ at the tip from which another wheat plant might grow. Or is nature so single-minded as that? Does she not, in her deep pit, her wallow, of forms, match all her many forms against one another to the death—or the life, whichever, death and life being all the same to her? Was wheat bred to make men, or men bred to make wheat? If the latter, then we have won, for only a few of us do this work now of cultivation and harvest. And consume the wheat, and throw the waste to our cattle, as casually as conquerors. But those who grow the wheat still wait on nature, on her sun and her nourishing or damaging rains, and know the terror or exaltation of her moods. And the rest of us hide from her in our own incurving shells, in the layers of walls and houses and streets and cities we have put between us and her, pale germs ourselves and as fertile.

Together the grains are shapeless, watery, making a slow-motion level wherever they are poured, with idle chips of straw and chaff marshaling ridge lines on the surface. You cannot hold wheat as you can hold corn; it slips between the fingers like water, sticks like drops of water to the hand; pours like water out of a truck or an elevator. Yet with an unwatery hardness, so that one grain in the bottom of a boot, like one pea under the mattress of a princess, can make the foot sore, demanding its single attention. Wheat creates a paradox which only wheat farmers understand: we cherish the discrete and do not comprehend liquidity: we can attend an ear of corn or an animal or another person, but nothing massed: the indiscriminate—water and air, sunlight, dirt, the undifferentiated bounty of our planet, we do not understand and cannot attend.

The wheat farmer understands; while our taps run and our chimneys smoke and our electricity flows, he will not deliberately waste a grain of wheat.

THE SURPRISING FACT IS THAT THE COMBINE HAS BEEN with us only a short time. Reaping—cutting the wheat in the fields—and threshing—separating the grains from the chaff and straw—were forever the basics of harvesting wheat, but before the two steps could be combined (you see: *combine*) into one continuous process, farmers and inventors went the long way around to perfect a device called a binder. The binder was the culmination of years of linear logic. Before machinery, men cut wheat, bound it into sheaves, loaded the sheaves onto a wagon, brought them into the barnyard, unloaded them, untied them, flailed them until the wheat broke loose, tossed the straw into the air to shake the wheat free of it, and blew the straw away.

Logically, therefore, to mechanize the harvest involved inventing (1) a machine to cut and bind the sheaves and (2) a machine that would sit in the barnyard and thresh the wheat. And that is what we did. Which makes as much sense as the little pop-up signal arms cars wore in the first days of turn signals (because that's how you and I signal a turn, right?), or the static gas pumps in service stations which in some places have been replaced by hoses dangling from above so that cars need not line up with the pump in order to be filled. (The standing pump made sense when gas was literally pumped by hand, but with electrical pumps why restrict the traffic to a line? Random access makes more sense.)

So we used binders. In fairness, the combine was thought of long before a power source became available that could practically operate its many parts. Not many farmers had forty mules available, much less land dry enough to support a fifteen-ton machine. But there were other options, particularly a device called a header, which cut off only the heads of the grain and left the useless straw standing in the fields to be plowed under as fertilizer. The header saved time in the field, saved the cost of twine to tie up the unnecessary sheaves, saved threshing time in the barnyard, but few used headers.

Everyone knows that Cyrus H. McCormick invented the reaper. The reaper was the forerunner of the binder. The reaper was a misdirection in the evolution of farm equipment. It had a sickle bar that cut the wheat at ground level and a reel that socked the stalks onto a back table where they were raked together and bound by hand into sheaves. The sheaves were stacked together into a shock and picked up later by wagon and taken into the barnyard. The reaper wasn't all bad: it cut labor time in half. The binder, its successor, did the sheaving automatically, carrying the stalks on a canvas belt from the back table up a ramp and into a canvas cradle where a tying arm knotted a length of twine around the bundle. The binder made one man and two horses the equivalent of six men working by hand. That meant speed; that meant efficiency; that meant larger crops and more income; that meant Junior could move to town. The history of agriculture, especially in America, is the story of how many people found ingenious ways to leave the farm for the city.

The other end of the reaper-binder system was the stationary thresher, a piece of American folklore as colorful and as short-lived as the longhorn trails. Set up the thresher next to the barn and build a two-story straw pile where children may play, and during harvest the ladies will serve bounties of fried chicken and cherry pie and chocolate cake to the crews of men. But it wasn't that pleasant, except perhaps for the children. Here is what one wife wrote about the man who invented the combine:

> I don't know what inspired him to build his one-man threshing machine. Maybe he had to pitch bundles of grain into the old-time thresher, or maybe he watched his mother trying to cope with the babies and prepare meals

for the hordes of hungry men needed for the harvest, and remembered the sleepless nights working against time. I only know my heart has long been filled with gratitude for the man who emancipated women from the drudgery of the harvest.

And this is Hamlin Garland, genteel chronicler of hard ways, describing the work of feeding the thresher:

> Will had worked unceasingly all day. His muscles ached with fatigue. His hands trembled. He clenched his teeth, however, and worked on, determined not to yield. He wanted them to understand that he could do as much pitching as any of them. . . . It seemed as if each bundle were the last he could raise. The sinews of his wrist pained him so; they seemed swollen to twice their natural size. But still he worked on grimly, while the dusk fell and the air grew chill.

The binder was a pretty thing, handsome as a sulky, especially the Deering models, which were blue and ivory and elegantly striped. The thresher, by contrast, was monumentally ugly, as its nickname—"the groundhog"—suggests. Long as a trailer truck, taller than a buckboard, it sported leather pulley belts, chain drives, rachet gears, levers, side compartments enough to make it seem some obese monster mounted on dainty, incongruous feet. You can see some of the real threshers of those days at the Agricultural Hall of Fame in Bonner Springs, Kansas. One there might have been named by Donovan or the Beatles: Yellow Fellow.

Before steam, before the internal-combustion engine, the groundhog was run by a great mill wheel called a sweep power to which could be harnessed as many as twelve horses. The horses walked around at two-and-one half revolutions per minute; the sweep power geared the 2½ rpms up to 205 rpms and a long pulley belt transferred the power to the groundhog. Not many farmers today would be able to hitch twelve horses to anything, because the intricacies of the harnesses, the subtle tensions of all those traces would be beyond their technical knowledge (although, in fairness, no horse farmer rip-van-winkled out of the past could even lubricate, much less repair, a self-propelled combine: to each age its own technology).

Most labor-saving devices accomplish the same end. They reduce the number of times something is handled, human hands being slow and expensive to maintain. Notice how many times, even with a perfected binder and groundhog, the wheat is handled, and notice also how many more opportunities the older system offers to shake loose and lose the grain than does modern combining.

In the early years of the twentieth century, the sweep power gave way to the steam engine, but the combine was not developed until after steam had its brief heyday and gave way in turn to the internal-combustion engine.

Now the combine seems to have been with us always, but as late as 1938 a million and a quarter binders still crossed the fields. That year combine production first equaled binder production. That was also the year the Massey-Harris company of Canada introduced a self-propelled combine. Not many farmers were interested: Why do we need another tractor, they asked, especially one we can use only two weeks a year? Like the computer's, the self-propelled combine's potential is not obvious until after you have bought one and begun looking for ways to maximize the expenditure.

The greatest test of the self-propelled combine came during World War II. The War Production Boards of the United States and Canada agreed in 1944 to allow Massey-Harris to build 500 self-propelled combines above and beyond its annual quota of new machines, and these 500 became the famous Harvest Brigade of that year. Large numbers usually yield little meaning. Here are some which translate back to those merely 500 machines: starting in Texas and California and working northward, as the summer progressed, all the way to the Dakotas and

Minnesota, the Harvest Brigade harvested 500,000 bushels of grain every day, the daily equivalent of 250 railroad boxcars, which is two long freight trains. They cleared during that eventful summer a million acres of grain, saved a third of a million man hours and a half-million gallons of critical gasoline, and added twenty-five million bushels of wheat and other grains to North America's stores. They harvested not only wheat but also oats, barley, flax, sorghum, alfalfa, onions, lettuce, beet and carrot seed, peas, beans, and corn. All that from 500 combines, and they saved half a million bushels of grain that would have been knocked down and lost by tractor-pulled combines because the tractor, which rides ahead of the combine attachment and a full tractor width to the right, destroys an outside strip when it opens up a field, and a self-propelled combine does not. The self-propelleds took over after the war, largely as the result of the Harvest Brigade's demonstration.

In the fields of Kansas, the combines are impressive machines. On the 6,000-acre* Paul Mears farm in Beloit, Kansas, four of Mears's own combines thresh out his three thousand acres of wheat. Later in the fall they will combine his corn and harvest his milo. Mears gets about thirty-five bushels of wheat to the acre in a good year; he farms land with enough ground water so that he can plant wheat every year. Farther west the ground water must be allowed to build up over two years before it will sustain wheat, so that every year half the land lies fallow. The annual rainfall in the Beloit area is about twenty inches a year; in western Kansas it drops to from eight to fifteen inches, a great American desert.

Mears is a tall, spare man whose story, though not typical of all Kansas wheat farmers, is certainly exemplary: he started out with a widowed mother and a bare 300 acres of farmland; over the years, with hard work and careful husbandry, he has amassed his 6,000 acres in three counties. He and his son Char-

---

*That is, 9.3 square miles.

lie now farm the land together, and Charlie has 400 acres as a start on his own farm.

None of Mears's four combines is younger than nine years old. "I hate to buy a new one," Mears says. "They make lots of changes on them, put a lot of shields on them, until you can't find anything. When you've run one for eight or ten years you get to know where everything is." The neighbors aren't cutting wheat today, he explains. The straw is too wet, too tough—the words are interchangeable. "But it's going to rain," he continues, "and we feel like we might just as well be putting in our time as standing around twisting our thumbs." The toughness of the straw makes problems in the combines; it wraps around sprockets and gears and axles until they can no longer turn. With so much dampness, the ground is soft, which is no great problem for the combines with their huge cleated tires, but would mire the heavy trucks if they followed the machines through the field as they usually do. Instead, the trucks wait at the edge of the field, and the combines must stop after each round to unload their grain bins.

On the front of a combine is a cutting table sixteen feet wide. A reel with wooden paddles drives the stalks of wheat into the sickle bar at the bottom front edge of the table; behind the sickle bar an augur running the full width of the table feeds the stalks in from both sides to the center back of the table, where pins on the augur and on the back of the table fork the straw into an opening about the size of an oven door. Behind this opening is the machine's most important component, a steel drum with narrow grooves wrapped completely around it which fit into the ridges of a smaller drum below. Ninety percent of the wheat is cracked out of its husks on this roller and dropped onto a screen below. The economies of wheat harvesting are never more obvious than in the design of the combine itself: all the rest of the big machine, all the screens and shakers and walkers, serve only to harvest out that additional ten percent which means the difference between profit and loss.

Walkers are parallel rows of toothed bars which move the straw toward the back of the combine, shaking loose additional grains of wheat as they go. The wheat shaken loose, and the wheat cracked loose by the roller, progresses across a series of screens which separate the chaff from the grains, cleaning away the waste. At the back of the combine, the straw hits a propeller mounted out in the open under the machine; the propeller blows the straw evenly into the swath behind the combine. In the meantime, the grain proceeds up a rubber-paddled conveyor to the combine's storage bin, which, on Mears's machines, has an eighty-bushel capacity. There the grain is stored until the combine unloads it through an augur into a waiting truck. With a sixteen-foot cutting table, a half-mile swath straight down a field represents one acre and about thirty-five bushels, so that Charlie could usually go down and back and collect a load.

The cutting table operates hydraulically, and Charlie, who knows how to get the most from a combine, continually shifted the lever that raised and lowered the cutting table as we drove through the field. You would think, watching a combine from a distance, that running the machine was merely a matter of steering it, but in fact a good driver, properly manipulating the cutting table, probably makes a difference of four or five bushels per acre in the harvest. If a patch of wheat is knocked down by the wind, Charlie quickly lowers the cutting table to pick up the downed heads; if the wheat is high, he lifts the table to avoid cutting more straw than necessary. At a low place in the field he lowers the table; as he approaches a rise he must raise the table or it may well dig into the ground. None of these operations is automatic on Charlie's combine; each requires a keen eye for the terrain, obscured as it is by the wheat stalks. From time to time Charlie stands to drive, looking straight down between the cutting table and the combine itself to check the height of his cut.

From the distance, a combine sounds like a roaring wind, but riding one you discover a distinct rhythm to which all its parts are attuned: do do do do *doot* do do *dodo* do, do do do do *doot* do do *dodo* do. Everything—the sickle bar, the six paddles of the reel, the augur with its five spirals on each side of the center, the roller, the walkers, the screens—everything is working to this rhythm, the sickle moving that many times, that many paddles going by, that many times the screw going around, each cycle lasting about three seconds.

Over to a truck, and Charlie cuts back his engine, drops his loading augur against the side, and feeds the grain into the truck bed. Another combine feeds into the bed from the other side. Unloaded, Charlie puts the big machine into gear, steers a tight circle, and enters the field again at a square corner left by the last combine. The combine seems accelerated at first, then, as you get used to its rhythms, steadies in for the half-mile trip down the quarter-section, do do do do *doot* do do *dodo* do, do do do do *doot* do do *dodo* do, the only sound you can hear, hypnotic. There are German philosophers who have argued that only the rhythms that farm work generates enable human beings to do such work. There are also German philosophers who have argued that even plants have feelings, feel pain when cut, feel ecstasy when caressed by the morning dew. Those are German fancies, but certainly the rhythms of a machine are lulling; one loses all track of other thoughts, becomes part of the machine oneself, a hand on the table elevation lever, another hand on the knob of the power steering wheel, eyes watching the wheat ahead as a sailor would watch the waves, catching the darkening that means the wheat is bent over, catching the slight change in height that means the ground slopes upward. So distracting are the rhythms of the machine, distracting as a fine carefree woman, that only late in the day do you notice that your back and shoulders are sore, your mouth dry, your eyes hot from the dust and concentration. The machine commands you: you only incidentally command the machine.

At the edge of the field, Mears keeps a tractor and disk at hand to disk under the straw as soon as the field is dry enough and as a precaution against fire, which the tractor could immediately disk under and put out. A wheat fire would be a sight to see; the wheat itself would burn fiercely with all its starch and oil. And soon the ground is covered with shiny yellow straw; I remark on it to Mrs. Mears when she brings our dinner—lunch—to the field in the trunk of the family Cadillac, and she says, "It does have a strange feeling—almost like walking on satin." The great strawstacks of old no longer exist since the wheat is threshed in the field, on the run, as it were. The straw Mears needs for cattle bedding he bails in a separate operation. The rest is returned with its load of nutrients to the earth.

Incredible quiet in a field when the combines are running down at the other end of a quarter-section, almost no sound at all except the rustle of the wheat itself. It's a five-mile drive from this section back to Mears's house, and no other occupied houses can be seen, though we passed many empty farmhouses and a few neglected one-room schoolhouses on the way out. The sky this morning is clear and blue except for a thrust of high, wispy cirrus clouds from the west, heralds of a warm front on its way and wet weather with it. It's raining in Denver; in two days it will rain in Beloit. Charlie says a farmer should be able to harvest all his wheat in one week, because that's the longest stretch of good weather you can expect to get, but he and his father have two weeks of work ahead. Wheat is a perverse crop, requiring so many months of growth, demanding rapid harvest. Corn can sit in the field all winter and not be damaged, protected by its thick raincoat of shucks, but rain soaks the grains of wheat, swells them like beans left overnight in a pot, and when the sun comes out the grains dry, turn white, and lose most of their moisture and most of their value in the process. The wheat we are harvesting today is too green; you can crush a grain between thumb and fingernail and produce a soft paste of endosperm. Each truckload taken in to Mears's on-site elevators is tested for moisture on a small machine. Charlie measures out a standard measure of the grain, pours it into the black box, sets the dial for WHEAT, and the electrical impedance of the wheat registers on a gauge as moisture percentage. The loads this morning run up to twenty percent moisture. Fifteen percent is better, says Charlie; ten percent is ideal. He backs the truck into a corrugated steel shed, lifts the bed, and dumps the wheat out the tailgate into a hole in the floor guarded with bars of tubular steel. Down pours the grain into an underground bin. Then he opens up a gate underground and an augur screws the grain into a dryer run from the power takeoff of a tractor behind the shed. Hot spots in the grain, caused by areas of wheat with too much moisture, would attract bugs. Drying helps eliminate the hot spots. In addition, a white plastic bottle drips a fumigant into the grain as it goes through the underground augur.

Mears stores most of his wheat in his own grain bins and takes it to town when the moisture and the price are right. Smaller operators deliver the grain directly from the field, and pay penalties if it is too moist or too dry. Mears has ten bins twenty feet high and seven bins thirty feet high clustered around the unloading shed, which sports a green tower—the elevator that carries the grain from the dryer up higher than the bins. Pipes from the elevator extend to the tops of the bins, so that by shifting a lever inside the shed Charlie can direct the grain into any bin he chooses. The bigger bins have blowers built into their sides at the bottom to continue the drying process. A lone chickadee, I notice, sits on one of the guy wires that steady the elevator. Wheat has a smell, even in its raw state: it smells like Wheaties, nutty, branny, rich, warm—bread in the raw.

While Charlie unloads his truck, I walk around the Mears farm, delighted with its works. A modern working farm bears no resemblance at all to the picturesque farms of our past. Mears has built his wife a new brick ranch house, clean and centrally air-conditioned, but the rest of the farm is plain and practical. The old farmhouse has been converted into a bunkhouse for the hired hands who help with the summer's harvesting; it sits gray and weathered north of the new house, with old machines littering its yard. Across from the new house rises the complex of grain bins and elevators, and behind that complex is a vast muddy feedlot, for Mears fattens cattle there in the winter on the corn and milo he grows.

Next to the feedlot on the north is another galvanized metal shed, this one a big repair shop with a peaked roof and white front. Inside the shop, every variety of tool and part; a motorcycle, probably Charlie's; an oil grid in the floor running the length of the shop. Wood tools; a variety of saws of all sizes and shapes; a rack with different sizes of metal washers on it; fifty boxes the size of cheese boxes filled with bolts; blacksmith tools; hammers; plastic milk bottles cut out to hold bolts, nuts, filters, valves, screws, springs, drills; electrical wires; spark plugs; oil filters. A refrigerator filled with animal pharmaceuticals—vaccines, hypos, drenching equipment. Posts with old inner tubes hanging over them; an arc welder and sections of pipe; welding rods in a homemade metal stand; chains: small chains, fine chains, square-linked chains, pullchains; a differential pulley; oil pans and oil waste pans; a spotlight on a stand; hubs for tires; racks of wrenches on pegboard; racks of jars full of nuts and bolts; files; chisels; a modern hanging lamp screwed to the wall; a radio up on a beam; a broom. Pulley belts; grease guns with a variety of nozzles; electrical cords; multiple electrical outlets; a space heater hanging from the ceiling; tires; more oil pans; jacks; a hydraulic cylinder; and we are back around at the front door. You must be able to fix anything on a farm, and usually in a hurry, so that you rarely throw old parts away. The bolt or washer you junked yesterday may be the very one you need today.

Across from the work shed a barn with lean-tos built onto all three sides to extend its protection, and under the lean-tos two New Holland bailers, more equipment, a hay rack, a stack of more than a hundred tires, truck and automobile and tractor; more tools, then stacks of gears and pipes and transmissions—a junk sculptor's paradise. Paul Mears doesn't raise chickens; no ducks waddle contently through his barnyard. He's a large-scale farmer, and measures his crops by sections and his cattle by hundreds, and when he doesn't farm he usually travels. He is one of Kansas's Master Farmers, an award given annually to only a very few of the men who farm in that state of farms.

Out in the field, the harvest continues, and will continue for days after I have returned home. A combine breaks down and Mears sends out a call for a welding truck, which, directed by radio, soon appears, and right in the middle of the untraveled dirt road the welder and Mears's men remove the cutting table from a combine and weld a broken strut. My young son rides round and round the field at Charlie's side, as awed and dazed and happy as a child can be, his hair blowing like straw in the wind. From the distance the combines look like giant insects, though the aerodynamic lines of the Massey-Ferguson machines soften that effect; over in the next field some custom-cutters drive Gleaner combines, square galvanized-steel machines with enclosed, air-conditioned cabs, the most insect-like of all.

It's hard to remember, amid these horizon-wide fields of wheat, Kansas's hard-scrabble past. The fence posts around some of Mears's fields recall the difficulties settlers had on the treeless prairie: they're heavy splinters of limestone, a dirty yellow, planted upright in the ground. Charlie says they will stay in place forever if you don't bump them with your tractor. The abandoned buildings we pass on the way to the fields are limestone too, often enough, though I notice no bluffs in the area. Someone dragged those splinters of limestone out into the fields and built those fences, those old buildings, and fought grasshopper plagues and deadly blizzards and years of drought to start these farms.

During harvest time on a modern Kansas wheat farm, life isn't much easier: Mears will be out in the fields by eight o'clock every morning, and won't be back in until nine at night. The difference is that today such hours don't continue year-round as they did in the subsistence-farming years of the past. Wheat is profitable, but at thirty-five bushels an acre only economies of scale make it so. Our golden grain is mass-produced by farmers such as Paul Mears. It's good work, and hard work, and colorful if you stand back far enough.

# 11 / An Artist in Iron

*The name Eisenhower translates roughly as "iron" and "hewer."*
*To further refine the original German, I'm told, one should know*
*that* eisenschmidt *would mean blacksmith, while an* eisenhower
*was something of an artist in iron, a man who literally hewed*
*metal into useful and ornamental shapes, such as armor, weap-*
*ons, etc.*

—Dwight D. Eisenhower, in *At Ease*

"SOMETHING OF AN ARTIST IN IRON." DWIGHT EISEN-
hower was that, though he did his best to hide his artistry
within the armor of a soldier. Huckleberry Finn disguised as
George Washington, he truly believed no one would ever find
him out. He worked at obfuscation with the usual Eisenhower

doggedness. Hints of his interior life turn up perhaps twenty times in all the 2,350 pages of his memoirs, which must be something of a record. The hints tell the story: despite his cool superiority to most of the cherished beliefs of mankind, his complete confidence in his ability to outgun all but a very few of the citizens of the world, his conviction that he could think more clearly and act more wisely than any other man of his generation, he found within himself a rebellion so physical that only a will as hard as his own could have controlled it.

SIGNS AND PORTENTS. "ALL HER LIFE A WOMAN OF peace, my mother was born close to war and the clamor of battle. Growing up, she could see its ravages in a devastated land and in broken bodies. If her hatred of war arose out of childhood memories, she had justification. War's tragedy, inescapable in its waging and in its aftermath, was no tale she had read or heard. She knew it of her own seeing and pondering." Ida Elizabeth Stover, Dwight's mother, left Virginia on her own, at fourteen, to follow two of her brothers by wagon train to Kansas and get an education. In Abilene she met David Eisenhower, Dwight's father, and soon enough they were married. David had forgone farming—he hated it—to open a general store in Abilene, but the business failed after the drought of 1887 because David and his partner carried too many farmers on credit. His partner ducked out with the few remaining funds and David was left to pay the creditors. Looking for work, he and Ida moved to Denison, Texas, two children in tow.

"I was born during a fierce thunderstorm and it was to that coincidence that [Mother] always blamed my liking for lightning and thunderstorms as a child." Born on October 14, 1890, the third of seven sons, one of whom died in infancy. Five would grow up to success and prosperity. One would grow up to history.

*Why* must always be the question. The beginning was auspicious enough. A mother born into a burned and salted Civil War valley who knew her own mind at fourteen and crossed half a continent to make it up. A father who had failed in business through an excess of generosity and who would never be generous again. A fierce thunderstorm. A birth. Strong medicine.

WE ARE ALWAYS CHILDREN FIRST. HIS TWO GREAT METaphors were his father and his mother—war and peace, attack and supply, masculine and feminine, sternness and joy. He lived as a man within the gigantic limits of their lives, waging war as his father would have waged it, with a cold and unrelenting ferocity, waging peace as his mother would have waged it, with patience and unfailing optimism, but with shrewdness too.

Ida Elizabeth gave him his looks, handsome, blond, blue-eyed. She also gave him his freedom. "Mother was by far the greatest personal influence on our lives." "Her serenity, her open smile, her gentleness with all and her tolerance of their ways, despite an inflexible loyalty to her religious convictions and her own strict pattern of personal conduct, made even a brief visit with Ida Eisenhower memorable for a stranger." And a lifetime memorable for a son. He shaped her manners and customs and habits into the public Eisenhower, the serenely smiling mother of the nation.

David Eisenhower gave us the other Ike, the man of controlled and completely confident violence. Here is that Ike, years later, when Khrushchev is raging about the U-2* at the Paris Summit, staring the Russian down with the confidence of a hard country boy: "The length of his explanation and the emphasis he gave to this subject clearly indicated that he was determined to keep me out of Russia. His document was repetitious, and at one point he became so vehement that I could

---

*The U.S. spy plane the Soviet Union had recently shot down.

not help grinning. He happened to notice this, and thereafter kept his eyes glued to the text of his speech."

David was dark, black-browed, stern, violent. "With his family of hearty, active boys," Ike wrote later, "I'm sure that strict discipline was necessary for survival. He certainly was never one for spoiling any child by sparing the rod. If the evidence showed that the culprit had offended deliberately, the application of stick to skin was a routine affair." The culprit, often enough, was young Dwight, a rebel until long after West Point from any duty he thought impractical, ill-conceived, or citified, however hallowed by custom.

But David administered his most memorable beating to Dwight's older brother Edgar. When his father found out that Edgar had been skipping school to earn some spending money, he marched home for lunch and abruptly, without explanation, began to beat the boy with a harness strap. Dwight, twelve years old, had seen beatings before, but none like this one. He tried to pull his father off his brother. "I don't think anyone ought to be whipped like that, not even a dog," he told his father. Later he would rationalize the beating because it convinced Edgar he should stay in school. But Ike remembered that piece of fatherly brutality all his life. It and other experiences like it taught him to be tough even as it saddled him with a rage he would always have trouble controlling. The serene Dwight D. Eisenhower, be it remembered, smoked *four* packs of cigarettes a day until a physical breakdown in the late 1940's convinced him he should quit—which he did then, with characteristic Eisenhower guts, cold turkey.

IKE'S BROTHERS. HIS FIRST TEAM. THE OLDER ONES PRO-tected him from bullies until he was old enough to protect himself, and from them he learned the value of superior force. Fight fair when the stakes are low, but two against one will usually stop a fight that needs stopping. "Ed, Earl, and I were the hot-tempered and quarrelsome element, while Arthur, Roy, and Milton were always credited with more tractable natures." Earl and Milton paired off, born only eighteen months apart. Dwight and Edgar paired off, both outwardly anti-intellectual, hell-raisers, naturals. In 1944, Ike would write Edgar from Europe: "I have heard that a man named Kenneth Davis is writing a biography. I wish that all such things would wait until a man really had leisure to think up some really good tales to tell about his boyhood. If they gave me time and did not check up too closely on fact I could make you and me look like Tom Sawyer and Huckleberry Finn." Then a sly thrust at Edgar: "Which would you rather be?"

Blood poisoning from a splinter in his leg sent young Dwight into a two-week delirium. "The doctor came two or three times a day and only occasionally was I conscious—usually when he used his scalpel to explore the wound." Now the team was working. Dwight overheard the doctor discussing amputation with his parents. He called in Edgar. "I . . . made him promise to make sure that under no circumstances would they amputate my leg." He told Edgar: "I'd rather be dead than crippled." Edgar stationed himself outside the bedroom door. No grim-faced father intervened then.

During most of Dwight's childhood, the Eisenhowers lived in a small four-bedroom house in Abilene. His mother "skillfully assigned us to beds in such a pattern as to minimize the incidence of nightly fights." She rotated their chores and adjudicated their disputes, with the threat of massive fatherly retaliation always in the background. The brothers stuck together, despite disputes. They even helped each other through college, Dwight working nights for Edgar at the Belle Springs Creamery in Abilene, winching up 300-pound cans of ice and studying for West Point on the side. The thickness of life with his brothers would shape his future choices of staff and companions. He was always shy and undemonstrative with women, preferring the company of men. Men he could measure, knew the temper of their cutting edges, the shape of their patience, the force of their intelligence.


A PHOTOGRAPH: SIX BOYS AROUND A ROUGH CAMPING table, white tent in the background before a screen of cotton-woods. Battered Thermos on the table, tin cups and plates. "While we were in high school, a group of us decided to camp on Lyons Creek, about twenty miles south of town, and so far as I know the only clear-water stream in that part of Kansas. . . . We planned to be gone two weeks." All the boys in the picture wear good school shirts and pants except Dwight. He wears a blue work shirt and bib overalls, socks that might once have been white, muddy, low-cut shoes. The others look around tentatively from their places at the table; he, bold foreground, faces the camera from his camp stool, tousled hair, collar up negligently in back, the consideration of a grin warming his face, shirt and overalls wrinkled, shirtsleeves too short for his lanky arms, big hands lolling in his lap, a kitchen towel dangling from one hand, legs spread-eagled and heels parked against the ground, a stamped tin cooking spoon nonchalant in an enameled pot camped between his feet. He looks, as he intended, like one hell of a fellow. "I could make you and me look like Tom Sawyer and Huckleberry Finn. Which one would you rather be?"


"MEN OF DESTINY ARE OFTEN HARD TO TELL FROM other men," Richard Rovere wrote at the beginning of Eisenhower's campaign for the Presidency. Winston Churchill, sick in his childhood bed, prodded his counterpane into hills and set clever tin soldiers to engage the enemy. Dwight Eisenhower read Greek and Roman history, committing its battles to his total memory. "Such people as Hannibal, Caesar, Pericles, Socrates, Themistocles, Miltiades, and Leonidas were my white hats, my heroes. Xerxes, Darius, Alcibiades, Brutus, and Nero wore black ones." Hannibal, master of exotic technology and the surprise attack, he liked the best of all. "This bias came about because I read one day that no account of Carthaginian history was ever written by a friendly hand. . . . For a great man to come down through history with his only biographers in the opposite camp is a considerable achievement. Moreover, Hannibal always seemed to be an underdog, neglected by his government, and fighting during most of his active years in the territory of his deadly and powerful enemy." He read so hard his mother locked his books away. He found the closet key and went on reading whenever she left the house.

Hannibal would not be his only hero. He collected them as other boys collect marbles, seeking always a finer agate. "My hero was a man named Bob Davis. He had long been a traveler, a fisherman, hunter, and guide. He was also a bachelor, a philosopher, and, to me, a great teacher. Bob, about six feet tall, a little stooped, quiet and gentle, was in his fifties when I knew him, roughly from age eight to sixteen. He never seemed to be annoyed when I went along on expeditions to the Smoky Hill River. . . . We spent weekends together on the river, with my mother's blessing." Bob was illiterate. Bob taught Dwight poker. "So thoroughly did Bob drill me on percentages that I continued to play poker until I was thirty-eight or forty and I was never able to play the game carelessly or wide open. I adhered strictly to percentages." "Stress he could endure," wrote William Carlos Williams of George Washington, "but peace and regularity pleased him better. There must have been within him a great country whose wild paths he alone knew and explored in secret and at his leisure." Fisherman and hellraiser, rider of rafts down flood-swollen Abilene streets, trapper of mink and camp stew specialist, Eisenhower would guard his great country as carefully as Washington. It gave him a way of looking aside, a comic perspective on the life of men in the world. If the greatest thing in the world is to be Huckleberry Finn, then it is no great thing to be King or Emperor or President. High office and heavy responsibility must even seem total poverty to a spirit lusting for the wilderness. Then the men who occupy those offices can be no more than ordinary men. And since he was at least as much as they, he could see past the office to the men, and past the men to the function.

His trick was not to let us know his contempt for the works of men, his topsy-turvy value system. Sometimes we caught him at it, as sometimes, if you are quick enough, you can see Old Nick's cloven foot there on your best friend even though he switches it from left to right almost faster than the eye can follow. Ike let a dinner guest see that foot at the White House once. The guest asked him why the United States had not interceded for the French in Vietnam, and he gave the honest answer: "Because nobody asked us." Perfectly honest answer. Best reason he knew for staying out of a stinking jungle war nobody could ever win. He let it slip by because he suspected no one would believe that the solution to a major international problem could be, in its principle, so simple. "Practical problems," he was candid enough to admit in *At Ease*, "have always been my equivalent of crossword puzzles."

NO ONE SEEMS TO HAVE UNDERSTOOD THAT HE WAS A brilliant man. He was not an intellectual, and perhaps that fact confused people of intellect who assume intelligence must always breathe an air of the salon. But his memory was phenomenal, his ability to reason of the highest caliber. We have Richard Nixon's word for that. Nixon wrote of Ike in *Six Crises*: "He could be very enthusiastic about half-baked ideas in the discussion stage, but when it came to making a final decision, he was the coldest, most unemotional and analytical man in the world."

"In grammar school," Ike tells us, "spelling was probably my favorite subject either because the contest aroused my competitive instincts or because I had learned that a single letter could make a vast difference in the meaning of a word. . . . Arithmetic came next because of the finality with which an answer was either right or wrong." But he saw no point to Spencerian penmanship, that ornate Victorian conceit, and, typically, never bothered to learn it. Preciosity annoyed him, activated the violence he so scarcely contained. Here he defends his taste and scoffs at Spencerian in the space of two subtle sentences: "Although I began, in my late fifties, to paint in oils, fascinated with colors, my handwriting remains angular and slurred at best. My hand was made less for the use of the pen than of the ax—or possibly the pistol." They were huge hands, it's true, hands from which he clipped the nails with shears.

Still in rebellion from duty, not yet willing to don the armor of his family name, the rigid mask of his father, he did no better than he should have at West Point. And yet he had his moments. Forced to demonstrate a problem in integral calculus to which he knew the answer but not the solution, he invented a new solution in the last minutes before he was called to recite. The instructor accused him of cheating. Cadet Eisenhower prepared assault and battery, but an associate professor of mathematics turned up in time. Ike's new solution was simpler than the old. It was incorporated into the Point's procedures.

Later, accepting his duty, he would enroll in the Command and General Staff College at Leavenworth, Kansas, and graduate first in his class of 275 hand-picked officers. He would repeat the feat at the Army War College. That is how generals are made, and by then he was prepared to command.

ALL HIS LIFE, BELIEVING IT A WEAKNESS, HE WOULD DISguise the great country within him, giving his mother's friendliness to the public world and his father's toughness to the practical problems of command. They were studied roles, both of them, calculated to misdirect. He feared nothing so much as exposure. To be known for what you are when no outward sign reveals you—that would be terror to reckon with. It happened only once. As a young cadet, on furlough from the Point in civilian clothes, Ike traveled to Chapman, Kansas, to umpire a baseball game. He arrived early enough to eat lunch, and after lunch he wandered into a shooting gallery:

> I thought it would be fun to try a few shots at the moving targets. As a complete stranger in Chapman, and dressed in ordinary clothes, I could hardly believe my ears when I picked up a rifle and heard a man standing nearby say to another:
> "Okay, now Mister, you've been bragging about your shooting. I just happened to see this soldier boy come in here and I'll bet you ten dollars that he can beat you on any target and in any kind of shooting you want."
> Although nothing had been addressed directly to me, when I heard this astonishing statement—nothing I was wearing identified me as a cadet or soldier—unaccountably, and for the first time in my life, a fit of trembling overcame me. My hands shook. Without a word, I laid down my rifle, having already paid for the shells, and left the place without a backward glance.
> Never before or since have I experienced the same kind of attack.

An attack of anxiety at being so easily discovered, and you can believe it was severe. The Eisenhowers weren't the sort of people who paid for shells and then failed to use them.

The armor allowed little personal expression. "Ike was not a demonstrative man with any of his family," his wife Mamie wrote after his death, "—not even with me." His rare personal gestures worried him. When John graduated from West Point in 1944, Ike couldn't resist sending the graduating class a brief message of congratulation. As Supreme Commander he was well within his right to do so. But he cabled the message to the Superintendent of the Point with a preface. "I am most diffident about making such a suggestion and ask you, in considering it, to turn it over well in your mind, and *don't let me do*

*anything that would appear either ridiculous or egotistical."*
Those are *Ike's* italics.

He believed he should not directly assert his personality in
his work. "His greatest aversion," wrote Emmet John Hughes,
one of Ike's speech writers, "was the calculatedly rhetorical device. . . . All oratorical flourishes made the man uneasy, as if
he feared the chance that some hearer might catch him *trying*
to be persuasive." Yet Ike knew how to write ornately if he
chose to. "Let me tell you something," he said to another of
his speech writers, Arthur Larson. "You know that General
MacArthur got quite a reputation as a silver-tongued speaker
when he was in the Philippines. Who do you think wrote his
speeches? I did."

He knew his ability. "My God," he wrote to himself in 1942,
"—how I hate to work by any method that forces me to depend
on anyone else." This iconoclasm from the man who became
the most skillful delegator of authority the nation has ever
known. He could delegate because he was absolutely certain
he was in charge, and qualified to be. "The fact remains," he
told Larson about John Foster Dulles, his Secretary of State,
one day, "that he just knows more about foreign affairs than
anybody I know. In fact, I'll be immodest and say that there's
only one man I know who has seen more of the world and
talked with more people and *knows* more than he does—and
that's me."

CONFIDENT OF HIMSELF—EVEN ARROGANT OF HIM-
self—he assumed others would trust him too. If they did not,
then he would not do his duty. He would return to the wilderness within him, become a cowboy in Argentina, a crack journalist, a teacher at a cow college. These were all his dreams at
one time or other. None of them came about. He didn't want
them to. They were huckleberry alternatives to the challenges
he wanted but didn't want, wanted but couldn't ask for. They
were also bargaining weapons. At West Point, preparing to

graduate, he was called before a Colonel Shaw to discuss his commission. Shaw hesitated to commission him at all because his disciplinary record was less than shining and his knee so weak from a football injury that he might have to be retired early at government expense.

"When Colonel Shaw had finished, I said that this was all right with me. I remarked that I had always had a curious ambition to go to the Argentine (as a reader of geographies, I was curious about the gauchos and Argentina sounded to me a little like the Old West), and I might go there and see the place, maybe even live there for two or three years."

That gave Ike the offensive, moved the shoe to Shaw's foot. Shaw discovered the need then to find a place for a young man who had cost the United States four years of education. He offered Ike the Coast Artillery. Ike considered the Coast Artillery a graveyard for officers, and refused. Shaw offered him the Infantry. That was more or less what he wanted. He accepted.

He prepared himself to be Supreme Commander—invented the job—but didn't ask for it. He prepared himself to be president but came back to campaign with almost as much reluctance as Churchill ascribed to him during the war when he told Lord Moran, "Ike had not only to be wooed, he had to be raped." Campaigning, Ike told Emmet Hughes: "If they don't want me, that doesn't matter very much to *me*. I've got a hell of a lot of fishing I'll be happy to do." He *wanted* both jobs, or rather, the responsible adult in him wanted both jobs. But he expected those who assigned the jobs to want *him*. That was the least the War Department and the people could do if they expected him to be always bolting away his wilderness, like a fly rod he could never find time to use, locked up there in its case, accusing him. "What more do they want from me?" he asked his friends while agonizing over the question of a second term. "I've given all of my adult life to the country. What more must I do?" But he took on the second term anyway because of two scruples: he believed that he was better qualified than any Democrat to pursue peace, and sometime in his young manhood he must have promised himself on his mother's behalf to do as much for peace as he knew he would one day do for war; and he would allow no man to believe he gave up the presidency because of a mere physical debility, a mere heart attack. And so he ran.

HIS SERVICE IN THE CANAL ZONE SEEMS TO HAVE marked the turning point of his young life. Prior to that assignment he had played as hard as he had worked. Now, with his firstborn son lost to scarlet fever, he was ready for a change. For three years, in Panama, one more hero guided him before he became a hero himself and learned to look upon men of great ability with respect tempered with equanimity: General Fox Conner, commander of Camp Gaillard. While Mamie fought bedbugs and listened to the jungle whisper its nightly obscenities ("Mamie," he told her years before, "there's one thing you must understand. My country comes first and always will; you come second"), Ike devoured Conner's books and rode out on reconnaissance to be tutored by firelight. Conner drilled him in tactics, debated him in philosophy, speculated with him on the nature of man. After Conner's tutorials, Ike was always number one in his class.

> Our conversations continued throughout the three years I served with him in the isolated post of Camp Gaillard. It is clear now that life with General Conner was a sort of graduate school in military affairs and the humanities, leavened by the comments and discourses of a man who was experienced in his knowledge of men and their conduct. I can never adequately express my gratitude to this one gentleman, for it took years before I fully realized the value of what he had led me through. And then General Conner was gone. But in a lifetime of association with great and good men, he is the one more or less invisible figure to whom I owe an incalculable debt.

If he was the greatest, Fox Conner was far from the only teacher in Ike's life. Beginning with Bob Price, the Smoky River trapper, and passing beyond Conner to George Marshall and John Foster Dulles, Eisenhower picked—or was picked by—men of calm and wisdom, men older than he, benevolent fathers as it were, who could find in him an intelligent and respectful son to raise up. Of his own father Ike would write, at the time of David's death, "I'm proud he was my father! My only regret is that it was always so difficult to let him know the great depth of my affection for him." The quieter men he chose for teachers. He could learn war *and* peace from them. He fed his immense intelligence on an equally immense inner violence, for if Huckleberry Finn was hidden, easily grinning, within the armor, so also was the anger of his father. Ike's temper was legendary. It seems to have been a calculated instrument, something he used when he needed to and controlled when he did not. Superior force was always his style. The anger supplied the necessary fuel. Did *he* change the code name of the Normandy invasion from the lighthearted ROUNDUP to the blackly feudal OVERLORD? But Normandy offers only one example. He ended the Korean War by passing the word to Mao through Nehru that unless the North Koreans got down to business at Panmunjom he would use the atomic bomb on China. He cooled Lebanon with one of the largest contingents of troops ever deployed by the United States in a friendly country in peacetime. He assaulted the Soviet Union with sweeping proposals to turn over both countries' nuclear materials to the United Nations,* to open the skies, to share space.

Yet the man of violence and superior force was not a war lover. A war lover, like Patton, is a killer, and Ike could not be a killer because he had been raised, as his mother told a biog-

---

*Playing percentages all the way. "Our technical experts assured me that even if Russia agreed to cooperate in such a plan solely for propaganda purposes, the United States could afford to reduce its atomic stockpile by two or three times the amount the Russians might contribute, and still improve our relative position."

rapher, to "choose good." The biographer paraphrases Ida: "They were told that everyone has it in him to know right from wrong, good from bad; that he is free to choose which he will have, and, if he chooses wrong, not even God can avert the consequence." Ida resolved the paradox simply. "War will never bring peace," she told the biographer, "but so long as there are those who make war, someone has to go to our defense." That is how you kill without being a killer.

Field Marshal Alan Brooke once made the mistake of accusing Ike of giving American forces the lead in a World War II battle for "nationalistic considerations." It would have been obvious to anyone but an Englishman that the artist in iron would never be guilty of basing a decision on anything so irrational as nationalism. Ike reacted. "I am certainly no more anxious to put Americans into the thick of the battle and get them killed than I am to see the British take the losses. . . . I have not devised any plan on the basis of what individual or what nation gets the glory, for I must tell you in my opinion there is no glory in battle worth the blood it costs." The violence, you see, simply fed his reason.

It's instructive to look at the way he handled George Patton. Patton got his *identity* from battle, and from nowhere else. Ike understood Patton's personality perfectly well. Nearly every time he refers to Patton in his memoirs he finds something humorous and slightly askew about the man. "When I returned to Camp Meade in the autumn [of 1920] many changes had taken place. Senior officers of the Tank Corps who had seen action in France were back. Among these men the one who interested me most, and whom I learned to like best, was a fellow named Patton. Colonel George S. Patton was tall, straight, and soldierly looking. His most noticeable characteristic was a high, squeaking voice, quite out of keeping with his bearing."

Ike, the practitioner of iron control, would tolerate from Patton displays of temper, hysteria, and public megalomania for which he would have court-martialed any lesser man. Because he knew Patton's ability, and so long as he could apply it to his larger strategies, he would use Patton the way the K-9 Corps used its dogs. "The finest leader in military pursuit that the United States Army has known." That was his estimation of Patton, and no lesser estimation would explain the length to which Ike was willing to bend his principles to keep Patton on. Old Blood and Guts might frighten his men. He didn't frighten Eisenhower. He reminded him of the rebellious Dwight whom David Eisenhower had more than once disciplined with a belt. Ike substituted, for the belt, the public confession and the personal apology, devices at least as painful to Patton. But Ike the realist also defended Patton to anxious mothers and angry World War I veterans who wrote the Supreme Commander from the States:

You are quite right in deploring acts [in this case, slapping a soldier hospitalized for battle fatigue] such as his and in being incensed that they could occur in an American army. But in Sicily General Patton saved thousands of American lives. By his boldness, his speed, his drive, he won his part of a campaign by marching, more than he did by fighting. He drove himself and his men almost beyond human endurance, but because of this he minimized tragedy in American homes. Had he weakened or wavered for one second he would have given the enemy time to organize—and we would have paid for that mistake in American lives.

He liked Patton personally. He didn't indulge him, because future discipline wouldn't allow it, but at least, with careful thought, he could construct an artwork or two. The irony of giving Patton, a man who lusted to command, a fake army complete with command headquarters, field equipment and radio traffic, to decoy German attention from Normandy to Calais, could not have been lost on either man. It was a joke; it was also good planning. Ike made Patton wait and sweat. When he finally unleashed him, Patton went like hell. But the Supreme Commander found no room for personal feelings after the war. When Patton flapped once more while commanding the Third Army in Berlin, comparing the Nazi party with the Republicans and Democrats, Ike relieved him of command and set him to assessing the war, far from anxious mothers and keen correspondents.

IF HIS STAFF EXPECTED DRAMA IN THE VICTORY ANnouncement, it did not yet know Ike. He announced the German surrender with characteristic restraint, saying nothing to draw attention to himself or to gloat over a fallen enemy. He cabled the Combined Chiefs of Staff: "The mission of this Allied force was fulfilled at 0241, local time, May 7, 1945." That day and afterward it was business as usual at headquarters. "We had no local victory celebrations of any kind," Ike writes emphatically in *Crusade in Europe*, "then or later."

His celebrated Guildhall Address, delivered in London in 1945 at the time he received London's honorary citizenship, enlarges on his feeling about the war. The man who grew up on heroes and became one himself asserts boldly that heroes, in the usual sense of the word, don't exist.

First he assesses himself as history usually assesses successful commanders:

> Humility must always be the portion of any man who receives acclaim earned in blood of his followers and sacrifices of his friends.
>
> Conceivably a commander may have been professionally superior. He may have given everything of his heart and mind to meet the spiritual and physical needs of his comrades. He may have written a chapter that will glow forever in the pages of military history.

The diffident "may have been" and "may have given" and "may have written" hardly disguise the superlatives the Supreme Commander knew history would erect to his work. They hardly disguise the pride part of him felt at having earned such an assessment. But he had read history before, and had lived it these past hard years, and learned a darker truth:

> Still, even such a man—if he existed—would sadly face the fact that his honors cannot hide in his memories the crosses marking the resting places of the dead. They cannot soothe the anguish of the widow or the orphan whose husband or father will not return.

Then he draws the guideline he thinks historians ought to follow:

> The only attitude in which a commander may with satisfaction receive the tributes of his friends is in the humble acknowledgment that no matter how unworthy he may be, his position is the symbol of great human forces that have labored arduously and successfully for a righteous cause.

Which is to say, heroes are people who do their jobs right at a time when their jobs spearhead a great historical movement.

We know from Vietnam what a cynical command fighting an ill-conceived war for a less than righteous cause can do to an army. We know from My Lai. Will we ever be able to determine the part that Eisenhower's courage and humility contributed to make his battlefield relatively more humane?

THE EISENHOWER OF THE PRESIDENCY WAS NOT A DIFferent man from the Eisenhower of Abilene and of the war. The principle of the continuity of a man's personality ought to be axiomatic, but during his presidency many believed otherwise. Ike was said to be indecisive; he was said to be lazy; he was assumed to be naive. He was none of those. He faced different circumstances, and his discipline and experience could not alter them all. He had always required a clear mandate; he got one from the people, but not from the system. "Nominating Dwight Eisenhower," wrote Richard Rovere after the 1952 Republican National Convention, "was an act of hard sacrifice and self-denial for most of the delegates here. It was clear from the time the first throngs began to gather in the lobby of the Hilton that a lot of them, including many who wore 'I Like Ike' buttons the size of saucers, really didn't like the General at all and were supporting him only because they had been sold on the Taft-can't-win theory. . . . They accepted the hateful argument. Twenty years is a long time to be out of office." Arthur Schlesinger, Jr., once described Eisenhower as the man who would go down in history as the president who saved the county from his advisors. It is also true that he saved the country from the radical conservatism of the Republican Party.

The opposition of his adopted party would continue as long as Eisenhower was in office, expressing itself in a defeatism that gave Ike decreasing minorities in both Houses of Congress when it was not expressed in open hostility. He learned to live with it, hamstringing though it sometimes was, but he never liked it. That's why he encouraged young people to join him in Modern Republicanism: he knew he would never convert the Ancient.

From sandlot baseball and West Point football he learned the functions and uses of a team. The word has fallen into disrepute, not least because he overused it, but it deserves more than sneers. A team put men on the moon, as a team discovered America. A team won World War II. More than one Regular Army officer, watching young Eisenhower pin on general's star after general's star, would complain bitterly to his friends that Ike's staff, not Ike, was responsible for the Allied victories. But Ike picked that staff, trained that staff, coached that staff until it was the kind of instrument that could prevail in a multi-national coalition such as had never been successful before. He picked a team for Washington, too, and if his team did not play as well in that byzantine stadium, he is not entirely to blame. He didn't train its members. All-star games never do quite measure up.

THE ACHIEVEMENTS OF HIS PRESIDENCY WERE THOSE you would expect of a soldier and a son of small-town Kansas folk: the St. Lawrence Seaway, the interstate highway system, the National Defense Education Act, the nuclear submarine, the Polaris missile. He did not go to Hungary's aid during its 1956 revolution for what seemed to him the most obvious of reasons: he would have had to supply our forces by air, a disastrous situation. He did not openly attack Joe McCarthy for a reason he believed equally obvious: an executive attack might have driven the Senate to close ranks around its most vicious member and might have made a martyr of McCarthy within the Republican Party itself.

He gave us eight years of peace, with more provocation to war than was ever visited upon either John Kennedy or Lyndon Johnson.

In the last years of John Foster Dulles's life, Dulles became one of Ike's heroes, though by now the president had learned to temper his hero-worship with judgment. He came to like everything about Dulles except his fanatical anticommunism. Nothing is more revealing of Ike's purpose as president than his decision, hard upon Dulles's death and contrary to all Dulles's cherished legalisms, to undertake an exhausting personal campaign to bring peace to the world before he passed it on to the next man. On the endpapers of *Waging Peace*, the second volume of his memoirs, the lines of that odyssey seem to tie together all the continents of the Free World. Yet Ike's last campaign had a curious quality of anticlimax, as if the Supreme Commander, preparing for retirement, were making one final review of his troops. His troops—the peoples of the world—turned out by the millions to attend him.

WHAT PARTISANS RIDICULED AS INDIFFERENCE AND drift, he saw as deliberate dissent from the political philosophy of Franklin Roosevelt and Harry Truman. A modern liberal, confronting the kind of conservatism Eisenhower represented, sees incompetence or special privilege. But conservatism has its strong philosophic roots, going back through the Protestant ethic at least to St. Augustine. Liberalism has its roots as well, going back through humanism at least to the heresy of Pelagius, the monk who believed man could perfect himself without the grace of God. Both systems are only theories about the nature of man, not proven truths, and the Augustinian theories held sway in the United States for most of the years of its founding and growth. It remains to be seen if they are minority theories. In the person of Dwight Eisenhower they attracted overwhelming majorities.

Eisenhower was not a naive man. He argued, at the end of *Waging Peace*, that if the nation moved in the direction of his conservatism, "then the future would hold encomiums for my administration as the first great break with the political philosophy of the decade beginning in 1933." But if, he said, the nation moved in the direction the Democratic Party had been leading it, "then the growth of paternalism to the point of virtual regimentation would so condition the attitude of future historians that our time in office would be represented as only a slight impediment to the trend begun in 1933 under the New Deal." Discounting his uncharacteristic rhetoric, the president's point is clear: he knew what he was doing, and knew that whether or not you agreed with what he was doing would depend on your political philosophy.

RETIRED AT LAST TO GETTYSBURG, LIVING IN HIS PEACE-ful wilderness, he published the most extraordinary book ever written by an American president, *At Ease: Stories I Tell to Friends*. In that collection of observations and anecdotes, the Eisenhower who practiced indirection becomes candid, the Eisenhower some thought ordinary proves wise. Many of the things he would not talk about while in command he now discusses simply and directly, with the humor of Prospero. And demonstrates thereby the depth of his self-knowledge. Sometimes he reminds us of the secret movements of human events:

> Behind every human action, the truth may be hidden. But the truth may also lie behind some other action or arrangement, far off in time and place. Unless circumstances and responsibility demand an instant judgment I learned to reserve mine until the last proper moment.

Sometimes he sounds like a wise but melancholy philosopher:

> In my experience with Blackie [a horse he trained that no one else believed trainable]—and earlier with allegedly incompetent recruits at Camp Colt [whom he also trained]—is rooted my enduring conviction that far too often we write off a backward child as hopeless, a clumsy animal as worthless, a worn-out field as beyond restoration. This we do largely out of our own lack of willingness to take the time and spend the effort to prove ourselves wrong: to prove that a difficult boy can become a fine man, that an animal can respond to training, that the field can regain its fertility.

George Marshall named the battlefronts of World War II *theaters;* the Eisenhower of *At Ease* reveals his awareness of the large shape of the drama:

> The tragedy of it all was immense. From the Sunday morning when unarmed church parties of our men died under hundreds of Japanese bombs and shells to the final days when men, women, and children of Japan perished under two bombs at Hiroshima and Nagasaki, millions died. The

loss of lives that might have been creatively lived scars the mind of the modern world.

Emmet Hughes could not have been the first to notice, behind the open grin and the hearty manner, the "wide and unblinking eyes." But in *At Ease* the man seems finally at peace with himself.

HE ORGANIZED AN ARMY AND RAN A WAR AND GUIDED the strongest nation in the world for eight hard years, but what he thought he really wanted to do was to be a cowboy in Argentina. His hand, he said, was made to hold a pistol, not a pen. In the twentieth century the pen controls the pistol. He regretted it, but he always looked the truth square in the eye, and he wasn't about to flinch from that one. Even though it meant hiding his deepest feelings from the world. He didn't give a damn about school, but he learned to be first in his class. He didn't give a damn about discipline, but he learned not only to live by its rules himself but also to confer its life-saving strength on whole armies. He didn't give a damn about offices and position and rank, but he took them all on because he believed he could handle them better than anyone else available. He did his duty: it was a duty to which he came with the greatest reluctance, knowing as he did that the world of men can be handled as a machine or dug in like a garden, knowing that the modern world had chosen to become machine-like, knowing that he himself, like his mother before him, preferred gardening. But knowing also that he could handle any machine the world might put in front of him, a rifle, a tank, an army, a nation. Having learned machines from his father. "My David didn't like gardening and such," Ike's mother told her biographer. "Books. Machines. That's what he liked. At home, in what spare time he had, he opened a book and was lost. He didn't worry one speck because I didn't read my eyes blind, like he did. I didn't worry because he didn't dig in the dirt every minute he possibly could, like I did. We just let each other enjoy ourselves." Ike hardly enjoyed working the bloody machines, but he had no choice. When he retired to Gettysburg he worked hard at farming. He wanted, he said, to leave the place better than he found it.

He liked best of all a maxim which Robert Frost inscribed in a book of poems at a time when, Ike said, "many people . . . thought I was moving too slowly about matters close to their hearts." Frost's maxim:

The strong are saying nothing until they see.

We can hardly do less now when we consider measuring the campaigns to which he devoted his life.

# 12 / Watching the Animals

*The loves of flint and iron are naturally a little rougher than those of the nightingale and the rose.*

—Ralph Waldo Emerson

I REMEMBERED TODAY ABOUT THIS COUNTRY LAKE IN Kansas where I live: that it is artificial, built at the turn of the century, when Upton Sinclair was writing *The Jungle*, as an ice lake. The trains with their loads of fresh meat from the Kansas City stockyards would stop by the Kaw River, across the road, and ice the cars. "You have just dined," Emerson once told what must have been a shocked Victorian audience, "and how-

ever scrupulously the slaughterhouse is concealed in the graceful distance of miles, there is complicity, expensive races—race
living at the expense of race."

The I-D Packing Company of Des Moines, Iowa: a small out-
fit which subcontracts from Armour the production of fresh
pork. Can handle about 450 pigs an hour. No beef or mutton.
No smoked hams or hotdogs. Plain fresh pork. A well-run out-
fit, with federal inspectors alert on all the lines.

The kind of slaughterhouse Upton Sinclair was talking
about doesn't exist around here any more. The vast buildings
still stand in Des Moines and Omaha and Kansas City, but
most of the operations are gone. The big outfits used to operate
on a profit margin of 1.5 percent, which didn't give them much
leeway, did it? Now they are defunct, and their buildings,
which look like monolithic enlargements of concentration-
camp barracks, sit empty, the hundreds of windows broken,
dusty, jagged pieces of glass sticking out of the frames as if the
animals heard the good news one day and leaped out the nearest exit. Even the stockyards, miles and miles of rotting weathered board pens, floors paved fifty years ago by hand with brick,
look empty, though I am told cattle receipts are up compared
to what they were a few years back. The new thing is small,
specialized, efficient houses out where the cattle are, in Denver, in Phoenix, in Des Moines, especially in Texas, where the
weather is more favorable to fattening cattle. In Iowa the cattle
waste half their feed just keeping warm in the wintertime. But
in Iowa or in Texas, the point of meat packing today is refrig-
eration. It's cheaper to ship cold meat than live animals. So the
packing plants have gone out to the farms and ranches and
feedlots. Are even beginning to buy up the ranches themselves
so that they won't have to depend on the irregularities of farmers and cattlemen who bring their animals in only when the
price is up or the ground too wet for plowing. Farmhouses
stand empty all over America. Did you know that? The city
has already won, never mind how many of our television shows

still depict the hardy bucolic rural. I may regret the victory, but that's my lookout. We are an urban race now, and meat is something you buy shrink-wrapped at the supermarket.

There are no stockyards outside the I-D Packing Company. The pigs arrive by trailer truck from Sioux City and other places. Sometimes a farmer brings in two or three in the back of his pickup. Unloads them into the holding pens where they are weighed and inspected, goes into the office and picks up his check. The men, except on the killing floor, are working on the cooled carcasses of yesterday's kill anyway, so there's time to even out the line. Almost everything in a packing house operates on a chainline, and for maximum profit that line must be full, 450 carcasses an hour at the I-D Packing Company, perhaps 300 heavies if today is heavies day—sows, overgrown hogs. Boars presumably escape the general fate. Their flesh is flavored with rut and tastes the way an unventilated gymnasium locker room smells.

Down goes the tailgate and out come the pigs, enthusiastic after their drive. Pigs are the most intelligent of all farm animals, by actual laboratory test. Learn the fastest, for example, to push a plunger with their foot to earn a reward of pelletized feed. And not as reliable in their instincts. You don't have to call cattle to dinner. They are waiting outside the fence at 4:30 sharp, having arrived as silently as the Vietcong. But perhaps that is pig intelligence too: let you do the work, laze around until the last minute and then charge over and knock you down before you can slop the garbage into the trough. Cattle will stroll one by one into a row of stalls and usually fill them in serial order. Not pigs. They squeal and nip and shove. Each one wants the entire meal for itself. Won't stick together in a herd, either. Shoot out all over the place, and you'd damned better have every gate closed or they'll be in your garden and on your lawn and even in your living room, nodding by the fire. They talk a lot, to each other, to you if you care to listen. I'm not romanticizing pigs. They always scared me a little on the farm, which is probably why I watched them more closely than the other animals. They do talk: low grunts, quick squeals, a kind of hum sometimes, angry shrieks, high screams of fear.

I have great respect for the I-D Packing Company. They do a dirty job and do it as cleanly and humanely as possible, and do it well. They were nice enough to let me in the door, which is more than I can say for the Wilson people in Omaha, where I first tried to arrange a tour. What are you hiding, Wilson people?

Once into the holding pen, the pigs mill around, getting to know each other. The I-D holding pens are among the most modern in the nation, my spokesman told me. Tubular steel painted tinner's red to keep it from rusting. Smooth concrete floors with drains so that the floors can be washed down hygienically after each lot of pigs is run through.

The pigs come out of the first holding pen through a gate that allows only one to pass at a time. Just beside the gate is a wooden door, and behind the door is the first worker the pigs encounter. He has a wooden box beside him filled with metal numbers, the shape of each number picked out with sharp needles. For each lot of pigs he selects a new set of numbers— 2473, say—and slots them into a device like a hammer and dips it in non-toxic purple dye. As a pig shoots out of the gate he hits the pig in the side with the numbers, making a tattoo. The pig gives a grunt—it doesn't especially hurt, pigskin is thick, as you know—and moves on to one of several smaller pens where each lot is held until curtain time. The tattoo, my spokesman told me, will stay on the animal through all the killing and cleaning and cutting operations, to the very end. Its purpose is to identify any animal or lot of animal which might be diseased, so that the seller can be informed and the carcasses destroyed. Rather too proud of his tattooing process, I thought, but then, you know the tattoos I am thinking of, the Nazi ones.

It would be more dramatic, make a better story, if the killing came last, but it comes first. We crossed a driveway with more red steel fencing. Lined up behind it, pressing into it because they sensed by now that all was not well with them, were perhaps a hundred pigs. But still curious, watching us go by in our long white canvas coats. Everyone wore those, and hard plastic helmets, white helmets for the workers, yellow helmets for the foremen. I got to be a foreman.

Before they reach their end, the pigs get a shower, a real one. Water sprays from all angles to wash the farm off of them. Then they begin to feel crowded. The pen narrows like a funnel; the drivers behind urge the pigs forward, until one at a time they climb onto a moving ramp. The ramp's sides move as well as its floor. The floor is cleated to give the pigs footing. The sides are made of blocks of wood so that they will not bruise, and they slant inward to wedge the pigs along. Now they scream, never having been on such a ramp, smelling the smells they smell ahead. I don't want to overdramatize, because you have read all this before. But it was a frightening experience, seeing their fear, seeing so many of them go by. It had to remind me of things no one wants to be reminded of any more, all mobs, all death marches, all mass murders and extinctions, the slaughter of the buffalo, the slaughter of the Indian, the Inferno, Judgment Day, complicity, expensive races, race living at the expense of race. That so gentle a religion as Christianity could end up in Judgment Day. That we are the most expensive of races, able in our affluence to hire others of our kind to do this terrible necessary work of killing another race of creatures so that we may feed our oxygen-rich brains. Feed our children, for that matter.

At the top of the ramp, one man. With rubber gloves on, holding two electrodes that looked like enlarged curling irons except that they sported more of those needles. As a pig reached the top, this man jabbed the electrodes into the pig's butt and shoulder, and that was it. No more pain, no more fear, no more mud holes, no more sun in the lazy afternoon. Knocked instantly unconscious, the pig shuddered in a long spasm and fell onto a stainless-steel table a foot below the end of the ramp. Up came another pig, and the same result. And another, and another, 450 an hour, 3,600 a day, the belts returning below to coax another ride.

The pigs aren't dead, merely unconscious. The electrodes are humane, my spokesman said, and, relatively speaking, that's true. They used to gas the pigs—put them on a conveyer belt that ran through a room filled with anesthetic gas. That was humane too. The electrodes are more efficient. Anesthesia relaxes the body and loosens the bowels. The gassed pigs must have been a mess. More efficient, then, to put their bodies in spasm.

They drop to the table, and here the endless chain begins. A worker takes the nearest dangling chain by its handle as it passes. The chain is attached at its top to a belt of links, like a large bicycle chain. At the bottom the dangling chain has a metal handle like the handle on a bicycle. The chain runs through the handle and then attaches to the end of the handle, so that by sliding the handle up the chain the worker forms a loop. Into the loop he hooks one of the pig's hind feet. Another worker does the same with the other foot. Each has his own special foot to grab, or the pig would go down the line backwards, which would not be convenient. Once hooked into the line, the pig will stay in place by the force of its own weight. Now the line ascends, lifting the unconscious animal into the air. The pig proceeds a distance of ten feet to where a worker standing on a platform deftly inserts a butcher knife into its throat. They call it "sticking," which it is. Then all hell breaks loose, if blood merely is hell. It gushes out, at about a forty-five-degree angle downward, thick as a ship's hawser, pouring directly onto the floor. Nothing is so red as blood, an incandescent red and most beautiful. It is the brightest color we drab creatures possess. Down on the floor below, with a wide squeegee on a long handle, a worker spends his eight hours a day squeegeeing that blood, some of it clotted, jellied, now, into an open drain. It is cycled through a series of pipes directly into a dryer, later to be made into blood meal for animal feed.

The line swings around a corner, high above the man with the squeegee, around the drain floor, turns again left at the next corner, and begins to ascend to the floor above. This interval—thirteen seconds, I think my spokesman said, or was it thirty?—so that the carcass may drain completely before further processing. Below the carcass on the ascent is a trough like those lowered from the rear of cement trucks, there to catch the last drainings of blood.

Pigs are not skinned, as cattle are, unless you are after the leather, and we are after the meat. But the hair must be taken off, and it must first be scalded loose. Courteously, the line lowers the carcass into a long trough filled with water heated to 180 degrees. The carcass will float if given a chance, fat being lighter than water, so wooden pushers on crankshafts spaced equally along the scalding tank immerse and roll the carcasses. Near the end of the trough, my spokesman easily pulls out a tuft of hair. The line ascends again, up and away, and the carcass goes into a chamber where revolving brushes as tall as a man whisk away the hair. We pass to the other side of the chamber and find two workers with wide knives scraping off the few patches of hair that remain. The carcasses pass then through great hellish jets of yellowish-blue gas flame to singe the skin and harden it. The last step is polishing: more brushes. Our pig has turned pink and clean as a baby.

One of the small mercies of a slaughterhouse: what begins as a live animal loses all similarity as the processing goes on, until you can actually face the packaged meat at the exit door and admire its obvious flavor.

The polished carcasses swing through a door closed with rubber flaps, and there, dear friends, the action begins. Saws. Long knives. Butcher knives. Drawknives. Boning knives. Wails from the saws, large and small, that are driven by air like a dentist's drill. Shouts back and forth from the men, jokes, announcements, challenges. The temperature down to fifty degrees, everyone keen. Men start slicing off little pieces of the head right inside the door, each man his special slice, throwing them onto one of several lines that will depart for special bins. A carcass passes me and I see a bare eyeball staring, stripped of its lids. Deft knives drop the head from the neck, leaving it dangling by a two-inch strip of skin. Around a corner, up to a platform, and three men gut the carcasses, great tubs of guts, each man taking the third carcass as it goes by. One of them sees me with my tape recorder and begins shouting at us something like "I am the greatest!" A crazy man, grinning and roaring at us, turning around and slipping in the knife and out comes everything in one great load flopped onto a stainless-steel trough. And here things divide, and so must our attention.

My spokesman is proud of his chitterling machine. "I call them chitlins, but they're really chitterlings." It's the newest addition to his line. A worker separates the intestines from the other internal organs and shoves them down a slide, gray and shiny. Another worker finds one end and feeds it onto a steel tube flushed with water. Others trim off connective tissue, webbings, fat. The intestines skim along the tube into a washing vat, shimmy up to the top of the machine where they are cooled, shimmy back down where they are cooled further, and come out the other side ready for the supermarket. A worker drops them into wax buckets, pops on a lid, and packs them into shipping boxes. That's today's chitlin machine. They used to have to cool the chitlins overnight before they could be packaged. Now five men do the work of sixteen, in less time.

The remaining organs proceed down a waist-high conveyor next to a walkway; on the other side of the same walkway, the emptied carcasses pass; on a line next to the organ line the heads pass. By now all the meat has been trimmed off each head. A worker sockets them one at a time onto a support like a footrest in a shoeshine parlor and a wedge neatly splits them in half. Out come the tongues, out come the brains, and at the end of the line, out come the pituitaries, each tiny gland being passed to a government inspector in white pants, white shirt, and a yellow hardhat, who looks it over and drops it into a wax bucket. All these pieces, the brain, the tongue, the oddments of sidemeat off the head and carcass, will be shipped to Armour to become "by-products": hotdogs, baloney, sausage. You are what you eat.

The loudest noise in the room comes from the big air saw used to split the carcass in half down the backbone, leaving, again, connections at the butt end and between the shoulders. Other workers trim away interior fat, and then the carcasses proceed down their chain to the blast freezer, fifty miles an hour and twenty-five below zero, no place for mere mortals, to be chilled overnight.

Coming out of the freezer in another part of the room is yesterday's kill, cold and solid and smooth. A worker splits apart the two sides; the hams come off and go onto their own line; the shoulders come off and go onto theirs, to be made into picnics, shoulder roasts, trotters. Away goes the valuable loin, trimmed out deftly by a worker with a drawknife. Away goes the bacon. Chunks and strips of fat go off from everywhere in buckets carried on overhead hooks to a grinder that spins out worms of fat and blows them through a tube directly to the lard-rendering vats. Who uses lard any more? I ask my spokesman. I don't know, he says, I think we export most of it. At the end of all these lines men package the component parts of pig into waxpaper-lined cartons, load the cartons onto pallets, forklift the pallets into spotless aluminum trailers socketed right into the walls of the building, so that I did not even realize I was inside a truck until my spokesman told me, and off they go to Armour. Processing an animal is exactly the opposite of processing a machine: the machine starts out with components and ends up put together; the animal starts out put together and ends up components. No clearer illustration of the law of entropy has ever been devised.

And that is a tour of a slaughterhouse, as cheerful as I could make it.

But the men there. Half of them blacks, some Mexicans, the rest whites. It gets harder and harder to hire men for this work, even though the pay is good. The production line keeps them hopping; they take their breaks when there is a break in the line, so that the killing floor breaks first, and their break leaves an empty space ten minutes long in the endless chain, which, arriving at the gutting operation, allows the men there to break, and so on. Monday-morning absenteeism is a problem, I was told. Keeping the men under control can be a problem, too, I sensed: when the line broke down briefly during my tour, the men cheered as convicts might at a state license-plate factory when the stamping machine breaks down. It cannot be heartening to kill and dismember animals all day.

There's a difference, too, between the men who work with the live animals and hot carcasses and those who cut up the cold meat, a difference I remember from my days of butchering on the farm: the killing unsettles, while the cold cutting is a craft like carpentry or plumbing and offers the satisfactions of craftsmanship. The worker with the electrodes jammed them into the animal with anger and perverse satisfaction, as if he were knocking off the enemy. The worker at the guts acted as if he were wrestling bears. The hot workers talked to themselves, yelled at each other, or else lapsed into the strained silence you meet in deeply angry men; the cold workers said little, but worked with deftness and something like pride. They knew they were good, and they showed off a little, zip zip, as we toured by. They used their hands as if they knew how to handle tools, and they did.

The technology at the I-D Packing Company is humane by present standards, at least so far as the animals are concerned. Where the workers are concerned, I'm not so sure. They looked to be in need of lulling.

Beyond technology is the larger question of attitude. Butchering on the farm when I was a boy had the quality of a ceremony. We would select, say, a steer, and pen it separately overnight. The next morning several of us boys would walk the steer to a large compound and leave it standing near the concrete-floored area where we did the skinning and gutting.

Then the farm manager, a man of great kindness and reserve, would take aim with a .22 rifle at the crosspoint of two imaginary lines drawn from the horns to the opposite eyes. And hold his bead until the steer was entirely calm, looking at him, a certain shot, because this man did not want to miss, did not want to hurt the animal he was about to kill. And we would stand in a spread-out circle, at a respectful distance, tense with the drama of it, because we didn't want him to miss either.

The shot cracked out, the bullet entered the brain, and the animal instantly collapsed. Then the farm manager handed back the rifle, took a knife, ran forward, and cut into the throat. Then we hooked the steer's back legs through the Achilles tendons to a cross tree, dragged it onto the concrete and laboriously winched it into the air with a differential pulley. Four boys usually did the work, two older, two younger. The younger boys were supposed to be learning this skill, and you held your stomach together as best you could at first while the older boys played little tricks like, when they got there in the skinning, cutting off the pizzle and whipping it around your neck, but even these crudities had their place: they accustomed you to contact with flesh and blood.

And while the older boys did their work of splitting the halves with a hacksaw, you got to take the guts, which on the farm we did not save except for the liver, the heart, and the sweetbreads, in a wheelbarrow down to the back lane, where you built, with wood you had probably cut yourself, a most funereal pyre. Doused the guts with gasoline, tossed in a match, and Whoosh! off they went. And back on the concrete, the sawing done, the older boys left the sides hanging overnight in the winter cold to firm the meat for cutting.

By now it was noon, time for lunch, and you went in with a sort of pride that you had done this important work, and there on the table was meat some other boys had killed on some other ceremonial day. It was bloody work, of course, and sometimes I have wondered how adults could ask children to do such work, but it was part of a coherent way of life, as important as plowing or seeding or mowing or baling hay. It had a context, and I was literary enough even then to understand that burning the guts had a sacrificial significance. We could always have limed them and dumped them into a ditch. Lord knows they didn't burn easily.

I never saw our farm manager more upset than the day we were getting ready to butcher five pigs. He shot one through the nose rather than through the brain. It ran screaming around the pen, and he almost cried. It took two more bullets to finish the animal off, and this good man was shaking when he had finished. "I hate that," he said to me. "I hate to have them in pain. Pigs are so damned hard to kill clean."

But we don't farm any more. The coherence is gone. Our loves are no longer the loves of flint and iron, but of the nightingale and the rose, and so we delegate our killing. Our farm manager used to sleep in the sheep barn for nights on end to be sure he was there to help the ewes deliver their lambs when they tired after long labor. You saw the beginning and the end on the farm, not merely the pre-packaged middle. Flint and iron, friends, flint and iron. And humility, and sorrow that this act of killing must be done, which is why in those days good men bowed their heads before they picked up their forks.

# 13 / A Scientific Cooperation for the Welfare of the Sick

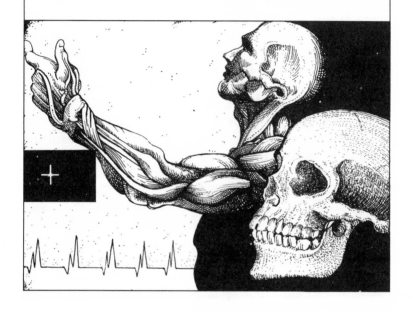

THERE IS NO INSTITUTION ANYWHERE IN THE WORLD quite like the Mayo Clinic. A private group practice (surrounded by an implementing Foundation) of some 700 salaried physicians and medical scientists that in one recent year registered 255,190 patients, trained 842 residents and medical students and directed the investment of more than $40 million in medical research, Mayo has modest imitators but no obvious antecedents and no immediate kin. Its uniqueness is of original design. In contrast to many other twentieth-century institutions, it remains scrupulously faithful to the intentions of the men—of the family—who founded it. But besides inten-

243

tion it is also a product of historical accident, of the increase of surgical success at the turn of the century with the introduction of aseptic technique. Accident and intention intersect in the lives of the founding Mayos, father and sons: the Clinic to which they gave their fortunes and their name is the lengthened shadow not of one man but of three.

The father, the "Old Doctor," William Worrall Mayo, was born to the wife of a ship's captain, in a lineage thick back to the 16th century with physicians, in Lancashire, England, in 1819. His father died when he was seven; he saw the excitement of hungry mobs in grimy Manchester before he was grown. He determined to study medicine, and studied it in Manchester, such as medical study was in those days, and honed his practice on the urban poor. He learned chemistry from no less a scholar than John Dalton, the gaunt, awkward schoolmaster who revived atomic theory from its doldrums. It was the high point of young W.W.'s education. "Father was always talking about Dalton," patiently attested one of his sons. The Old Doctor was ever a wanderer; at 25, in 1845, he took ship and wandered to America, establishing the Mayos on these shores.

There was never any dearth of disease in those days before modern sanitation and modern medicine. We no longer know that horror. Cancer today, viral pneumonia that carries off the elderly, polio for those of us who were parents or children before Salk, when every movie theater and every swimming pool was thought to be a menace, only hint at the suffering and the brutal mortality. Medicine was severely limited. It could palliate. It could cut, but only the surface of the body and the extremities, and even those at deadly risk. W.W. Mayo worked first in medicine at Bellevue in New York. Then he worked as a tailor in Buffalo. He may have felt he did equal service at either trade. A few years later, practicing medicine again in Indiana after studying it further in Missouri, suffering the recurrent fever of what was in those days an endemic midwestern disease, he announced, "Hell is a place where people have malaria," and made his way to Minnesota, more or less to stay.

He was a small man, an intelligent man, fierce, contentious, stubborn. He took democracy to heart and bluntly spoke his mind. He married a woman of fortitude, Louise Abigail Wright, who sometimes operated a millinery business. She had need: her husband doctored, edited a newspaper, captained a steamboat, surveyed the territory, even attempted to farm, but he seldom made much money. She lost a firstborn son at six weeks, bore two daughters, lost a third daughter at one year. In June, 1861, she bore W.W. Mayo another son, William James, in the farmhouse her husband had built with his own hands near LeSueur the summer before. Will was the first of the Mayo brothers to be.

The next year W.W., his wife and every other able-bodied soul in the neighborhood fought down a Sioux uprising at New Ulm. Thirty-nine Sioux were hanged at Mankato for their rebellion, among them a giant named Cut Nose who had once tried unsuccessfully to separate little W.W. from his horse. After the hanging, W.W. separated Cut Nose from his skeleton, cleaned it, articulated it and hung it in his office for a lesson in bones.

The family made one final move. W.W. signed on as examining surgeon for the Civil War draft—he got into trouble giving private examinations after hours for a fee, though the practice was legal—in Rochester, Minnesota, a small town in the southeastern corner of the state, settling there in 1864. After the war, on July 19, 1865, was born the second Mayo brother, Charles Horace. W.W. proposed another shift, and even went up to Minneapolis for a time to practice doctoring in the big city, but his long-suffering wife refused to be removed any more, and after three months her husband came home and dropped anchor. He would wander again in old age, east and west across the world.

William James and Charles Horace. Dr. Will and Dr. Charlie.

Will was fair, with blue eyes, Charlie dark. Will was orderly, demanding, publicly stiff; Charlie was casual, unpressed, warmhearted. Observers would say later that the two brothers seemed to have divided up one personality between them, as identical twins sometimes do, though Will was the elder by four years. It became a system that worked—the hard guy and the easy guy, the threatening detective and the detective who offers you a smoke. Together they got the job done. But first they were children growing up in frontier Rochester, hunting arrowheads, fishing, canoeing on the Zumbro River, riding out to club down a mess of passenger pigeons from the millions that roosted in migration in the trees beyond the town.

"We were reared in medicine," Will said later, "as a farm boy is reared in farming." The comparison was exact. They worked for their father from their earliest years, graduating from sweeping out the office and holding the buggy on house calls to administering anesthesia and finally to assisting in kitchen-table surgery. W.W. had his books (and Cut Nose dangling there beside his desk for anatomy instruction); he didn't mind at all mortgaging his house one year to assemble the $600 he needed to buy an improved microscope; but Will and Charlie learned medicine first of all through their backs and eyes and hands. Their father was the master under whom they apprenticed. That was the tradition in medicine then, the old craft tradition of experience and example. It would weaken with the rise of formal medical schooling, but it was one of the proven methodologies that worked its way into the Mayo Clinic's design: an "endless chain," Dr. Will would call it. Hardly anyone ever operated at Mayo without a crowd of visiting surgeons and, later, resident fellows, looking on—the surgical suites were designed from the beginning especially for observation—and the Clinic today, one institution among hundreds, yet graduates some two percent of all the residents trained in the United States.

Will went to medical school at the University of Michigan, Charlie at the Chicago Medical College, by their father's plan, to bring back a broader range of medical knowledge than one school alone could offer (although the rumor still persists among physicians that Charlie, always an antic spirit, was sent down from Michigan for skipping rope with the intestines of his first-year anatomy cadaver). To graduate, Charlie needed certification that he was over 21 years of age and of good moral character. His impatient father supplied the necessary document succinctly: "To whom it may concern, This is to certify that Chas. H. Mayo is over 21 years of age and is of good moral character." They all taught each other. Pooling information was one of the secrets of their success.

It needs to be said that the young Mayos were not prodigies. They were good, and they got to be very good, "a wonderful surgeon" and "a surgical wonder," as a colleague characterized them—Charlie the surgical wonder for his innovative versatility at operations all over the body. They got to be very good by observation and cautious innovation and hard labor.

They began their careers in days still pioneer, driving out by horse and buggy or riding the convenient trains, fighting Minnesota weather and worse. On a country call in January 1885, in gathering dark and drifting snow, Will decided to leave his buggy and cross the last mile of woods on foot. Two wolves found him out. He ran for his life, shouting and brandishing his black bag. The wolves only left him at his patient's door.

The Mayos were workhorses. They examined and operated seven days a week from early in the morning until, most days, eight or nine at night. "A guest at Mayowood," writes Dr. Charlie's son, referring to the sprawling estate Dr. Charlie established outside of Rochester, "commented . . . that he had just seen Father remove a cataract, tonsils and a goiter, resect ribs for empyema, perform a gastroenterostomy, which is an operation joining the stomach and intestine, shorten the round ligaments for prolapse of the uterus, correct bowlegs and finish off with his operation for bunions—before lunch." Lunchtimes contrasted at the Mayo brothers' homes. Dr. Will stationed a secretary at a nearby table and dictated correspondence while he ate, leaving his shy wife to cope with the inevitable distinguished guests. The Will Mayos had no children. Dr. Charlie, by contrast, despite his prodigious surgical schedule, made the noon hour an occasion to see his several sons and daughters. After eating, while the children swirled noisily around him, he managed an upright quarter-hour nap.

Both brothers took turns going off to observe other surgeons wherever exceptional men performing exceptional work could be found—in Boston and Philadelphia and New York, but also in Europe and in England. They were open-minded. They read journals and attended meetings, worked up monographs and reports. They served voluntarily as physicians to Minnesota's "lunatic asylums" in exchange for the experience of performing any necessary surgery and autopsies. They sought and got appointment as surgeons to the railroads for that experience too and for the free passes that carried them to patients out in the country beyond Rochester and to medical meetings in the East and the South.

There was a reservoir of suffering humanity in the Upper Middle West then—at the close of the nineteenth century—as everywhere else in the world. The dam that confined it was medical ignorance, ignorance that was just giving way. Anesthesia first, then antiseptic technique, finally the superior gloves and gowns and sterilization of aseptic surgery began to make healing possible. Gynecology was one of the first fields of surgical practice to benefit, with operations to repair the damage of repeated childbearing. Hernia, a minor problem today that was then painful, chronic and sometimes fatal, was one of the next, and appendicitis another. "A son of Ole Nelson of Rock Dell," the Rochester newspaper reported one day, "was taken ill recently with inflammation of the bowels, and was very low, when an operation was performed by the Drs. Mayo, assisted by Dr. Witherstine. A gangrenous portion of the bowel was removed, and the patient is well on the road to recovery. This is the eighth successful operation of this character to be made by the Drs. Mayo." Appendectomy breached what had been, before asepsis, the sacrosanct confines: the abdominal interior. Such surgery had been a sentence of death only a few years before.

The Mayo brothers didn't often originate the new surgical procedures. What they usually did was refine them, perfect them, perform them in incredible numbers and with observant care and reduce their mortality until finally they became routine. Ten gallbladder operations in 1895 became 75 in 1900 and 324 in 1905. In 1905 the Mayos performed 2,157 abdominal operations in all. They were boyish-looking men when they were young, dressed in country suitings. When they showed up at Eastern medical meetings with their careful reports, claiming to have performed hundreds of operations in a town of six thousand souls (in 1904 they reported jointly on 1,000 gallbladder procedures when many surgeons had not yet performed ten), they were sometimes taken for charlatans. They evolved a stock answer for doubters: "Come and see." Eventually the doubters did, and went away convinced.

Long before patients visited them from everywhere in the world, the Mayos healed the sick around them: the chronic gallbladders and infected appendixes misdiagnosed as "colic" and "stomach disease" and "dyspepsia"; the tens of thousands of goiters in those regions without iodine in their soil (the Mayo Clinic treated 37,228 cases of goiter between 1892 and 1934); the ovarian cysts that grew so large, filling with fluid, that women sometimes wore special harnesses their husbands made for them to hold their abdomens up (the largest ever removed at Mayo, in 1920, weighed 139.5 pounds) but that no one had dared to remove except in extremity. These the Mayos worked night and day to heal, and the word went out that, almost alone in those parts at first, they could. "As I look back over those early years," Dr. Will said later, "I am impressed with the fact that much of our success, if not most of it, was due to the time at which we entered medicine." And that is part of the story, the fortuitous part, but not by any means the whole.

The Mayos, father and sons, practiced careful, progressive, increasingly scientific medicine, but so did others, and others founded no unique clinic. The brothers had something more: ambition, business sense, an eagerness to enlarge and systematize a rapidly expanding practice. Just out of medical school, Will told a Rochester judge who made the mistake of asking him his plans, "I expect to remain in Rochester and to become the greatest surgeon in the world." The Doctors Mayo kept one common checking account throughout their lives; they became millionaires while still relatively young men; they hired competent business help, competent investment advice. They were generous men. No patient at the Mayo Clinic ever pays more than he can afford. But they had little of their father's profligate inconsistency with collections, and Will especially could be indignant with deadbeats. When he accepted the presidency of the American Medical Association in 1905, at 44, he named medicine "the most holy of all callings," condemned fee splitting, foresaw schools for advanced training, and proposed that "all hospitals should have competent individuals whose business it is to see that no one secures free treatment who is able to pay."

The brothers earned their money, built magnificent houses, owned fine automobiles, yachts for weekends on the nearby Mississippi and thousands of acres of prime farmland, traveled the world. They gave most of what they had back to medicine and left their heirs far from rich. Dr. Charlie's farm disasters in particular were legendary. A $20,000 Holstein-Friesian bull acquired to improve his dairy stock died two weeks after he bought it; his flock of geese flew off with its wild kind during the autumn migration; his chickens wouldn't lay; his Guernseys proved to be tubercular. "I am not a farmer," he told a visitor. "I am an agriculturist. An agriculturist makes his money in town and spends it on the farm, while a farmer makes his money on the farm and spends some of it in town." Of guests at dinner he would ask, "Which will you have, milk or champagne? They both cost me the same."

The Clinic grew naturally out of the practice. A tornado that devastated part of Rochester in 1883 made obvious the town's need for a hospital. A congregation of teaching sisters there, the Sisters of St. Francis, undertook to raise the funds and build one. Dr. Charles Mayo performed the first operation at the new St. Mary's Hospital of 45 beds on September 30, 1889, with Dr. W. J. Mayo administering anesthesia. From the beginning the hospital's medical staff consisted entirely of Mayos and, in time, Mayo partners. St. Mary's was where all that new surgery got done, there and in hotels outfitted oddly with surgical suites. The hospital built its first addition in 1893; another addition before 1900 brought it up to 134 beds. It is an institution of nearly 1,000 beds today, and the Mayo Clinic still supplies its professional staff.

The practice enlarged apace. The doctors expanded their offices in downtown Rochester to accommodate the increase. They took in partners—surgeons at first, several of them relatives, and later internists who handled diagnosis. Surgical practice still predominated over medical, by necessity. Medical research would eventually change the balance. Sixty-six percent of the Clinic's fellows were surgeons in the years 1930–35; the percentage dropped to 31 over the next five years.

Early on, the Mayos realized that their straight partnership arrangement would have to give way to something more conserving of the partnership's assets, or it would fragment whenever a doctor died. They convinced their reluctant partners then to exchange their valuable share of the group's total assets for only the equivalent of one year's income, to be paid to their heirs when they died. Thus the group became self-perpetuating: that was the key to its conservation, and still is. It acknowledged universal usage and became the "Mayo Clinic" in 1909; by 1912 it registered 15,000 patients; by 1914, 30,000. By then the Old Doctor was gone, victim of a farm accident. He died in 1911, when he was 92.

The Mayo brothers could hardly evolve so successful a practice without making a name for themselves. They won friends

throughout the world; necessarily, they also discovered ene-
mies. In 1914, the same year the Clinic's first specially designed building opened its doors, they proposed to donate $1.5
million of their common fortune to a graduate school of medicine of the University of Minnesota to be established at Rochester. They might as well have proposed to rob the state. De-
nunciations and hostile petitions flew. They were accused of
graft, of self-advertisement, of splitting fees and grabbing prof-
its and worse. The hostility, much of it from Minnesota doctors, culminated in a bill introduced into the state legislature
forbidding the university-Clinic affiliation that actually passed
the state senate, though it died in the house. The bill came up
again in 1917, by which time affiliation was well under way.
Supporters drafted Dr. Will to defend his generosity.

He told the legislators and the packed hearing room that his
father had been an inspiration. "He taught us that any man
who has physical strength, intellectual capacity, or unusual opportunity holds such endowments in trust to do with them for
others in proportion to his gifts." It seemed to be the idea of
some persons, he said, "that no one can want to do anything
for anybody without having some sinister or selfish motive
back of it." He said, bluntly: "If we wanted money, we have it.
That can't be the reason for our offer. . . . Now let's call a spade
a spade. This money belongs to the people, and I don't care two
raps whether the medical profession of the state likes the way
this money has been offered for use or not. It wasn't their
money." Last of all he quoted Lincoln, *sotto voce*: "'That these
dead shall not have died in vain.' That line explains why we
want to do this thing. What better could we do than help young
men to become proficient in the profession so as to prevent
needless deaths?"

The opposition slunk home. The Mayo Clinic began its continuing work of training young doctors in residence.

The two brothers took their turns at fame, as at everything
else. Dr. Charlie followed Will to the AMA presidency in 1917.
They alternated serving in Washington during the First World

War and ducked as much publicity in the popular press as they could. They even asked their lawyers if they could sue for libel for excessive praise. The lawyers saved the story for their grandchildren.

The distinguished editor William Allen White caught another moment of Mayo modesty in a commencement line:

> We were standing in line at Columbia University in the City of New York at Commencement in June, 1910, wearing borrowed academic gowns and about to receive degrees. Around us were a lot of notables whose faces we recognized. But we were put side by side and we looked at each other like a couple of dogs for a minute. Finally Dr. [Will] Mayo said to me, "I don't know what I'm doing here," and I said, "You've got nothing on me, neither do I." Then we both grinned and he said, "Who are you?" And I said, "To tell you the truth, I am just a country editor from a little town in Kansas called Emporia and my name's White." He grinned again and said, "Well, all right, I am just a country doctor from a little town in Minnesota called Rochester and my name's Mayo."

They collected honors and honorary degrees everywhere; the ornate documents, some of them illuminated and struck with ancient seals, still cover the walls of the old board room in the Plummer Building, nineteen stories complete with tower and carillon, that was opened to house the ever-expanding Clinic in 1928. They traveled; Dr. Will saved a bullfighter in Mexico City one morning by deftly cutting down and tying off a torn artery; in Lima a local collector made him a gift of an Inca chief's skull. Well-meaning acquaintances suggested that one or the other of them run for governor of Minnesota and even for president of the United States. The Mayos so consistently credited each other when either was praised—"my brother and I" was the inevitable qualification—that someone said if Dr.

Will were elected president "he would probably accept the office in the name of his brother and himself."

They managed modesty in the face of it all. The story everyone has heard, even today, recalls a self-important millionaire who buttonholed Dr. Will in the Clinic lobby and asked, "Are you the head doctor here?" To which Will is said to have replied, distracted or deadpan, "No, my brother is the head doctor. I'm the belly doctor." They had divided their surgical territory years before. "Charlie drove me down and down until I reached the belly," Dr. Will claimed. Dr. Charlie did surgery on eye, ear, nose, throat, bones and joints, brain, nerves and neck, but his specialty, if he could be said to have had one, was thyroid work, surgical procedures which he had developed independently or greatly improved. Thyroidectomies totaled one-tenth of all operations performed by Mayo Clinic surgeons between 1911 and 1921. Thyroxin was first isolated in 1914 at Rochester. (There would be other research triumphs later—most notably cortisone in 1936, for which its two discoverers, Drs. Edward C. Kendall and Philip S. Hench, received the Nobel Prize in 1950—and steady progress in basic science as it relates to medicine, but the Mayo Clinic's forte since its earliest days has been patient care more than research.)

Charts published in a 1926 Historical Sketch of the Mayo Clinic that Dr. Will supervised dramatize the Clinic's expansion: from more than 8,000 operations in 1910 to nearly 24,000 in 1924, the increase most notable in operations on the liver, the uterus and the appendix. Thyroid operations declined precipitously after 1919, reflecting medical understanding that iodine was vital to the health of the gland. Stomach procedures declined as medical treatment of ulcer came in. Medical treatment of disease began to make a dent; hospitalized medical cases rose from fewer than 500 in 1912 to more than 10,000 in 1924.

Dr. Will performed his last operation in 1928, his 68th year, when he discovered increasing tremor in his hands. "I want to stop while I'm still good," he told his secretary. His younger brother was forced from surgery a year and a half later by a retinal hemorrhage. A series of strokes followed for Dr. Charlie.

Giving up surgery was hard. But what has been hardest of all for many other founders—relinquishing control of their institutions—appears to have been easier for the Mayos. Dr. Will had been the administrator, always consulting privately in his decisions with his brother; in 1932, at the age of 71, he resigned from the Mayo Board. His advice continued informally to carry the force of law until he died, but gradually the Mayo Clinic became essentially self-administering through a structure of physician committees responsible to the governing board, a medical democracy that reinforces the coordination of group practice that is central to the Clinic's continuing success. Dr. Will defined the ideal: he called the Mayo Clinic "a scientific cooperation for the welfare of the sick," and that it was and is.

Dr. Charlie died first, of pneumonia, on May 26, 1939, not long after Dr. Will had been operated on for cancer of the stomach. Dr. Will followed his brother in two months, dying on Charlie's birthday as if to link them even in death.

Dr. Charlie's eldest son, Charles W. Mayo, "Dr. Chuck," maintained the continuity of family on the Mayo Clinic Board and in its operating rooms until his retirement at 65 in 1963 (he was killed in an automobile accident in 1968 as his younger brother Joe had been at the age of 34, in 1936). But his was only one vote, and since he was something of a maverick it was often a vote that stood alone. Dr. Chuck's son, another Charles, trained at Mayo but practices elsewhere today. In the third and fourth generations the family has dispersed.

Yet it is clear that the values of the Mayos still anchor the enormous institution that the Mayo Clinic has become. Patients are still not questioned about finances until after they have been treated. The Clinic remains conservative about publicity, and though it now cooperates with bona fide journalists, it hardly ever issues a press release. Staff physicians receive salaries, not shares of profit, and still receive only one year's income as their share of the group practice if they resign. In return their time is their own, including time for study, for professional meetings, for writing and research. Patient records are still scrupulously maintained. An entire building has been set aside for them by now, housing more than 3.5 million dossiers that blow from building to building as needed in pneumatic tubes.

"The Mayo name is on the Clinic," Dr. Chuck wrote in a memoir of his life, "on the origin of group medicine, on a number of surgical instruments, curved clamps and dissecting scissors, invented by my father and me, on a type of bedside tray that is seen everywhere, on a universally used operative procedure in gynecological surgery that is called the Mayo operation, on a tiny vessel Father discovered that marks the division between the stomach and the duodenum and is known as the vein of Mayo; and, of course, on the ubiquitous Mayo diet."

A certain reserve pervades the clinic air, a midwestern reserve that may be the unwitting source of the occasionally heard canard that the clinic is more interested in the disease than the patient, is mechanical and cold. Nearly 1,000 patients a day register at the Mayo Clinic; without system it would rapidly falter to anarchy; and there are those who find any system chilling. The test is whether or not people are healed. Presumably they are: they increase in numbers annually.

"They helped everyone his neighbor," the surgical society of the Mayo Clinic resolved upon the Mayo brothers' deaths. They did. Through the agency of the institution that their sturdy genius shaped, they still do. To which the Old Doctor, W.W. Mayo, would add sharply, as he did when he heard his sons too frequently praised, "Why not give me some of the credit? They are mine and I trained them."

# 14 / A Friend's Suicide

A FRIEND OF MINE KILLED HIMSELF SOME YEARS BACK, three months after leaving the Middle West for New York. Conrad Knickerbocker was, as we say, a talented man. In four short years in Kansas City he had established himself as a successful middle-management businessman. In his spare time he became a book reviewer for the *New York Times Book Review*, appearing more often in the front of that periodical than in the back, a distinction he appreciated. He reviewed books for *Life*, too, one of the first to be awarded that burden. At the library one day, before he became successful, Knick discovered a Canadian novelist who interested him—Malcolm Lowry—and made him his own. Like Knick, Lowry drank far too much,

believed in the supernatural, and wrote with a grace of complication beyond the ordinary. Knick's first essay about Lowry appeared in *Prairie Schooner*, the journal of the University of Nebraska. A later essay, about looking for traces of Lowry in
England, was written for *Esquire*. The magazine turned it
down because it assumed more knowledge of Lowry than *Esquire* thought its readers possessed. That essay appeared in the
*Paris Review*. *Esquire* bought a short story about what it was
like not to have been a soldier in World War II. Another short
story appeared in a paperback anthology called *Black Humor*,
a term Knick liked to claim he coined, and perhaps he did.
While accomplishing these first works, he also contracted to
write a biography of Malcolm Lowry and a novel. And published, again in the *Paris Review*, a long, lucid interview with
William Burroughs that revealed Burroughs for the first time as
more than merely a madman.

By daylight, Knick worked full time—very full time—as
manager of advertising and public relations for Hallmark
Cards. He was responsible for all company publications. He co-
ordinated the production of six Hallmark Hall of Fame television specials each year. He personally wrote press releases and
promotional copy for Hallmark's many cultural projects, and
one year organized a major exhibition at Kansas City's Nelson
Gallery of Art that involved hundreds of letters, deals, cajol-
ings, the transformation of a cathedral-sized hall into an intimate and religious experience, and much more.

Knick did all these things and always had time to talk, marvelous talk blown with gags and metaphor, marvelous talk
edged with irony and loaded, I see now, with bitterness, but not
simple bitterness. There was nothing simple about my friend.

He did all these things despite the fact that he found himself,
from time to time, drunk beyond comprehension, standing in
the middle of a Kansas City street in the middle of a Missouri
winter wondering where he was and who he was and how he
had arrived there. Friends tell me he was vicious when he was
drunk. I never saw him that way, didn't know until after he was

dead that he was seeing psychiatrists and dropping in on AA meetings and blowing his mind in the middle of streets. I choose to think he chose to spare me.

If his story is to be believed, Knick once found himself drunk at three in the morning in a black whorehouse in Chicago wondering how he could get out alive, and called a friend, a powerful man in Chicago, who sent down his tough black chauffeur and his tough black Rolls-Royce to bail Knick out. He wrote about it later in the manner of J. P. Donleavy, and if he'd had Donleavy's sense of humor about himself, instead of Malcolm Lowry's self-pity, he might have lived.

He sorted through an extraordinary collection of lives. He was born in pre–World War II Berlin. His father was H. R. Knickerbocker, the distinguished international correspondent, the very man who introduced Sinclair Lewis to Dorothy Thompson. The childhood didn't go well, as it usually doesn't. At six, I am told, Knick was seeing an analyst in England. From six to nine he attended an English public school. An Englishman who knows that experience tells me that it must have been hellish to be in one of those schools a term at a time; this Englishman says he waited with something like violence for his father to pick him up on Fridays and give him a humane weekend before delivering him again to the school for a week; but Knick lived there week in and week out, while his father corresponded and his mother searched the Continent.

After the divorce, mother and son moved to Topeka, Kansas, where she went to work writing publicity for the Menninger Clinic. He was sent to a military school in Missouri. If his writing is a measure, he preferred to remember his summers in Topeka. Where, at Edelblut's Drug Store, you could always get cigar boxes to keep your comic books in. Where the man who fixed his bike and helped him start a stamp collection had escaped the war because he sported an undescended testicle. Knick went to Harvard after the war and graduated with honors. His father, along with a crowd of other international correspondents, was killed in an air crash in 1949. Knick joined the Air Force and went through OCS at Lackland Air Force Base in San Antonio, Texas. He graduated toward the end of the Korean War, and got out without much service during the general demobilization. He married a savvy country girl in Missouri whose family owned a small-town newspaper, and he ran the newspaper for a time, until the marriage broke down following the birth of their first child. Soon after, he arrived in Kansas City with $25 in his pocket. Got a job with the Skelly Oil Company for a while, and came over, with undoubted relief, to Hallmark.

After so many bad starts, his writing moved ahead. He decided his time had come. He lunched with Clifton Daniel of the *Times* and sealed his fate: he would become a daily reviewer for the Times at the same salary he had earned at Hallmark, good pay for three book reviews a week. He sold his Kansas City house in twenty-four hours, bought a pre-Revolutionary house in New Jersey ("I bought a pre-war house" was his joke) and moved East. Three months later he was dead.

The day Knick killed himself, his review of *Papa Hemingway*, by A. E. Hotchner, appeared in the *Times*. It was his intended epitaph. This is some of what it said:

Much later on, it began to get bad, but there were signs before that. Hemingway said it took him 20 years to face his father's suicide. One Christmas, his mother sent him the revolver with which his father had killed himself. "I didn't know whether it was an omen or a prophecy," Hemingway said. It turned out to be both.

Hemingway also said, "The worst death for anyone is to lose the center of his being, the thing he really is." Mr. Hotchner's harrowing account of the author's last years shows how Hemingway lost that center and was unable to recover it. By 1960, he had begun to have delusions that the Federal Government was tapping his telephone and intercepting his mail.

The following year, he became deeply depressed over his

inability to finish his book of Parisian memoirs. One day at his Idaho home, his wife found him with a shotgun in his hand and a note propped up on the gunrack. Hospitalization followed. The last time Mr. Hotchner saw the author alive, he said, "If I can't exist on my own terms, then existence is impossible." The merit of Mr. Hotchner's book lies in the fact that it not only makes that statement credible, but inevitable and tragic.

And with those words in print, and a decent wife, and two children who had his red hair and his tension and his good mind, Knick walked out of his pre-Revolutionary War house on a sunny Saturday afternoon, cold sober, to his garage, mounted a .22-caliber rifle somehow against his chest or near it, moved the trigger and shot himself in the heart. He was moribund when his wife found him, and dead on arrival.

Back in the Middle West, those of us who knew him, personally or in business, gathered round. We had not yet experienced the fact of his death, only the announcement. We responded, it seemed to me, as if Knick had tricked us, pulled off another surprise in his endless repertoire of surprises. The question was, why had he killed himself? He, as many said, had so much to live for. He had just moved from business to what most thought was his goal: to write, to be a writer. He was successful, writing for the nation's most prominent newspaper. He was working on a biography and beginning a novel. He was married, with two children to prove it. He had seemed, at Hallmark, a successful executive. His boss, a bulldog of a man, but canny and competent, said he must have been crazy. Said it several times, as if to convince himself that people don't go around shooting themselves unless they are different in kind from you and me: crazy.

His literary friend said he was worried when he left for New York, said he probably shouldn't have taken on the big world. Another associate, who knew alcohol from bitter experience, said the drinking was a good part of the problem.

He was too wound up. He wasn't getting on with his novel. Lowry's widow was censoring the biography. His wife was a problem. All these explanations I heard. And, again and again: he shouldn't have left the Middle West.

This is what the *Kansas City Star* wrote:

Conrad Knickerbocker's tragic death deserves to be mourned in the literary meaning of the words. Death in that sense is not itself tragic; it is the end of tragedy, a release for the man.

I last saw him for a few minutes at one of those absurd big literary champagne dinner parties in New York. "Do you like it here?" I asked, meaning his new position on the New York Times as book reviewer and with freedom to comment at will on the nation's cultural scene.

"I hate it," he said, and spread his arms. "I hate New York. I wish I was back in Kansas City."*

But I said "Hang on, guy, you've got it made."

He did have it made. Apparently. When he wrote his first review for The Star sometime in 1959 he started on a literary career that soon showed promise of distinction. He did not write long for The Star alone. Soon after his review of John Barth's now classic "The Sot-Weed Factor" (only his review was quoted for years in advertisements) he was invited more and more to review for national magazines and newspapers. His short stories began to appear in national and international magazines. He began work on what might have been the definitive biography of Malcolm Lowry, with assistance of Lowry's widow. He signed a contract for the novel he was writing.

Then the New York Times called him to write reviews and gave him freedom to report on whatever of the nation's cultural life attracted his interest. He had it made. He achieved the position for which, whether consciously or

---

*He didn't: he was kidding.

not, he had been working. He had fame. He moved to New
York.

And he hated New York. He wanted to come home.

Over this epitaph, as subtitle to a section of the *Star*'s book
page called "Books of the Day," appears this sentence:

> The best fiction does not come from the eastern seaboard,
> Warren French points out in a review of "Prize Stories
> 1966"; most of them can be described only as "vindictive."

The Lowry essay appeared posthumously in the *Paris Review*, and George Plimpton, a classmate of Knick's at Harvard,
managed a Freudian slip, confusing Knick's name with Lowry's, and that confusion was certainly part of it. Suicides need
models, people to meet when they cross over.

I couldn't imagine the act. I knew the man only as mentor,
and thought he was immortal. I thought, as I listened to the
others talk—Kennedy's assassination was not so far behind—I
thought: that he had seen his future unfolding before him,
good reviews and unexceptional sales, a prize or two, literary
acclaim in his fifties, genteel decline. It isn't too hard to pre-
dict once you understand it as a game. I thought: his wife. But
however good or bad she may have been with him, he had lived
with her for years. I thought, once I knew of it: his drinking.
But he had been drinking for a long time. I read Karl Menninger's study of suicide, *Man against Himself*, and thought then
as I think now that the catalyst must have been his father's
fame, which Knick was on his way to equalling. But no multi-
plicity of explanations troubled the Middle West. One explanation sufficed: he should never have left. It's safe here, and
there is room here, and the bad cities of the coasts, the Sodoms
and Gomorrahs, can't swallow you up. I talked to no one who,
after he had sifted the case, really believed otherwise, except a
few close friends. Despite the hundred cases of Dr. Karl.

I was a pallbearer. I cried, finally, when I felt my friend's weight inside the coffin and understood that he was dead. We loaded the box into a black Cadillac like the ones he had, with J. P. Donleavy, written about, long and lean and low and smiling. Then we pallbearers—AA men, the literary man, a doctor, myself—got into another Cadillac for the ride out to the cemetery. The day was gray and cold, as they say. With a blustery wind out of the northwest. Knick had a brief but honorable funeral in an honorable Episcopal church, the suicide slurred over as a minor aberration. He would be buried in holy ground.

The driver of the pallbearers' car pointed out as we got in that each of us had individual thermostats beside our seats. The literary man did most of the talking as we drove in procession behind the widow, to cheer us up, I suppose. The literary man asked the driver what the most expensive coffin might be, and the driver, fresh up from Dallas, where they make the metal boxes we are buried in, the depositories, the School Book Depositories as it were, said the most expensive coffin was a monster called the Sarcophagus, weighing several thousand pounds, moved to the hearse on an appropriately decorated dolly. And no worms shall corrupt until the Judgment Day. The factory, he said, sent along special shock absorbers for the Cadillac as part of the package. Then the literary man asked if the cemetery toward which we were proceeding was top-drawer in Kansas City and the driver said it was one of the best. I disliked that question until I thought about it later. Then I realized that it was the sort of question Knick would have asked and cared about.

We buried him on a hillside in a new section of the cemetery. While a small tractor with a power shovel crossed the road near us with miniature wagons, three or four, each carrying one grave's load of dirt. The wind brought tears if we had none. No question any longer of what we were crying about. A friend was dead, and something of all of us with him, including our envy of him in life and our envy of him in death. The day before he died his analyst told his wife he was better, and that is how deep we all are, and that is how deep we should be buried. Weep for us and lower us into the basal granite, the magma, of the earth: the grave is too shallow, and who could bear a resurrection?

The priest in his white wrapping opened a pre-packaged vial of sterile dirt and dispensed it onto the coffin, and the widow wept, and the redheaded children stood white before the grave. We left him there all alone. That was the hardest part for me. I suppose I thought he was still alive inside his bronze box, roaring as he often roared, or weeping as he must often have wept.

Was Knick crazy? Had he fatally outdone his father? Had he mistakenly left the Middle West behind? All the explanations were valid and all the explanations were wrong. I spent a year pretending he was alive and well in Argentina, for he loved to parody the Nazis, acting out his anger in his black but humorous way, signing his more intimate memos at proper Hallmark Cards with a massive *Reinhard Heydrich* and a swastika. He made no sense at all to some people, though they had to admire his business ability; he offended others who thought him arrogant beyond belief; he charmed others with his wit and intelligence and ironic patient impatience with sloppiness of mind or body.

We shared Thanksgiving that year with Knick's widow and his children, and I heard his six-year-old son disputing with my four year-old son. "My father is dead." "No, he's not," said my son, unwilling to comprehend. And vehemently, the other boy, with his father's anger: "Yes he *is*. He's *dead*." *Having* to believe, as his father had to believe, the worst, so that he could at least consider the better, if only to scoff, if only to wish. "Kansas City is a hideout," Knick liked to joke. "There's nothing else to do here in the evenings, so you write."

And now my friend settles into private myth. After all the explanations are made, one remains, part of the myth, no longer repeated as his splendor is no longer seen, as he is no longer discussed except as reference for a slash of insight, a moment of truth: that he killed himself because he left the Middle West behind and went to the big city, to the terrible East. What everyone forgets is that, entirely despairing of it, Conrad Knickerbocker shot himself in the heart, counting on the loss of blood to kill his massive, hungry brain.

# 15 / An Excursion on the Prairie

ONLY FOOLS GO OUT LOOKING FOR BEAUTY. IN THE worst of times, soon after my divorce was final, in late spring, I decided to drive to Oklahoma from Kansas to see the annual dances of the Osage Indians, dances I had been told were still authentic, and to meet the aging chronicler of the Osages before he goes, a man born in 1895, part Osage, former member of the Tribal Council, an author, an elegant man, an Oxford man. I thought vaguely that a trip to the country would do me good.

Like my own predecessors, but five hundred or a thousand years earlier, the Osages came from the Ozarks, from the Ozark border. Lived in villages along Missouri's Osage River, the river they called the Place-of-the-Many-Swans. To most people the Ozarks means outhouses, but those are not their chief distinction. They are the only mountainous country between the Appalachians and the Rockies. They exist because a swell of rock, a batholith, rose up under the region a billion years ago and rivers and creeks etched their meanders into the swell. The batholith rose up slowly, without vulcanism. The chronicler of the Osages, John Joseph Mathews, believes that the tribe postulated no Hell because it had never seen a volcano, and he is probably right. Hell is Vesuvius, or Krakatoa, or a hydrogen bomb. The Osages postulated only death and resurrection. And learned to survive the midwestern tornadoes by clinging to the sumac bush. They did not survive the encroachment of the white man, however, and eventually removed to Osage County, Oklahoma, and would have languished there, but oil was found on their tribal lands, and today pumps like earth-shattering mosquitoes suck Osage oil and deliver it to the Phillips Petroleum Company, headquartered at Bartlesville. The oil saved the Osages, people say, but we shall see. Shall see if anyone is saved on this lickerish continent where man arrived so late and with such grandiose expectations.

The graffiti have changed in the rest stations of small Kansas towns. The walls no longer bear Neanderthal sketches of breasts and mingled genitals nor bardic verses of adolescent celebration but requests for urgent meetings: MEET ME HERE SUNDAY NITE 9 P.M. SUCK; HANDSOME COUPLE HUSBAND WELL-HUNG WANT TO MEET, etc., and, plaintively, I'M NOT SO YOUNG ANYMORE BUT I'VE GOT, etc. Swingers in farm towns of five hundred souls seem possible but unlikely even under a harvest moon; it's more likely that the illustrators and versifiers of old have been reading the classified in counterculture periodicals, and in the smallest of towns kids walk the streets with hair to their shoulders and *Rolling Stone* blares from every Kwik-Shop and drugstore. The revolution is total, we're all into it now, but in southern Kansas the revolution is attenuated by distance from the urban centers of its origin to long hair and Rolling Stones and MEET ME HERE

SUNDAY NITE and gatherings of the thin Kansas marijuana from fields left unguarded by the KBI, the Kansas Bureau of Investigation, the same that solved Capote's murders long ago. The KBI announced to the press shortly before I left for Oklahoma that it would stake out the marijuana fields as it did each summer, but that it didn't have enough men to stake out them all. The marijuana is poor anyway, volunteer stands left over from the days when Kansas grew hemp for the manufacture of rope. Kids still crop it, however, and the men of the KBI guard it through the moonlit summer nights like children watching over a fairy ring, waiting for the elves to come by.

In early evening I arrived in Pawhuska, the county seat of Osage County, where the Osage Indian Agency is situated high on a protective bluff, and found a motel of six rooms, the second-best in town. The girl at the desk left me in the midst of registration, slipping into the kitchen of the Taco Hut next door to fill an urgent order. The smell of burning corn blew back, corn the Indians devised. We call them Indians; they almost always called themselves the People; the Osages called themselves the Little Ones, hoping the gods of the universe would thus overlook their arrogance. The Osages and dozens of other tribes were concentrated by government fiat long ago in Oklahoma: the old maps, the maps of Oklahoma before the Oklahoma Run, before the territory became a state, show a patchwork of reservations. The Indians felt crowded, blasted; we felt them confined and thanked God. That was not exactly a standoff. The arguments continue about what we did. We thought the Indians another and most dangerous species of animal and we cleared the land: that is what we did. The Indians, the People, being human, thought otherwise. They thought we took their birthright away.

That is not exactly what the Osages thought. Deeply religious, they feared their faith had failed them. Feared that Wah-Kon-Tah, the Eternal Mysteries, despising their lack of faith, had turned away. Once the Osages commanded Missouri, Arkansas, Oklahoma and Kansas, pushing back the Caddos and the Apaches to the south and west, holding in thrall the smaller tribes to the north and east. They found in the creatures of the Ozarks and the prairie the qualities to which they aspired, the qualities that made them powerful: in the beaver, the fresh-water mussel, the white pelican, the brown bear, the wapiti, the deer, the owl and most of all the buffalo wisdom, virtue, industriousness, courage, long life. They divided into clans, each clan taking its sacred tradition from one of the creatures, sparing only the buffalo, so important to their economy that the nearest they could approach its sacredness was the Buffalo Face clan—only its face, not the animal whole. They were a fierce people, and because they lived on an ecotone, an interface between forest and prairie, and could crop the best of both worlds, they found the protein to make them strong and tall, averaging six feet or more in their best warriors at a time when white Europe averaged a little over five, able to walk seventy miles in a day, adept at horses when horses came, adept at guns, fusils, when fusils came upriver with the people they called the Heavy Eyebrows, the French trappers of pre-Revolutionary America.

So long as Spain and France contested their territory, they were courted, a valued border guard between two nations extended on overlong lines of supply, but when the English came, the people they named the Long Knives for the swords they wore, and even more when the Americans came, they began to lose ground, because the Spanish and the French only traveled through, but the Anglo-Saxons stopped and settled, parceled out the earth that the Osages thought belonged to Wah-Kon-Tah. Lesser chiefs and Nobodies traded the land away, signed treaty after treaty, and the Cherokees in top hats and cutaways pressed in, adept at the ways of Washington. The Osages never lost their land in battle, as other tribes did, and they were paid for their treaties more than most, but the land fell away nonetheless, and became, they said, like a shriveled old woman, and eventually, in the late nineteenth century, they removed reluctantly to Oklahoma, suffered the embarrassment of having to buy land in the Cherokee Strip that once had belonged to them by right of conquest, and settled in. They had been overwhelmed by bodies, white bodies like a horde of maggots that took up occupancy on their lands and could not be dislodged no matter how much neolithic frenzy they displayed, no matter what fierce and false masks they painted on their faces, no matter how many scalps they took. Scalps brought the Long Knives, and more treaties, and more pittances to replace the bounty they had once enjoyed. They never knew starvation, but they knew want, and if they went undefeated in battle, they learned defeat in council, because the more their ways failed them the more they increased their worship and the more Osage they became. When other tribes dressed for council cannily in white men's clothes, the Osages still swaggered in their buckskins, gorgets of shell at their necks to symbolize Grandfather the Sun shining at noon, roaches of deer hair or softened porcupine quills on their heads, cascades of bone or necklaces of eagle or bear claws over their chests, and the whites thought them unregenerate savages, and the Anglicized Indians of the other tribes thought them a shame, though a dangerous shame, not to be trifled with. The Osages were never a tribe to be trifled with. They had an essential arrogance, Mathews says, and though he denies he means the word pejoratively, I have my doubts. They had the arrogance of a people who never had to fight on their home ground. They were most American in that: neither have we, except with each other.

I found John Joseph Mathews, at the cocktail hour of my arrival, in the room he shared with his wife at the better motel. They had lived there most of a year, ever since a serious operation brought her into town from the stone house Mathews had built with his own hands long ago on his ranch on the prairie, too far from town for safe convalescence. Mathews was drinking Wild Turkey, and I joined him, his wife preferring rum and orange juice, the juice on doctor's orders for the potassium it contained. The man reclined on his bed on one elbow, beneath the elbow a folded blanket, in exactly the posture of the old Osage chiefs in the faded photographs taken long ago by the Bureau of Ethnology. He is a tall man, a big man, was dressed in a blue jumpsuit, his forehead Shakespearean and capped with fine white hair, his voice firm and commanding, with a touch of Oxford at the edges. Fifty years ago he failed to appear at Oxford until months past the beginning of term. The hunting had been good in Wyoming that year. His Oklahoma sponsors were scandalized, but the dons at Oxford understood: a chap doesn't come away to term when the hunting is good. Mathews was navigator of an aircraft in the First World War. After Oxford he hunted his way through Switzerland and down to North Africa. In North Africa one evening, making camp, he was suddenly surrounded by burnoosed Arabs on horseback firing their rifles into the air. He asked his guide if they were safe. "Joy-shooting," his guide said, and invited the Arabs to supper, but Mathews, young Mathews then, remembered another day, when he was a boy in Osage country and a crowd of Osage braves found him out on the prairie and surrounded him on horseback and fired their rifles into the air, and the two rounds of joy-shooting came together in his mind and he asked himself what he was doing in North Africa when he ought to be at home.

He went back to Oklahoma then and began his work of chronicling the history of the people among whom he had grown up. The old men of the tribe sought him out as they never would have done at an earlier time, young as he was. They were afraid, Mathews said, that their oral histories, histories passed down verbatim through hundreds of years, would be lost, and with the loss of their tribal memory, the record of their collective lives. So they allowed Mathews to take notes, and later to tape-record the histories they had learned from their fathers, and their fathers from their fathers before them, preserving every gesture and inflection as they had been taught, so that, for example, Mathews could still pull at his collar contemptuously when he described how badly the first white men the Osages had seen, nearly four hundred years ago, stank, an affliction the Osages attributed to the strange cut of their clothes.

An early novel set among the Osages was a Book-of-the-Month Club selection in the 1930s, and later came a Guggenheim and other fellowships, and in 1961, after two decades at least of work ("I had been working on that book all my life," Mathews told me), he published a detailed history of the tribe, exhaustive and exhausting and touched with a sense of irony so subtle that at times it can take your breath away. *The Osages: Children of the Middle Waters* was nothing less than a history of America from the Indian point of view, without bitterness but spring-loaded with the kind of humor that is still an Osage trademark, humor that finds its finest expression in the spectacle of proud men and proud nations making fools of themselves, though there is, for the Osages, a double irony in that.

Here is a contingent of Osages visiting Paris in 1827:

It was reported that at Saint Cloud, Little Chief's face was painted with blue and red when they met the King, and after paying their respects to the Dauphin and the Dauphiness, they had breakfast with the Captain of the Guards. They were invited everywhere, and were taken to the theater so often that they became bored, even with all the glasses in the theater on them continually.... Certainly they would have given no sign of boredom. On the Neosho and formerly at the Place-of-the-Many Swans, one had to sit for hours listening to the chieftain and the warriors of many *o-do'n*, and to the long medicine talk of the missioners, where one sat passively with closed eyes, behind which one could escape to thrilling personal experiences. Here at the theater in Paris it was not unlike the medicine talk of the Black Robes saying mass. They did not close their eyes.

And a little later in the same visit:

The French women seemed to have been fascinated by the warriors, and Big Soldier said that he had been "married" three times while in France.

Finding this man in a small Oklahoma motel room was like finding Gibbon or Herodotus there, and Mrs. Mathews was no less remarkable, her voice lilting and her face still beautiful, surrounded by abundant gray hair. The elderly in America seldom carry such a freight of dignity and courtliness and pride. Halfway through my life, I stored the Mathewses away somewhere, knowing how much I might need their memory at a later time.

The Osages hold three separate rounds of dancing each summer, the first at Grayhorse, a village a day's walk southwest of Pawhuska that was once an Indian subagency, the second at Pawhuska, the third at the small town of Hominy. I planned to go to the Grayhorse dances the following evening, but in the meantime I drove to the Pawhuska cemetery, north of the Agency, to walk that stone record of the Osage past. The cemetery spread across the east side of a treeless hill, a mausoleum rising above it as Lee's mansion rises above Arlington. It looked raw and new, perhaps because so few trees grew among the graves or because it lacked a fence, but in fact it was old, and I soon found stones that dated from the late nineteenth century. I also found stones cut from Ozark granite in the shape of arrowheads, small stones of dead children, stones with oval ceramic plaques glued to their faces carrying photographs of the deceased in full dance dress, the photographs protected under a clear glaze. I found a long row of Mathewses and stones with Osage names I couldn't pronounce.

The biggest stones marked the period of the Osages' greatest prosperity; in the third decade of the twentieth century, full-blooded Osages received as much as thirteen thousand dollars a year in oil royalties. Oil is the one fact about the Osages that most Americans know. I had visited Phillips Petroleum a few months earlier, and each of the men I talked to there told me the same story, apparently the only story about the Osages they had heard, that with his oil money in hand an Osage would buy a Cadillac without bothering to learn to drive, would smash it up on the way home and leave the shards lying and stumble to town to buy another Cadillac and eventually learn by doing and make it back to his ranch. It was a famous story, and perhaps it was true, but it put the oil money and the white feelings about the oil money in perspective. The oil money was conscience money, after all, and lo, the poor Indian, he didn't know how to spend it very well. In fact, the Osages accepted the oil money as their due, thanking God and Wah-Kon-Tah both that they had had the good sense to hold their mineral rights in community rather than allot them out to individuals as other tribes had done, but they hardly thought it compensation for Missouri and Arkansas and Oklahoma and Kansas, for the disappearance of the buffalo and their removal from the Place-of-the-Many-Swans. And the thing to do with money was to spend it, because a man showed his greatness in these latter days not by counting coup but by the value of the things he could give away. That would not make sense to a corporation executive; it would make sense to a Rockefeller, however, and the Osages in their pride were hardly less arrogant than the Rockefellers. The oil money comes to far less now, but the energy crisis of the mid-1970s encouraged new interest in the Osage fields, and engineers came in to open up old wells and explore for new ones. The Little Ones in their white men's graves would not know or care about that, dreaming of the sweet careen of their Cadillacs and the ripping of metal that laid them low—though in truth most of them died in their beds in honored old age.

"Budded on Earth to Blossom in Heaven," read an inscription on a baby's grave, and farther down the row was buried a descendant of Daniel Boone. Whites and Indians lay buried side by side in the cemetery, and Christian and Osage symbols and words marked the graves, votive lights next to arrowheads, names in English and names in Osage, the macaronic of change that the Osages were powerless to stop but had attempted to slow by incorporation. They were never "good Indians," but they were willing, to a point, to adapt, in the pragmatic belief that power was power and ought to be borrowed whenever it worked. An earlier generation had prayed to God and Wah-Kon-Tah both, had faced their dead to the east of Christianity rather than to the west of Wah-Kon-Tah, reasoning that so long as the dead warrior was painted correctly he could not lose the way to heaven. So the headstones in the cemetery faced west and the graves east, silent on the side of the bare prairie hill, and I could read the inscriptions without walking on the dead.

The Grayhorse dances were scheduled to begin at eight the next evening, and I drove out from Pawhuska under a blowing, overcast sky through mile upon mile of native prairie, fenced along the roadside and marked with oil pumps and Hereford cows and calves but otherwise undisturbed, crowded with wild flowers blooming opportunistically before the big bluestem grew to waist high and overtopped them. At the intersection with the road to Grayhorse the highway enlarged to four lanes divided, one of those major interchanges Oklahoma builds in the midst of nowhere to prove that it too receives a share of federal highway funds. There I turned south, drove through a small town, then turned east on a country road across one-lane bridges and railroad tracks, past the old stone subagency building to the sacred arbor. It was a tin-roofed pavilion with open sides and a dirt floor. Mathews had told me to find the Whip Man, and after asking around I did. He was not yet in dance costume; stocky, handsome, with gray in his hair, he wore expensive western clothes—hand-tooled boots, gray pants, an embroidered gray shirt, a massive turquoise-and-silver buckle on his belt.

The dances had become important to the Osages again, the Whip Man said. People had lost interest in them a few years ago, but now they were being revived. There were white hobbyists now who came to the dances from all over the United

States, and so long as they danced authentically they were allowed to dance along with the Indians. I started at that; I had expected the dances to be confined to the Osages themselves. We can't do that, said the Whip Man; we're so intermarried now that we'd have to keep our own kin out if we didn't let any whites in. Intermarriage had changed things, he said; he was intermarried himself, and more and more Osages were intermarrying as time went on. Pretty soon you won't be able to tell the Indians from the whites, he said. Women were allowed to dance now, too, though he wasn't sure he liked them in the dance out of costume, in shorts and halters sometimes.

You won't see any feather-dancing here, though, said the Whip Man; the Osage dances were quiet and sober, no applause, no showing off for the crowd. The difference between the dances was subtle, the songs were different but you'd have to know Osage to tell the difference. The Whip Man said he had a different costume for each night, including one of purple satin made for him by a woman in California that he was saving for Saturday night. He pointed to a woman on the other side of the pavilion. She kept the sacred drum, he said, and spent maybe four thousand dollars a year to feed all the people who came to the dances and to give them beef and groceries and blankets at the Sunday-afternoon Giveaway. The expense was too much for her, and she was having to give up the drum. The Whip Man excused himself to go speak with her, and I took a seat in the bleachers at the west end of the pavilion.

The dances were scheduled to start at eight, but they didn't start until after nine: Grayhorse was running on Osage time now. The west and east stands filled with visitors; the Osages had benches—church pews, their family names painted on the backs—to the north and south of the dance floor, a dirt floor that had been raked smooth and sprinkled with water to keep down any dust that might be kicked up by the dancers, though dust wasn't likely after the storms that had blown through that day, and the sky was black now above the arbor with new storms coming. The railings outside the pavilion were lined with cars, and many of the Indians, Osage or visiting kin, would stay inside their cars throughout the evening, watching the dances through windshields beaded with rain. And when I looked back from the row of cars to the dance floor the sacred drum was in place in the center, surrounded by middle-aged men and a few boys, the drummers and their apprentices. They wore no costumes, only cowboy hats and windbreakers and jeans. They were not even Osage, I learned later, but Pawnee, professional musicians with voice and drums.

The Whip Man stepped onto the dance floor a little after nine. He was dressed now in moccasins, black pants, a long, square-cut black shirt, with sashes down his back and front and at his sides, with a fine porcupine roach on his head tied under his chin and held in place by a headband. He carried a riding crop and an eagle-feather fan, and he was accompanied by an elderly Osage in buckskins wearing a brimless beaver hat, a pillbox. The Osage who would lead the dancers, a representative of the Tribal Council, came in on the other side from the Whip Man with a younger man in full costume but wearing glasses; the younger man looked like a Tulsa executive, which he probably was. Then the dancers filed in, most of them in their teens and early twenties, all of them in brightly colored costume pants and shirts—blue, red, purple, even flowered prints—and elaborately sashed. A few of the youngest wore sneakers instead of moccasins. With no obvious signal from the Whip Man, the dances began, the drummers singing falsetto, *Hi, ya, hi ya ya ya, hi, ya, ya ya ya*, setting up a simple rhythm on the drum. The Whip Man stepped out and the man from the Tribal Council on the opposite side and then the dancers circled the drum counterclockwise, standing upright, making no fancy twists and twirls, the only obvious variation in their walk around the drum the pattern of their steps. The young men danced with more vigor than the old, but the old men knew the steps and the songs and would dance every dance throughout the evening, not sweating like the young, only stepping unblinking around the drum. The songs changed from dance to dance, and the rhythms of the drum, but the changes weren't even obvious, and despite the singers and the beating drum we might have been watching a troop of mimes. At the end of each dance, an ending that also went unmarked, no tonic beat of the drum to signal it, the dancers returned to their benches and then the tail dancers added a coda, three young men dancing out from the benches to the drum, arriving at the drum on the last beat and walking slowly back as the next dance began. The dances seemed to come in sets, two or three at a time, and between sets water boys carried white enameled buckets down the line and the dancers drank from a common dipper, sharing that too.

An elderly woman sat in the center of the dance floor next to the circle of drummers, and halfway through the evening I saw her silently weeping, for the Osages or for her clan song: the dance songs were accounts of clan honors, the Whip Man had said, accounts of the great deeds of each clan. A boy no more than six or seven years old was presented with his first roach by the man from the Tribal Council and then seated on a new blanket below me in the stands, and his father, who was blond, took pictures of him with a flashing strobe. The old man in the beaver pillbox carried a wooden flute, and during one dance he began playing it, raising it above his head and lowering it to his chest, dancing with high steps like Pan, making bird whistles with a wooden flute, playing it for one dance only and then subsiding into the plain step he had danced before, the flute silent through the rest of the evening. No one applauded, as I had been told they would not, no more than they would applaud in church, but the storms that blew over pounded the tin roof of the arbor with rain and the rain sounded like the applause of a multitude, sounded like the applause of a crowd of Osage ghosts coming down from the sky, and the roof leaked the driving rain, making puddles on the dance floor that the dancers avoided without seeming to see them. As the dances beat on, a few women and girls draped with shawls or blankets danced in a wider circle outside the main body of male dancers, and some of them wept. A small, gray woman who had been seated in a place of honor below me at the edge of the dance floor—she had given away a hog to the young dancers, the man from the Tribal Council announced in English at one point in the evening—stood and danced in place, her tiny feet moving up and down.

I saw no hobbyists, though I might not have known what they looked like. The dancers were all dark and all had black hair except for one man's dancing children, a red-haired boy and a blond girl in full costume. A young woman, a beautiful young woman, danced with her baby, which could not have been more than two weeks old; she was the wife of the best of the tail dancers, the dancers who perform a coda at the end of each set, and she showed him the baby after the dance with obvious pride, as if it had been inoculated, as if the rhythms of the dance had been embedded in its bones.

The dances ended as abruptly as they had begun and the dancers filed out and the drummers took away the drum. Having played Indian once in the Boy Scouts, having danced with dyed chicken feathers on my tail, I sat through the evening in a daze. The Osage dances grew from another dimension, somber, dignified, giving no quarter to the audience, dances danced not for pay or prize or for condescending crowds at the rodeo but simply to keep the line open to what was left of Wah-Kon-Tah. They had the rigidity and the density of the Roman Catholic mass before it went modern, and so they also had the glory. The Cherokee Trail of Tears extended from Tennessee out to the Panhandle, but the Osage trail of tears went around a dirt dance floor in the middle of the Oklahoma prairie under a pounding line storm. There was as much pain in the one as in the other, and as much memory. Mathews had only hinted at the depth of that memory in his book. I wondered that night, and I wonder now, what will become of it, what we do with memories, painful and glorious, when they no longer serve, as my own no longer served, as the Osages' hardly any longer served, had been reduced to a book and three rounds of dances and the lingering tales of the elderly. "Part of the melancholy of the past," Lionel Trilling once wrote, "comes from our knowledge that the huge, unrecorded hum of implication was once there and left no trace—we feel that because it is evanescent it is especially human." Human, and vulnerable, and as fragile as the bodies in which it is lodged.

I saw what would become of the memory of the American Indian the next day. I drove to a place near Bartlesville called Woolaroc, a game ranch and country estate and museum and organizational center built years ago by the late Frank Phillips, who founded Phillips Petroleum. Woolaroc means WOOds, LAkes and ROCks. It's a gaudy Oklahoma San Simeon, though its gaudiness is more of the spirit, so to speak, than of the flesh. Tourists who come to northeastern Oklahoma do not come to see the Osage dances. They come to see Woolaroc, on the rolling prairie hills south of Bartlesville.

Frank Phillips was a collector, on a scale commensurate with his wealth. He collected travel junk, Indian artifacts, bad paintings and bad sculpture, awards. He collected animals. Once inside the gate at Woolaroc I was required to stay in my car until I reached the museum, acres away, as if on safari through a Kenyan game park, because the ranch was stocked with free-roaming animals: buffalo, first of all, and Scotch Highlands cattle shaggy as musk oxen, antelope, odd Himalayan climbers, bighorn sheep, llamas, deer, grazers and browsers all and not a predator in sight larger than the hawks that circled overhead. The bighorn sheep stand sentry on ten-foot outcroppings of Oklahoma limestone and must wonder why the summers get so hot. Spotted less than discreetly among the groves of trees along the way were full-sized imitation tepees that looked from a distance as if they might be made of Portland cement.

The museum, in the center of the ranch on a prominent hill, was a large building made of native limestone, entirely devoid of windows, its massive metal doors decorated in Art Deco and surrounded by mosaics of Indians in battle dress. Inside, past the central foyer dominated by a life-sized bronze of Phillips himself standing under changing colored lights, the building housed an excellent, if somewhat eclectic, collection of Indian art and artifacts that Phillips had assembled through the years: flexed mummies, flakes and points and scrapers from pre-Columbian times, extraordinary Navaho blankets hung from the walls, a photographic essay on Phillips's archaeological adventures—he was a trim man with a big nose and he excavated some of Oklahoma's larger mounds in jodhpurs and English riding boots, and paid for a good job and got it—and farther into the museum a birch-bark canoe, pottery, reed baskets so finely woven that they took years to make, the bead-and-bonework of the Plains Indians, the turquoise-and-silverwork of the Navaho. Mixed among the Indian artifacts were artifacts from a comic Byzantium: the head of an African elephant, wall after wall of bad paintings of cowboys and Indians, bad bronzes of the noble pioneers who settled the West, including one pioneer woman whose dress the wind and the sculptor had so revealingly fitted to her body that her mons and her navel and her nipples all stood boldly in view, Oklahoma pornography in the name of Western art. But down in the basement of the museum I found the mother lode, the dream museum of a self-made man, an airplane in one room that flew transcontinental back in the 1930s, wingspan a good twenty or thirty feet, with Phillips's name on the side, and surrounding the plane in the cases that lined the walls the odds and ends of a wealthy man's travels: Jivaro shrunken heads; a complete collection of bodhisattvas in cheap brass turned out in some Calcutta factory, bad porcelain from China, bad ivory from Japan, netsukes, pots; and down one long wall a tribute to man's inhumanity to man, a collection of knives and swords and shillelaghs and machine guns and rifles and pistols and what have you, from the primitive to the modern—the primitive and the modern, as the collection made clear, never having been far apart in the war department, all of us capable of a neolithic frenzy now and then. The ultimate room was the last room in the basement of the museum, which displayed awards, citations, keys to cities, plaques and certificates given to Frank Phillips over the years, including a selection of the presents he received on his sixty-sixth birthday (it was Phillips 66, remember?); including, embalmed under a bell jar, a blackened piece of birthday cake.

However lurid his taste, it seemed to me after touring his museum that Frank Phillips felt some affinity for the Indians whose oil had made him wealthy. What his successors have done with that personal tradition is another question. Across the road from the museum I found a modern building with a two-story stained-glass window in its north wall. The window depicted the two paths the boys of America might take, the high road of virtue or the low road of excess and vice, and an Indian chief picked out in lead and glass stood at the fork pointing the way. The building is national headquarters for a program called the Y-Indian Guides, a program that is the chief recipient of funds from the Phillips Foundation. Inside the building I listened to a tape that explained how the program came about: the director of the YMCA thought it up while attending one of the Y's annual father-son banquets. He liked the way those banquets brought fathers and sons together, he said, liked the closeness they engendered and the enthusiasm they evoked, but it seemed to him that once a year wasn't enough, that if the Y could do anything it could find a way to build relationships between fathers and sons that would last all the year through. The presumptuousness of the notion seemed to have escaped the director of the YMCA, and the insult to the American Indian seemed to have escaped him as well. A display in the middle of the headquarters caught the tone of the program: a rotating model of an Indian dance, little carved Indians tripped and twirled by wires poking up from under the turntable. The girl at the novelty counter near the front door turned the model on whenever visitors went by, and ten wooden Indians danced.

A patio with a food counter and a row of vending machines extended beyond the back door of the building. I went out to find lunch, and when the woman behind the food counter saw me coming she turned on a recorder and a reedy version of "Home on the Range" began to play from a hidden speaker. The food counter sold only one item, barbecued buffalo burgers, and since I had never tasted buffalo before, I ordered a buffalo burger and got a can of Coke from a vending machine and settled down on a rock to eat. Two swans waddled toward me from a pond beyond the patio, but the woman behind the food counter came sweeping out with broom in hand and they retreated sullenly to the water's edge. I finished my lunch—the buffalo meat tasted strangely sweet, though that may have been barbecue sauce—and looked for a trash bin, and from around the corner of the food counter a tape began playing that I hadn't heard before. I followed the sound. It came from a stuffed buffalo that stood behind a low picket fence speaking in a rollicking Western voice, a John Wayne voice. "Hi," it said, "I'm Buffo. People call me a buffalo, but I'm really a bison. Buffo likes to keep America clean, so feed me all your papers and pop cans. I can eat everything you give me. Just put your paper and your cans in Buffo's mouth and he'll eat them up." Buffo went on to narrate the history of the buffalo in America, casually mentioning that all the buffalo, all sixty million of them, had been killed by the second half of the nineteenth century because they were so useful to men for food, for hides, for leather and robes, for smoked tongues and tenderloins, and even more casually mentioning that the Indians had also found the buffalo useful, but failing to mention that the Indians had somehow contrived not to kill off all but a handful of America's largest native animal in the process of using it. I fed my papers and my pop can to Buffo, through his black plaster mouth. He sucked them up eagerly and they clanked back through his body and disappeared. Buffo was threaded with a pneumatic tube that ingested trash. I wondered where the junk went after it popped down his throat, so I walked along Buffo's flank to where his hind quarters butted against the wall of the shed, and found my answer. Walt Disney would have contrived to pop the pop cans out Buffo's hoof or along an unseen inner thigh, but the people who ran the Y-Indian Guides were more forthright: Buffo had a black plastic tube projecting from his anus through the back wall. In that unnatural natural way he rid himself of the detritus of white civilization, shitting trash and pop cans into the bin beyond the wall.

I remembered then a story that Mathews had told me. Frank Phillips, it seemed, aware in his later years of how much fame and glory money can buy, decided to make himself available for physical resurrection, and in the mausoleum at Woolaroc where he is entombed he caused a handle to be placed on the inside of the door, and had a telephone installed, in case he should wake up and need to use it. Mathews remembered taking picnics to Woolaroc and sitting on top of Phillips's mausoleum eating lunch, hoping the phone would ring. I remembered that, and I remembered the heavy cement grave covers over some of the Osage graves at Pawhuska, and I thought about Buffo and the Y-Indian Guides, about the dimming Osage dances now filling up with white hobbyists, about the loss of memory which is upon us all, the loss of memory that is also the loss of a usable past, and it seemed to me that the Osages who covered their graves with cement to keep themselves permanently buried, to make sure they would not again be removed to some more blasted place, had the right idea, though it wasn't much help to the living. I drove back to Kansas that night. Through the glass wall of my apartment I can see the prairie sky.

# 16 / The Community
of True Inspiration

IOWA CITY, IOWA. POPULATION 33,443. THE UNIVER-
sity of Iowa houses, has housed since the middle thirties, the
Program in Creative Writing and, more recently, the International Writing Program. The one major literary award that has
escaped its students and faculty is the Nobel. Paul Engle,
Rhodes Scholar and poet, founded the writing programs. Here
he writes about an earlier utopia:

> Men and women have always come to Iowa with hope. In
> the 1850's came a group of Germans calling itself The
> Community of True Inspiration, who believed that God

286

still spoke directly to man. They settled between Iowa City and Grinnell and built seven little Amana villages in the medieval manner, the families living close together in communities and going out to work in the fields. They had the wisdom to realize that the Lord could best be served with good land rather than poor, and took up 26,000 acres of rich bottom soil and wooded hills along the Iowa River. They ate in communal houses (five times a day, in leisure and abundance, with excellent grape and dandelion wine brought out to those working in the fields at noon). All property save clothing and furniture was held in common. Each adult received a tiny sum known as "year-money" for odd expenses, the least-skilled worker in the hog house receiving the same housing and maintenance as the most responsible farm head. God was worshipped not in churches but in houses without cross or decoration and no music save the unaccompanied human voice grandly ringing out the hymns written by their own brilliant prophet Christian Metz.

They flourished in their isolated, abundant and devout life until the wicked world came to them by newspaper, paved road, car, radio, and the young people began to yearn for the things they saw others having, like bicycles and Sunday baseball.

Bill Murray, an Irishman, came over when he was twenty and learned America in the army. Now he teaches in the Writers' Workshop and writes novels in the summertime. Small, spare, with a tentative mustache hooked to his upper lip and the tired eyes writers wear in America, he sits at his desk in a miniature office jammed with books. Two identical copies of Evelyn Waugh on the desk amid scattered papers. "Today we went over this student's story. Often enough they go at each other tooth and claw, but today everyone liked the story. I had been hesitant when I first read it, and wasn't sure I liked it. Then I realized what he was getting at. He was writing like Beckett. I liked it better then."

I smoke. He smokes, Marlboros, holding his cigarette between thumb and first finger like a jeweler's screwdriver. "It's a great boost to the ego. The boy felt good for the praise. But I had to balance that, do you see? So I asked him, toward the end of the class, if he had sent it anywhere. I didn't know that he had. He said he had sent it out six times and it had been returned. That's the test, do you see? He'd sent it to the *New Yorker* and *Atlantic* and *Harper's* and to some of the lesser periodicals. It had come back without even any personal comment, simply rejection slips. I could have told him not to send it to the *New Yorker*, it wasn't their kind of thing at all. But the test so far as I'm concerned must be if something is publishable. That's what we look for. It's hard. The market for short stories in the United States is small. And if you are to become a professional writer, that is the market you must consider. If he had only sent it to one publication it would be a different matter, but six different professional editors—that means something, do you see? They can't all be wrong. Something must have been wrong with the story."

Enter then a young man, thick curly hair over his neck, a bush jacket, a knapsack slung on his shoulder. "Mr. Murray, I'm Daniel Kramer. Did Mr. Engle mention my seeing you?" Confusion. Murray doesn't know who Kramer is. Behind Kramer a shimmer of wine in the hall. Kramer hesitating, turning halfway to the door. "This is my wife." Pretty round face, dark hair, wine-colored wet-look coat. "Perhaps I'd better come back later when you are free." "If you wish."

"That happens often," says Murray, contemplating the jeweler's Marlboro. "So many of them wander through, especially in the summer, wondering what we are like, what we can do, can we be trusted with their talent. They may have been editor of their college literary magazine or they may have half a novel in their knapsack, or a sheaf of poems. They come in the door with this hesitation about presuming and stand and wonder if they might talk, and all the time you see this form hovering behind them in the hall and they wonder if they should make the introduction and then finally they say, 'Oh, and this is my wife,' and this pretty girl steps forward. She is concerned, do you see, she has married this man and he may be a great novelist or a great poet someday and she wants to protect him but not to seem intrusive. She will take good care of him, too.

"The very difficult thing for these students is that they must become critics of their own work. I tell them they are not here to write but to make fiction. The words don't make it—the fiction does. Sometimes the discussion becomes so intense that they almost come to blows. I was nearly killed once in a classroom." The voice, small lappings of Irish at its shores, quivers with remembered fear. "Choked to unconsciousness. Quite an experience. There's something of an encounter group in these sessions, yes. That's part of it. They must know themselves better. They get here and they've all been successes wherever they came from and then they discover that everyone else has been a success too. It's a blow, and some don't recover. Two or three of their stories have been dissected and they simply disappear. To where I don't know. Back to where they came from, perhaps, or somewhere else. And we're not making great writers. No one can do that. Most of them become teachers of writing at colleges, I think. We haven't kept track of them later. Should do a study on that, probably. We know more about the poets—lots of prizes. What at least we have taught them is to be excellent readers. I would hope they at least would be better teachers of writing than an academic might, more sympathetic, more willing to understand what the writer is trying to do without reference to the classical models only."

IN A HALLWAY, DISCOVERED: PAUL ENGLE, AMERICAN novelist Mary Carter, Daniel Kramer and his wife. Kramer turns out not to be a student at all, but a photographer sent out to record writing in Iowa City. Mary Carter, from Oregon, slim and trim as a young adjutant, a face styled from the Apache by *Vogue*. Plans made to meet. A party Friday night for the foreign writers and visiting poet George Garrett, who is being considered for administrative head of the Program in Creative Writing.

KRAMER (to Mary Carter): Do you teach here?

MARY (laughing): I'm a Jewish mother! What does that make you, Paul?

ENGLE (roaring): I'm a Jewish grandmother!

*On a stairway, discovered*: Engle stopping to talk with a woman dressed in forest green and cobalt blue.

ENGLE: How are you? I haven't seen you for months. Where have you been hiding?

SHE (*conspiratorially*): I have a long story to tell you that I guarantee will make you gurgle.

ENGLE (*roaring*): Now what could you possibly tell me that would make me *gurgle*? I don't *gurgle* every day, you know!

SHE (*adagio*): I finished my thesis. He returned it without comment. He said he could think of nothing to add.

ENGLE (*sly, glad*): Old——? Nothing to add? Why, he's gone senile! *I'd* have thought of something to add!

*She glides past, floating on her thesis.*

ENGLE (*aside, to me*): Extraordinary. She's a nun. She came here to do graduate work in her black nun's costume. Then her order modernized its dress and one day I saw this woman approaching me in a bright, colorful suit, very trim. I hadn't realized. She's quite a pretty woman, don't you think? Do you know what she said to me when I asked her how she liked secular clothing? She said she'd just gotten out of the habit!

*Exit Engle, striding across the flagstone floor of the English and Philosophy building like a farmer going to see someone about a horse.*

WEDNESDAY AFTERNOON, ROOM 412: GRADUATE POetry Seminar with George Starbuck (attended California Institute of Technology, Berkeley, University of Chicago, Harvard, graduated from none; military policeman in the U.S. Army;

*Bone Thoughts* published in the Yale Series of Younger Poets in 1960; *White Paper* in 1966; Guggenheim Fellowship; Prix de Rome from the American Academy of Arts and Letters). A large classroom, perhaps twelve students spread across the first two rows talking quietly among themselves. We sit in the back of the room, my wife Linda and I, and to our right sit Kramer and his wife to photograph Starbuck *in situ*. Also sitting in the back, a student apparently taking an exam. The transparency of American life: I am writing about writing in Iowa City; Kramer is photographing writers in Iowa City; Starbuck is a poet in Iowa City teaching young poets in Iowa City to write poetry in Iowa City; a quiet girl is taking an unrelated examination in the midst of all. No one waves for the camera; we no longer need two-way mirrors to observe; we all observe each other in Iowa City and observe each other being observed observing.

Starbuck is late, cleaning up the administrative desk that he detests so that he may teach his class and take off for a reading in Fargo, North Dakota. Fargo would hear the mermaids singing, each to each, as would Kansas City, Missouri, and Beaumont, Texas, and every other isolated town most of urban America believes illiterate. Poets wander throughout this land, meeting each other in airports and bus stations, fellow conspirators, crafty spies lofted like Daedalus on wings of poesy.

Starbuck is not Melville's sturdy hero. He strides in on long, bony legs, a crane wearing Baudelaire's skull-like head, the slightly flattened compact head that reveals the fused sutures of flat cranial bones, small quick fevered eyes, black hair close-shaved, dark gray polished cotton work shirt open at the collar, dark green wash-and-wear pants, skinny ankles bare above short black socks, great treads on unpolished black shoes, a workman poet with an anxious heartbeat and long-fingered hands.

He asks a girl to read her poem from a worksheet run off in purple ditto: "Every line / of your body is / familiar to me / as a death in April You / do not know / what I mean."

We can hardly hear the reading. Kramer is better off, needing only his single eye distorting reality through its multiple lenses, bee seeking nectar. She reads on: "I will remember / your mythology / in my life / long after god / is dead."

"I don't know what stance this line is taking," says Starbuck. "It could be rather witty, but I don't know how the wit is supposed to cut."

Words of discussion drift back: correlative / verbal level / clear / etched / modern metaphysical / ambiguity / intended / reversal / hard-edged / deliberate doubleness. A poem of its own of words Starbuck uses to describe the poetic dance that these children would learn as once they learned to skip and cartwheel and cry for loss. "I'd fallen asleep reading William Carlos Williams," says the girl in indifferent defense of her poem. "When I woke up I was in a sort of religious soft mood. I'm not too nuts about this poem really."

Another girl reads: *The Field Mice*: "With the first killing frost / they inhabit the walls. / Mornings the cat licks clean her fur and the small corpse / is still, already a museum piece / . . . The napkins folded like hands in our laps, / our tongues honed and ready." Starbuck: "That viewpoint on mice, that they hardly exist—I like that." A girl: "It's about what people do to others, isn't it? About families?" A boy: "A lot of ceremony in it." Starbuck: "I don't like 'honed and ready.' Is it redundant? It seems to me that the poem needs at least that much, at least something that strong, but this line seems too heavy, too hard." A girl: "*Honed.* I hate that word." Starbuck: "What's wrong with the word *honed*? Can there be something intrinsically wrong with a word? I'll have to start a list of words people don't like so that we can use them all in a poem at the end of the semester." A girl: "There's sexual animal imagery in this poem." Another girl: "Where do you see that? I suppose if you are an animal—" "*I'm* not an animal!" Starbuck: "The main thing that's happening in this poem is a progression of images—of *takes*—on things. It's nice. I like it."

Two silent boys chewing their fingers, covering their

mouths. They do not speak throughout the class period until one of them reads his poem.

My wife passes me a note: "How do they *grade?*" I shake my head. How do they grade? How can they bear that strangers free-associate around their work? How can the others interpret someone's poem in his presence? Starbuck treats them gently, coaxing ideas, holding in check a natural tendency to force his own meaning on the poem, holding in check a professional tendency to see these half-written poems for the apprentice works they are. "It is the falcon," a boy reads, "The multicolored falcon / of poetry, who sings no song, / Who steals no bread, / Who tortures to live."

Why are these children here? Why do they bring their intensity to this fragile and misunderstood work of combining words on paper to make a song? These sturdy boys, long hair, curly beards to disguise their youthfulness, these ethereal girls with their displaced, indirect attentions. Speaking strongly of another's poem, a girl unconsciously kicks off her shoes, reveals red plump feet, rubs them intimately together. These red-footed children, these tired overserious children, have come here not to learn a trade but to hope, like novices, that they have a calling, that theirs is a truly unbearable obsession, that the divine madness is truly upon them. Wallace Stevens, in a letter to his Dublin friend Thomas McGreevy: *It is quite possible to have a feeling about the world which creates a need that nothing satisfies except poetry and this has nothing to do with other poets or with anything else.* Emerson: *The highest minds of the world have never ceased to explore the double meaning, or, shall I say, the quadruple, or the centuple, or much more manifold meaning, of every sensuous fact.* And Emerson: *The signs and credentials of the poet are, that he announces that which no man foretold.* These are the stakes these children would play for, knowing that if they win the world will come around quickly enough, for the world has always honored poets despite what poets say, honored them above all others except the greatest leaders of the state. And these rude children with red feet know that.

> *The essential poem at the centre of things,*
> *The arias that spiritual fiddlings make,*
> *Have gorged the cast-iron of our lives with good*
> *And the cast-iron of our works. But it is, dear sirs,*
> *A difficult apperception, this gorging good,*
> *Fetched by such slick-eyed nymphs, this essential gold,*
> *This fortune's finding, disposed and re-disposed*
> *By such slight genii in such pale air.*

Wallace Stevens: *A difficult apperception.* That is what these children do not know, have not yet discovered or they would not be sitting in this comforting school. That writing is done out of pain, and no amount of writing will take away the pain: the pain is to be alive. And that writing is always an act of failure, that the essential poem does not exist and cannot exist, but only approximations thereupon. One sails to Byzantium; one never arrives there. And marriage comes, and children, and perhaps too much to drink, and perhaps ill health, and death certainly: poems cannot cure that; the test is, can that cure poetry? These are old thoughts, but they ought to be brought out again to balance off hard-edged takes on modern metaphysical ambiguities. Poetry is something children do the day they discover that the universe has no end. The night they dream of falling down a tunnel that extends into colorless infinity. Poetry cherishes particulars because particulars momentarily fix time. Its trick is to fix the particulars on the page in order to fix time on the page, a little dance, a frivolous pirouette. It is a lie, as all human works are lies. To be human is to lie. Nature doesn't lie.

A boy reads: "The machinery of nature reaches into its pockets / And pulls out a list / Of complaints against molecules. / They are everywhere, the list says, / They have no decency, they do not grow/ Old and die." That is what I meant.

A boy reads, one of those who chewed his fingers and did not speak, the cleverest boy in the class as you shall see:

> Rolanup
> Call the king
> for Rolanup the king of the friends
> full of the pullers and the book
> for the cooperation of Rolanup the cooker
> of sins, from the gypsy of the plantation
> who knows how to fish the green graves
> and the cheers.
>
> Rolanup my happy child, can I call you
> for the fair, the sandy eyes of Christ
> you lick for the Huns of the exit.
>
> Rolanup the blood
> Call the king see the prince of pain
> lap up the charred bodies from Sweden
> Rolanup my king.

Immediately this boy lights a cigarette, the first he has smoked. "I have to confess I don't understand this at all," says Starbuck. "Does anyone else?" No answer. "A legendary poem," someone says lamely. "It seems to me that this is about the birth of a northern Christ," says a girl. "A sort of call to battle," says Starbuck. "Could you tell us what you intended by it?"

The boy, clever boy, his head down as if in shame, shame not for the reaction his poem has received but for being in a place where people actually believe poetry can be discussed. "I can't say much about it. I sort of like it. I can't think of any solution, other than it progresses from prince to king. It's personal. I'm speaking to Rolanup—some imaginary king." Starbuck: "It's as if you made up a name and the name brings associations with it—like a three-year-old. But what is happening in the poem?" "I don't know." "Perhaps it's time you thought about it, about why it's a poem to you." "I don't know." "It doesn't look like scribbles from a poetic journal." "I don't know. I think I understand what you're saying. I have no reply. It's dangerous." Starbuck: "Are you going to go on and write four more?" The boy starts, quick flare of fear, regains control. "Why did you say four? I've got four more. I don't know why you said four." Starbuck: "Well, we'd like to see more sometime."

A girl says she doesn't feel like reading today. Our time is nearly up. Several other students read without discussion. The girl taking the exam, Kramer and his wife, are gone. "Well, that's it," says Starbuck. "See you next week." I walk to the front to thank him. He grins. "This is our distinguished visitor. He thinks what he saw today was typical of the way we work."

Yes.

IN THE EVENING, AT DUSK, ENGLE GATHERS UP HIS sheep, and visiting sheep, and visiting shepherds. I meet Hua-ling Nieh, author of two novels, two short-story collections, one collection of essays, and four works of translation in the Chinese, associate director of the International Writing Program, Engle's intimate friend, mother of two girls attending the University of Iowa, a lady lovely in her bones. We are then nine in Engle's station wagon, seven in Kramer's Chevrolet driving the twenty-five miles to the Amana Colonies for dinner: Engle; my wife Linda; myself; a Filipino novelist with a face and mustache like South Vietnamese vice premier Nguyen Ky's, but with warmth, not murder, in his eyes; Gaga, tiny tough Gaga, the name I knew her by, a Yugoslavian novelist who writes in Serbo-Croatian, a beautiful mole marking her mouth, a white fur cap on her head; and Hua-ling. We six face forward in the subway of Engle's station wagon. Three more face backward in the reversed rear seat: a Chinese poet arrived only the night before, former Chinese army sergeant, skilled Chinese boxer, collector of ancient songs, flat face and wide smiling mouth, wearing a woolly checked shirt; a Japanese poet in a gray, double-breasted suit, glasses, a Western head surrounding a Japanese face, grave, reserved; a Brazilian novelist only three days in town, slim, in a leather jacket, big nose, good smile, bemused eyes, once an engineer.

Following us, in Kramer's car, Kramer himself, with a book of pictures and words, all his, about Bob Dylan under his belt and a similar book on American middleweight writing champion Norman Mailer in the works; Kramer's wife and assistant and business manager and friend; a French poet, strange round pink head covered with a light fuzz of white hair, hints of albino, quiet; in the back seat another Chinese poet newly arrived with his striking wife and six-year-old girl of classical Chinese beauty and comical close-cropped boy of three. Meiwa, the little girl, will dominate the evening.

Our car fogs up. Engle recites the Amana story to us, gesticulating with one hand and steering with the other, pausing to swipe a paw across the steamed windshield, subwaying through the Iowa night. "They all lived together in these houses they built out of brick they made themselves. Each family had an apartment, and there were no kitchens because they ate in special houses set aside for that purpose. The Community of True Inspiration. They thought Protestantism too Romish. They were allowed to settle in Hesse for a while, but the pressure finally built up and they were asked to leave. They sent scouts over here—they had money, a good deal of gold, from selling their Hessian land—and the story is that the scouts sat on their horses on a hill overlooking this valley and pointed and said 'Amana,' which is supposed to be an old Hebrew word meaning 'This is the place.' They built the original colony and called it Amana, and as they grew in numbers they added little satellite colonies and called them West, East, North, South. Damn, I wish we had gotten an earlier start. I'd like you to see their houses. They were not allowed much beyond the creature comforts of food and a roof over their heads and warm clothes, but the esthetic impulse isn't easily suppressed, and they built marvelous solid furniture of oak and walnut. They expressed their love of color in gardens, lovely flower gardens. Sometimes they would grow flowers right up the walls of their houses—roses and the like—and completely cover the outside walls. They loved to eat—God! how they could eat—five meals a day, with plenty of wine on hand. Church was their only social activity. They were a practical people, a peasant people, and they believed that if there had been prophecy once it must still be possible to hear from God. They called their prophets 'Instruments'—just as if they were the tools of a solid peasant God. They did not approve of marriage, but they understood that the flesh is weak, and allowed it. Before two could become man and wife they might well be separated for a year to give them a chance to overcome this terrible weakness of the flesh, and if they had not, they were suffered to marry. They had no police force because no crime was ever committed here. If someone did something the community thought wrong, he would be called to task in church, and if he persisted he would be punished by expulsion from church until he saw the error of his ways. Which meant he would spend long hours at home alone, because everyone spent nearly every evening in church, and he would have to contend with the demons that assailed him when he was alone. My grandmother Louisa was one of them, and one day when she was working in her garden my grandfather, who was a captain of cavalry in the Civil War, rode through town and saw her. He asked her for a cup of water, and she got it for him, and then he said, 'When the war is over I will come back here and marry you.' And he did, though her parents were unhappy about it. 'Marrying outside,' as they called it, was a cause for sadness and some shame. So I have known these people through the years. I have a cousin here. I suppose I should write a book about them before it's too late. They've changed so much. They formed a joint-stock company finally, voted to dissolve the old communal-property idea and form a corporation in which everyone worked for a salary. Each adult got one share of Class A voting stock. It was worth fifty-four dollars when it was issued in 1932. It's worth much more than that now. Many of them now work for the Amana corporation, which got started when a member of the community invented a freezer. It's not directly connected with the community now. Some smart businessmen in Des Moines saw that it was a good thing and bought it out for less than the community should have allowed. They don't even get a royalty on their name."

We drive through dark streets seeing the outlines of large brick houses, and then to the Ox Yoke Inn in Amana. Settled in the basement bar of the Inn, we order drinks, the Brazilian novelist next to me sampling Amana grape wine, Paul across from me biting into a martini, Yugoslavian Gaga inexplicably sipping quinine water. A babel of languages, Chinese predominating after the necessary English, Chinese high and quick and ambient with proud humor. *Hsieh hsieh.* Thank you. My hands, plain American hands I seldom use in speech, levitate from my lap and begin gesticulating some universal tongue. I learn to smile wide meanings, to enunciate, to circumnavigate English, Sir Walter Raleigh on a global toot, hauling in a thought for a definition, following the definition to another discussion, returning to the original thought and reeling it out again, speaking English no longer nor any other language I know, and the others do the same.

Two drinks for us all, the waitress rushing like an Elizabethan maid before Falstaff's table, and then this Engle, this Instrument, this Christian Metz of his writers' Amana, herds us all upstairs to the Inn, where three tables have been joined to seat us for dinner. Thirteen places, bad luck, set crowded along the west side of the Inn, but we are sixteen with the two Chinese children. More places set, chairs moved closer together, and as if the places had been loaves and fishes there is suddenly room for us all. Five meals a day. "The largest man I ever saw was a member of the Amana colony," says Paul. "He weighed four hundred and fifty pounds." We are served ham diced and pickled with fresh onions in vinegar, cold sauerkraut, lettuce coated with mayonnaise, these the hors d'oeuvres before a mighty dinner. Mei-wa, Beautiful Girl, occupies a place at Paul's left next to Hua-ling, I at Paul's right, my wife dispatched as American Ambassador to the other end of the table to keep order and interpret menus since Kramer and his wife will be busy taking pictures. Mei-wa soon enough finds the big man out. Old Christian Engle raised two girls and adores daughters with a helpless adoration.

Mei-wa's eyes with their hooded corners slant upward to a whisper of brows; her hair is pulled back from her high forehead, and upon her crest of hair grow three white flowers, a child's crown. Her small nose turns up to emphasize its nostrils' flares of pleasure, and her mouth is tiny and expressive as an elf's bow. Her quick arms extend from puffed, lace-edged sleeves down to hands caught in the transformation between baby pudginess and the lithe fingers of a little girl; thin also are her legs, but not without some slight rounding of flesh.

*Triumphant child whose thought is instant act*, a line of Engle's. Will she eat some sauerkraut? No, it is sour. Will she drink some milk? Yes, it is cool. What does she want to eat? From Hua-ling a flurry of Chinese, from Mei-wa quick shakings of the head. She does not want steak. She does not want sausage. She does not want roast beef. Shrimp. She will have shrimp, french-fried in batter, dipped, curving plump knob, into red sauce. She will bubble her milk. She will drip milk from her straw into her water glass, and swirl white clouds and run and get her brother and give him some to drink. She will pick up her brother by the waist and carry him around to our end of the table. She will stand on her chair and dance, if she may have another shrimp for doing so. She will run to her brother, back now at his end of the table, and trade him a shrimp for a chicken leg, shrewd bargain but she prefers shrimp. She will sing, and she is only six, an aria from a classical Chinese opera about a girl who dressed as a boy and ran away from home, whom another boy fell in love with, who then returned home to her parents and an arranged marriage, whom the boy she loved then died of heartbreak for, who then visited his grave and the grave opened and the bodies disappeared and two butterflies flew away together.

And while this child, this princess, turns the evening to flowing crystal, Hua-ling heralds each act down the length of the table to Mei-wa's doting father and shy mother surrounding the little boy there, and my wife speaks Portuguese and Chinese and Serbo-Croatian by turns, though she knows only English and French. Christian Engle, sturdy Instrument, eats vast plates of food. The Japanese poet sits mostly silent, relishing his steak, as does the Filipino beside me. The Chinese former sergeant, as we finish our meal, asks permission through Hua-ling to sing a song. We become quiet, and he produces in a masculine baritone what must be a love song: it is, from the sixth century, when we broad-bottomed Saxons still roasted our meat over open fires.

Dinner finished, and Beautiful Girl goes on. Her mother is persuaded to sing, and does so in a voice rich with training. "She is music teacher of small children," says Hua-ling. "That's where the husband met her. He hear her sing and—" shrugging gently the beginning of love. The men become restless. Paul goes to buy the two children heavy bars of chocolate wrapped in shiny foil, and abruptly the men leave the table to do the same. They are homesick; their children are far away; they will buy some chocolate and send it to their children.

So it is possible to communicate. I am a Midwesterner. I have lived in the Midwest for most of my life. I have known no one of another language or another country. At the Inn I sense the checked hostilities of other tables around us—not the farm people, who look on with something like wonder at the motley gathering and with delight at the sparkling child, but from the businessmen out for the evening, over beyond the heavy central beams. Who are these people? Why are they dressed that way? What business have they singing? Who is the large man at the head of the table who laughs so loud?

But the warmth at the table, like the warmth of a fire kept going hot through a long evening so that now the entire fireplace radiates heat and the logs glitter and any wood piled on immediately catches flame, holds back the hostilities in the room. Sixteen people have sat at the Paul Engle Amana Colony boardinghouse table and experienced something like love.

We pile out to the cars, Linda and I joining the Kramers now, and beat our way to Paul's country A-frame for a party. Ahead of us, in Paul's car, caught in our lights, three serious faces— one Japanese, one Filipino, one Chinese—peer out through round holes wiped into the steamy rear window. We laugh and nudge each other, partly because of the evening, partly because we are Americans and cannot resist ironies, no matter how much we love.

THESE HAVE TAUGHT, OR LEARNED, OR WRITTEN, AT Iowa City: Paul Engle, Wilbur Schramm, Robert Penn Warren, Ray B. West, Paul Horgan, Eric Knight, Josephine Johnson, Hansford Martin, Walter Van Tilburg Clark, Robie Macauley, Herbert Gold, Harvey Swados, W. D. Snodgrass, Joseph Langland, James B. Hall, Oakley Hall, Thomas Williams, Verlin Cassill, Vance Bourjaily, Philip Roth, George P. Elliott, Henri Coulette, Donald Justice, Hortense Calisher, Curt Harnack, Calvin Kentfield, Philip Levine, Herbert Wilner, Walter Sullivan, Wirt Williams, Robert Lowell, Karl Shapiro, William Stafford, Andrew Lytle, Nelson Algren, Kurt Vonnegut, Jr., William Dickey, Bruce Cutler, Mary Carter, George Starbuck, Tennessee Williams. And more whose names I have not been able to track. And more whose names you would not recognize because they have not published in English.

DINNER AT HUA-LING'S HOUSE, A RANCH HOUSE SET back on a quiet street where others of the University faculty live. Paul must appear at a cocktail party in honor of George

Garrett, the poet from Hollins College who is being considered for the new position that will take the administration of the Program in Creative Writing off George Starbuck's back. Hua-ling will remain in the kitchen, cooking the curry, while Paul is gone, and I will sit alone in the living room under a lamp sipping bourbon. The weather has gone bad, a steady drizzle from cast-iron skies. Hua-ling brings me a book about China the size of a tabloid newspaper, three inches thick, bound in green-silk-padded boards. "We are the Jews of Asia," Hua-ling says. "We have no homeland. What you see in this book we may never see again. Much of it is being destroyed." All Hua-ling's th's are d's: I transliterate her words.

She returns to her curry, I to the book. In the gray twilight, under a lamp, I think I begin to understand the difference between the Japanese and the Chinese. The Japanese are a group people, as if they had been cloned from the same chromosomes, not separately bred. Each individual Japanese act must be considered in the light of its effect on all other Japanese in the world. Individuality remains, but refracted strangely through the group. The Chinese are individuals, like the Americans and the Russians, proud, racist, though with a stronger civilization behind them, so that they do not act so impulsively as we. "Western man *works* nature," the Filipino novelist told me the next day. "Eastern man *is* nature." I said that gave them intimacy. He said that gave us distance. We considered it a draw.

This book, this heavy book. An art and a culture so long in existence, so myriad, so exceptional, that I am staggered by it. Why would such a people come to Iowa City, Iowa? Except that Taiwan is not a pleasant place, any more than Hawaii would be if you could not return to the mainland where you were born. But Belgrade? Rio? Tokyo? Munich? Paris? The only possible answer is that these people come to Iowa City because Paul Engle brings them here. This is the place.

Paul returns and we eat curry, Hua-ling and I sitting on the floor, Paul on the couch. Paul leaves again to attend a reading

Garrett is giving. Hua-ling begins to tell me of the novel she is writing, growing more animated as she talks, chimes into bells into temple gongs, a novel about flight, a girl's flight from home and back home, from her husband and back to her husband. The Jews of Asia. In the third part the girl is hiding in an attic with her husband and her little daughter. She does not have to hide; her husband, not she, has committed a crime, a petty crime, stolen some funds from the firm he works for. The daughter does not bother to learn to walk; since the ceiling is low in the attic, she crawls on all fours. The man is cowardly, will not go out, does not want his wife to go out. She accepts that condition for several years, then begins to go out at night, eventually by day, becomes involved with a friend of her father's, an older man whose wife she has nursed and who first made love to her the day his wife died, in simple need. She coaxes the little girl then to go outside, as she has done, and the child discovers for the first time the beauty of flowers in the garden below the house. The child sneaks out at night to the garden; the police catch her in their spotlight and come up to find the family. The man is still weak, claims his identity card is in the hands of the welfare office; the woman reaches under the pillow and hands the card to the police. In the fourth part, the woman flies to America. Amana. This is the place.

Paul returns. He has not attended the reading, couldn't find a place to park. Went instead to his office and wrote some letters. Falls asleep sitting on the couch, man of sixty-three whose days and nights are filled with details, people, fundraising, time stolen in between to write.

AN AFTERNOON ALONE WITH HUA-LING WHILE PAUL prepares a party for his foreign writers. She wants to hear the tape I made at the I-D Packing Company in Des Moines on my way to Iowa City. It isn't a pleasant tape, and I worry that she wants to hear it out of politeness to me, because I had mentioned it the night before. No. "A writer should know of these things," she says. But before we listen to the sound of pigs being slaughtered, she plays for me part of an interview with Paul by a Czech writer, a woman, a poet.

"The writer cannot write only out of pain," Paul says. "We all have pain. The writing is not the pain. It is pain shaped by form. Without the form it is nothing. It isn't enough for the writer to have talent. We have had writers with great talents who could not realize that talent. Ezra Pound was such a writer. The great writer has talent, but what distinguishes him, what makes his writing great, is character. Robert Lowell, a great poet, afflicted with an emotional disorder that has never left him so that he still must be hospitalized part of every year, and yet great control, extraordinary control, all the toughness and depth of New England in his work. T. S. Eliot, a man who realized his remoteness from people, his loneliness and shyness, and made out of that remoteness a religious, distant, extraordinary poetry. It's a shame that he had to live in England. His work lost something there. I suppose the poet I admire most of all is William Butler Yeats, because he had this extraordinary sense of local place, the west of Ireland, and I have always had a similar feeling about this part of Iowa. Place means so very much in writing. The poets of the Southern school— John Crowe Ransom, Robert Penn Warren—evolved a tight, intellectual, metaphysical poetry out of the remembered experience of the Civil War. It is the poetry of a people who lost a war, hard, proud, refusing further compromise."

And there we stop the tape to listen to pigs squeal. Hualing's strength, listening to either tape: Jew of Asia, she has no place. She writes instead of flight. And what do I write of? The Middle West. A place so vast one must cut it out in little pieces, take it a piece at a time.

> *Mush is rough,*
> *Mush is tough,*
> *Thank Thee, Lord,*
> *We've got enough.*

We're late for Paul's party but happy for the afternoon. One other detail: Hua-ling taped my tape with my untaped commentary about the slaughterhouse. Wheels within wheels.

THE PARTY IS—A PARTY. WHISKEY AND ICE IN STYRO-foam cups, the kind you can bite little pieces out of if you choose, the kind that weep, comical that a thing so small and white and utilitarian can weep. The party may be the last time I will see the friends I have made here. Dan Kramer herds all the members of the International Writing Program out into Paul's yard for a group photograph, and while he is taking pictures I take one too with my bare eyes, a snapshot for a mental family album. This is that snapshot:

Light rain. Temperature about forty-five degrees, chilling. Little wind. Beyond the white rail fence, a bent stand of volunteer wheat. Dusk. The sky, enormous out here, swirled, shades of gray and glowing near-white, liquid. Dan's wife in her wine-colored coat. Green grass, grass green in November as Ireland's. Emerald grass. Dan braced atop a chair, one booted foot on each wooden arm, sturdy, steady. The foreign writers arranged in a wide group deeper at its center than at its edges, a fertile crescent. They have written hundreds of books, hundreds of poems, in all the languages of the world. Their countries have fought each other and lain with each other. It does not matter. They are writers. A small Polish man who appears arthritic, bent, the body of an old peasant, in a plain dark suit, dominates the left side of the grouping, stands slightly forward of the others, creates a foreground. He does not want to be missed. He smiles as someone smiles who has learned to smile that way for a still picture. Dan's camera could freeze him flying upside down through the air, but he does not know that, and so he folds his hands in front of himself and smiles that smile. Next to him, left of center and also in the front row, an Israeli writer still suntanned, a tall man, a handsome man. He talks as Dan works, noble head turned half back to see those across from him to whom he is speaking. He looks like a psychoanalyst on vacation. In the center, the exact center, of the photograph, Hua-ling. Wearing a red wool dress, her stocky and shapely body demanding that the dress behave as it was designed to, and it does. Behind her, towering up, Paul Engle in a houndstooth jacket, his voice booming quips to warm his sheep against the November chill. He wants to dominate the group; it wants to be dominated by him. Out in the country in Iowa, standing in the rain because an American photographer must take a picture, the group's link with all its places is Paul Engle, man of this place. He is the only American in the photograph. Gaga, tiny tough Gaga, wearing a red vest over a white shirt, wearing the pants in the family as she always does, complains humorously about the cold. An African black, bold and brown with a pointed beard, commands Dan to hurry. "Some of us are from the tropics, you know," he says. To the right, the Filipino novelist, the Chinese sergeant of poetry, a German, an Irishman blocked out in stone with a wicked twinkle in his eye. The French albino, his hair swirled like the sky. Far to the right, two men in dark suits who drift out of the frame and must be shooed back. A most solemn and ceremonial moment. Look right into the camera. Hold it. Thank you.

As the party ends, the Chinese poet consents to demonstrate Chinese boxing, and what he does is too swift for description except with one word: ballet. It would not be ballet against a human body. It would be instant death. "We have other ways, too," says the Filipino. "There is an art of spitting. The man trained in that art can peel an apple at ten feet." My God. Shall I say we put three men on the moon every month or two just to prove we can?

DINNER AT THE VANCE BOURJAILYS. I STARTED READING
*The Man Who Knew Kennedy* early that afternoon and knew
that it was a book I would finish. I knew Kennedy, but in
dreams only, like Barney, the narrator of Bourjaily's novel. The
night Kennedy was nominated I dreamed he and his father were
congratulating me on the steps of the White House. After his
election, I dreamed I had important information for him, wandered through the White House looking for him, made a wrong
turn and stumbled into a dark bar with a dirt floor covered with
sawdust, the bar filled with bulky, tough blacks. I backed out
fast enough, finally located Bobbie, who took me to a store-
room where he and Jack and I sat on tall packing crates and
talked with great seriousness of my information, whatever it
was. "What kind of people are we?" Helen, Barney's wife, asks
him that helpless question in Bourjaily's book. My wife asked
me the same question when Jack was shot. Perhaps everyone's
wife asked everyone that question when Jack was shot. Dinner
at the Bourjailys. On Halloween night.

We drive—Paul, Hua-ling, and I—through the country at
night, a long drive. Bourjaily has buried himself in deep country, buried himself so deeply that even Paul, who knows the
area cold, isn't sure of his turns. He asks Hua-ling to direct him
and she pleads confusion, but it is she at last who locates the
turn: "Here. These wild plum trees. Where we picked wild
plums once." She is right.

A small white farmhouse with a modern glass-walled living
room built into one side. Outbuildings. A barn. A shed. Some
sort of truck. Mud. Bourjaily greets us at the sliding living-
room door and hands us in to the bar. The house is efficiently
arranged for Americans: a big kitchen opening onto the living
room, a marble stand-up bar just inside the living room, then
a dining table already set for dinner, then a group of couches
and chairs around a raised fireplace. That is how an American
evening progresses, with trips back to the bar.

Bourjaily looks like someone who would be called Barney.
He wears a tattersall shirt and comfortable pants, whipcord

perhaps. He is not a tall man. Stocky. Something of a belly. A plain face with a big nose, humor in that face, sadness in that face. Weathered. Tanned. He hunts. Across one wall of the living room on racks and wooden pegs are arranged a variety of boots and weapons, a bandolier of blue shotgun shells. He does not apologize for hunting in *The Unnatural Enemy*, his book about hunting, but Barney does not hunt. Barney bird-watches. Bourjaily is a novelist, not a poet, and he looks like someone who says little and observes much. That is how he spends the evening. A poet needs only a few details. A novelist needs them all.

Patrician Tina Bourjaily wears a red dress with a LaCoste alligator where a shirtpocket would be. She is, tonight at least, languid, slow smooth gestures, slow smooth blinks. Perhaps she is tired. Her small daughter Robin sits atop the bar in black stretch pants and a blue-striped tee-shirt also marked with the LaCoste alligator. Robin is tired but unwilling to go to bed on Halloween night with guests for dinner. Expensive whiskey in an unpretentious house. Bourjaily has put his money into land, more than seven hundred acres of rich Iowa farmland. He knows where the values are. "No one has ever come trick-or-treating at our house," says Tina. "We're too isolated." Find a place and cleave to it.

George Garrett the legendary stands at the end of the bar. Bald, a glowing witty face, stocky as Bourjaily and about the same height but trimmer in his best gray suit. A Southerner. "The Radcliffe girls were naked on the stage," the first words I remember him saying. "We all went. A great disappointment."

Paul takes over. "Do you remember, George, the first time we met? It was after that reading at the Museum of Modern Art." Addressing us all now. "The Rockefellers, you know, don't drink. If you are a Rockefeller it is something you do not do. You do not even condone it in others. This particular Mrs. Rockefeller has a townhouse, and we went there after the reading, George and I, arriving rather before the others. She had allowed a bar to be set up on the ground floor. She has a pool in the floor opposite the entrance of the house, a decorative pool, and the only way you could get to the bar was by walking across the steppingstones of that pool. We were on the other side, the bar side, when suddenly the door was flung open and in walked Wystan Hugh Auden. He looked around and shook that great head of his and roared 'WHEA'S THE BLOOOODY BAA?' And then he saw it and walked into that pool without regard for the steppingstones, slogged right through the water and emerged on the other side soaking wet to his knees and proceeded to order a drink!"

Reading begets reading. "We heard Norman's reading in Carnegie Hall," says Tina Bourjaily.

"They wouldn't even consent to rent Carnegie Hall for one of Norman's readings these days," says Garrett.

"Yes," says Tina. "Those four-letter words seem tame these days."

"Perhaps if he undressed," I say.

"That would be a disaster," says Tina, blinking slowly. She goes to the kitchen and returns with a jar of pickled mushrooms. "We've been mushroom hunting today," she tells us. "This is from last fall. It's all one mushroom. They weigh as much as thirty pounds." They taste delicious. Mrs. Bourjaily canned them herself. I hope she knows her mushrooms.

Robin walks across the bar and knocks over a bottle of whiskey, which Paul deftly catches before it can bounce. We look at a book of mushrooms, and Paul bawdily seeks out one with the word *phallus* in its Latin name. He reads part of the description, lacing the words with double entendre. Its glans is bright red.

Robin cries at dinner, exhausted. Tina takes her on her lap, tired little girl. Vance serves beef and vegetables and today's mushrooms from a great hunter's pot. His voice has a strange twist in it, a deference, as if he were either shy or unsure of himself, and perhaps he is both. It's an attractive quality. Barney has the same quality. He's the only one in the novel who never knew Kennedy. He's not interested, as is his friend Dave

Doremus, in vast stakes, in vast power. He runs his woodwork factory, accepts his promiscuous wife, cares for his children, and keeps his head down. And survives. And this is what Barney, this is what Bourjaily, says about pain, the subject, ladies and gentlemen, of this chapter, and when I come upon the passage at the end of Bourjaily's novel the following week when I am still recovering from a difficult personal experience, it is exactly the thought I need. Barney, his daughter Mary Bliss, his sons Goober and Brad, are standing at Kennedy's grave in Arlington, and Mary Bliss has begun to cry: "I know I wished there were some way I could say the lines that came into my mind to a twelve-year-old girl and two boys, fourteen and seventeen, without sounding sententious. From the speech, of course, accepting the nomination, *we are not here to curse the darkness, but to light a candle.*" That's what I needed. Thank you, Mr. Bourjaily. You didn't sound sententious.

The rest of the evening went as such evenings go among intelligent adults in the United States of America: gathered around the fireplace, Tina sitting on the raised hearth with her feet tucked under her, leaning back against the bricks discreetly asleep; Bourjaily in an easy chair to the right, listening more than he talked; Paul asleep sitting beside me on the couch; Hua-ling awake next to him. Garrett was the star because he had come to Iowa City as a candidate, and candidates must take center stage. Having no one else in the group left to demonstrate himself to, he demonstrated himself to me. A reasonable, witty, well-traveled, articulate man. We talked about Truman, because I had just written about him; we talked about slaughterhouses, because I had just visited one. We talked about my preoccupations because Garrett is a gentleman, and that is what a gentleman does. At one point I asked Bourjaily about the destruction of the buffalo, theorizing that there must have been a great deal of death left over from the Civil War that got worked out in the West. A million buffalo a year for four years, until none were left, and Bourjaily's answer was so much more sensible than my death theories it startled me. "Market hunters," he said. "We still have them. They hunt to make a living."

That deserved a gesture, and leaving, I asked Bourjaily for one of his shotgun shells, and with amusement he let me take one, the Vance Bourjaily Memorial Blue Shotgun Shell, emblem of the evening, a Roman candle of sorts.

PARKED IN FRONT OF IOWA HOUSE, WHERE I AM STAY-ing, Paul proposes that I remain another day in Iowa City and go to the game. My wife has already returned home, and as I talk with Paul and Hua-ling I realize that I must return too, though the child in me wants desperately to stay. We say good-night; I get out of the car, and turn to watch these two generous people drive away. The car—Paul and Hua-ling—moves slowly around the traffic circle, a ceremonious and stately pavane. Then a long arm shoots out of the driver's window, waves, and they are gone.

And with them Amana. A haven, but a haven that must be an interlude for those who go there, a step in their progress toward whatever inevitable goal they may discover for themselves. A haven to be left, in good time, for the wicked world, for bicycles and Sunday baseball. Writers cannot adequately sing praise even in the spare churches of the Community of True Inspiration. They must slip home and see to the flowers growing up their walls. Or no flowers will grow, anywhere in the world.

# Index